The gothic novel in Ireland, c. 1760–1829

Manchester University Press

The gothic novel in Ireland, c. 1760–1829

Christina Morin

MANCHESTER UNIVERSITY PRESS

Copyright © Christina Morin 2018

The right of Christina Morin to be identified as the author of this work has been asserted by her in accordance with the Copyright, Designs and Patents Act 1988.

Published by Manchester University Press
Oxford Road, Manchester M13 9PL
www.manchesteruniversitypress.co.uk

British Library Cataloguing-in-Publication Data
A catalogue record for this book is available from the British Library

ISBN 978 0 7190 9917 5 hardback
ISBN 978 1 5261 6047 8 paperback
ISBN 978 1 5261 2230 8 open access

First published 2018
Paperback published 2021

An electronic version of this book is also available under a Creative Commons (CC-BY-NC-ND) licence

The publisher has no responsibility for the persistence or accuracy of URLs for any external or third-party internet websites referred to in this book, and does not guarantee that any content on such websites is, or will remain, accurate or appropriate.

Typeset
by Toppan Best-set Premedia Limited

Contents

List of figures	*page* vii
Acknowledgements	ix
Introduction: locating the Irish gothic novel	1
1 Gothic temporalities: 'Gothicism', 'historicism', and the overlap of fictional modes from Thomas Leland to Walter Scott	27
2 Gothic genres: romances, novels, and the classifications of Irish Romantic fiction	72
3 Gothic geographies: the cartographic consciousness of Irish gothic fiction	113
4 Gothic materialities: Regina Maria Roche, the Minerva Press, and the bibliographic spread of Irish gothic fiction	154
Conclusion	196
Appendix: A working bibliography of Irish gothic fiction, c. 1760–1829	201
Select bibliography	212
Index	228

Figures

1 Irish gothic texts and their generic identifiers — 81
2 The marketing cues of Irish gothic fiction — 82
3 Irish gothic novels and their primary geographic settings — 116
4 Map of the publication, reprint, and translation history of Roche's novels in the long nineteenth century (adapted from a map created using carto.com, map data © OpenStreetMap) — 166

Acknowledgements

This book has been the work of several years, over which time I have benefited from the assistance and encouragement of a great many people. The initial research for this project was made possible by a postdoctoral fellowship awarded by the Irish Research Council from 2010–12. I am very grateful to the Council for this funding, and to the School of English at Trinity College Dublin, which hosted me for the duration of my fellowship. My dear friend and former Ph.D. supervisor, Ian Campbell Ross, generously mentored me during this fellowship and over the course of the project as a whole. My particular thanks are due to him for his unfailing support of my scholarly endeavours over the years.

Research for this project was further enabled by teaching relief provided by the School of Culture and Communication at the University of Limerick (UL) in spring 2015. I am thankful to the School for this opportunity. Thanks are also due to my wonderful colleagues at UL, conversations and research collaborations with whom have undoubtedly strengthened the arguments presented here. I particularly want to acknowledge David Coughlan, Mike Griffin, Meg Harper, and Elaine Vaughan in this regard. I owe, moreover, a debt of gratitude to the members of an informal writing group that met occasionally to critique works-in-progress with coffee cups and chocolate bars in hand: my thanks to Cathy McGlynn, Patricia Moran, Maggie O'Neill, and Michaela Schrage-Früh. I am further indebted to colleagues outside of UL who have selflessly read, commented upon, critiqued, and helpfully discussed elements of continuing research over the years. These include – but certainly are not limited to – Graham Allen, Norbert Besch, Claire Connolly, Marguérite Corporaal, Aileen Douglas, Niall Gillespie, Moyra Haslett, Jarlath Killeen, Ed Larrissey, Barry Monahan,

ACKNOWLEDGEMENTS

Orla Murphy, Clíona Ó Gallchoir, Jim Shanahan, and Julia M. Wright. The late Diane Long Hoeveler was a real source of inspiration throughout this project, and it is only right that I remember her generous collegiality and groundbreaking research here.

Friends and family across the world have offered absolutely invaluable support – moral and otherwise – over the course of this project. Dani Blaylock, Dominic Bryan, Thérèse Cullen, Meg Hoyt, Ruth McCullough, Eveline Masco, Agnes Masengu, Jaele Rollins-McColgan, and Sara Templer have propelled me on through various stages of my research and have never, ever asked, 'Is the book finished yet?'

My most sincere thanks are reserved for Bruce Harper, who may well be able to recite this book from memory so permanent a feature has it become in our household. For good humour, continued interest (feigned and otherwise), technical assistance with 'graphs, maps, and trees', and long Sunday afternoons spent amusing Grace and Ryan while Mommy was at the library, I am deeply grateful.

Material originally printed in earlier versions in the collections Christina Morin and Niall Gillespie (eds), *Irish gothics: genres, forms, modes and traditions, 1760–1890* (2014) and Marguérite Corporaal and Christina Morin (eds), *Traveling Irishness in the long nineteenth century* (2017) is republished here with permission from Palgrave Macmillan. Reworked forms of arguments presented in the *European Romantic Review* and the *Irish University Review* are also reproduced here with permission from the editors. The full publication details are as follows:

'Theorizing "gothic" in eighteenth-century Ireland', in Christina Morin and Niall Gillespie (eds), *Irish gothics: genres, forms, modes and traditions, 1760–1890* (Basingstoke and New York: Palgrave Macmillan, 2014), pp. 13–33.

'Irish gothic goes abroad: cultural migration, materiality, and the Minerva Press', in Marguérite Corporaal and Christina Morin (eds), *Traveling Irishness in the long nineteenth century* (Basingstoke and New York: Palgrave Macmillan, 2017), pp. 195–203.

'"At a distance from [my] country": Henrietta Rouvière Mosse, the Minerva Press, and the negotiation of Irishness in the Romantic literary marketplace', *European Romantic Review* 28.4 (2017), pp. 447–60. See www.tandfonline.com.

'Forgotten fiction: reconsidering the gothic novel in eighteenth-century Ireland', *Irish University Review* 41.1 (2011): 80–94.

Introduction: locating the Irish gothic novel

Published in 1780 in a collection of tales titled *Novellettes, selected for the use of young ladies and gentlemen*, Elizabeth Griffith's little known but compelling short fiction 'Conjugal fidelity' narrates a domestic romance set against the backdrop of the 1641 Rebellion, or 'Irish Massacre'.[1] It tells of the troubled relationship between the Protestant Mr Pansfield – the descendant of 'an English family that had received a grant of some lands in that country [Co. Kilkenny] from Queen Elizabeth' – and his Catholic wife, Elvina Butler, as they weather the 'storms' then ravaging the country ('Conjugal fidelity', pp. 182, 186). In her 2006 chapter, 'The gothic novel', Siobhán Kilfeather identified the story as an early instance of Irish gothic fiction, but it has yet to receive serious scholarly analysis in studies of either eighteenth-century Irish or gothic literature.[2] It will seem an odd choice with which to begin a discussion of 'the Gothic novel' in Ireland, as promised by the title of this book. Yet, its continued neglect, driven by its failure easily to satisfy critical expectations for either 'Irish Gothic' or 'the Gothic novel', as detailed in this introduction, highlights the aims of this monograph: to interrogate scholarly preconceptions about the bodies of work associated with these monolithic terms and to draw a new conceptual map of Irish gothic literary production in the period 1760–1829.[3]

Widely used today as identifying labels for gothic literature produced in eighteenth- and nineteenth-century Britain and Ireland, 'Irish Gothic' and 'the Gothic novel' offer a helpful shorthand for referencing the shared themes, settings, and topoi that tie authors and texts together in recognisable gothic literary traditions. 'Irish Gothic' thus speaks of fiction that explores the mixed fears and desires of a minority Anglo-Irish population threatened

– imaginatively if not actually – by the unsettled native Catholics over whom they maintained precarious control.[4] It is typified by the novels of Victorian writers such as Sheridan Le Fanu (1814–73), Bram Stoker (1847–1912), and Oscar Wilde (1854–1900), although its origins are often traced to Charles Robert Maturin's *Melmoth the Wanderer* (1820). 'The Gothic novel', in turn, signifies '[a] strain of the novel' that developed in the latter half of the eighteenth century and enjoyed notable popular success before exhausting itself in the first few decades of the nineteenth century.[5] Commonly understood to begin with Horace Walpole's *The castle of Otranto* (1764), its defining characteristics include, as David Punter outlines, 'an emphasis on portraying the terrifying, a common insistence on archaic settings, a prominent use of the supernatural, the presence of highly stereotyped characters and the attempt to deploy and perfect techniques of suspense'.[6]

As terms, both 'Irish Gothic' and 'the Gothic novel' are valuable for the work they represent: the identification and scholarly recuperation of two interrelated bodies of popular fiction often overshadowed in contemporary critical responses and more recent analysis alike by literature considered more reputable and/or elite. We would do well to remember, though, as James Watt and Richard Haslam have both noted, that these labels are products of modern literary studies.[7] The inverted commas that so naturally envelop them, and which are used throughout this study, suggest their retrospective nature and underline their failure to offer a faithful reflection of eighteenth- and nineteenth-century understandings of the literature they describe. They also draw attention to the unfortunate – if largely unintended – homogenising effect produced by artificial categorisations that have successfully consigned to oblivion whole swathes of outlying literary production. This process of exclusion creates, in consequence, established gothic literary canons that now need to be interrogated to account for the texts – including 'Conjugal fidelity' – that have fallen victim to what Franco Moretti aptly terms 'the slaughterhouse of literature'.[8] These are works that are not generally considered gothic by the retrospectively defined 'rules' of 'Irish Gothic' or 'the Gothic novel' but which, when viewed through the lens of historical constructions of the term gothic, might reasonably be described as such. In their deviation from imposed gothic norms, 'Conjugal fidelity' and the other texts assessed in this study highlight the stark contrast between modern and historical perceptions of gothic literary production. In particular, as traced here and in the chapters that follow, these works reveal that the characteristics on which we base our current understanding of the literary gothic in Romantic-era Britain and Ireland simply are not those identified by contemporary readers.[9]

Griffith's 'Conjugal fidelity' is an excellent example of the jarring discord between historical and present-day understandings of the literary gothic. Despite its flirtation with the explained supernatural later associated with Ann Radcliffe (1764–1823), its description of a sublime natural world, its focus on a persecuted heroine trapped within patriarchal power structures, and its evocation of a past that continues to haunt the present, the tale flouts key assumptions about contemporary gothic literature. As a short story, it defies our positioning of the novel as the gothic literary genre par excellence, a privileging made evident in the very term 'the Gothic novel'. It further upsets our conceptualisations of 'the Gothic novel' in its lack of the medieval, Catholic Continental settings associated with eminent gothicists such as Walpole, Radcliffe, and Matthew Lewis (1775–1818). It more easily falls into the category of 'Irish Gothic', appearing to adhere to prevailing, psychoanalytic readings of the form in its use of the 1641 Rebellion as its setting. Griffith's depiction of this period in Irish history gestures towards the important role Protestant historiography of 1641 played in creating what Jarlath Killeen identifies as the quasi-fictional 'martyrology' and enduring identity-in-opposition that would both define the Irish Anglican community and underwrite Irish gothic literary production in the long eighteenth century.[10] Alongside annual, commemorative sermons preached on the anniversary of the outbreak of rebellion on 23 October 1641, repeated reprintings of Sir John Temple's *The Irish rebellion* (1646) over the next 150 years registered enduring Protestant paranoia over a recurrence of 1641-scale violence.[11] New editions of *The Irish rebellion* appeared 'in response to Protestant insecurities at critical periods in Ireland's history', as Charlene Adair observes.[12] 'Conjugal fidelity' seems similarly to react to the popular unrest and heightened social tensions caused by Irish entanglement in the Free Trade debate of 1778–81 and accompanying 'political dispute between the Irish patriots and the Castle government'.[13] Its depiction of spiteful Catholic priests prowling the 'wretched' Irish countryside in search of victims effectively manipulates Protestant fears of Catholic restlessness in the late 1770s ('Conjugal fidelity', p. 186). It correspondingly corroborates the imagology of a righteous Protestant people preyed upon by barbaric savages found in Temple's *Irish rebellion*.

So far, so 'Irish Gothic', but Griffith's tale strips the force from its anti-Catholic message with its characterisation of both Protestant and Catholic populations as culpable for the violence with which the country is beset.

Apparently burned to death in his own home by Irish rebels because of his status as a Protestant settler landowner, his brutal mistreatment of his wife, and his fatal attack on an Irish priest, Pansfield is far from an innocent victim. Instead, he is actively presented as an unsympathetic, if not hateful, character for much of the story. At the same time, his reconciliation with his wife shortly after she sees his 'ghost' and realises that he has survived the attack against him, coincident to his own personal reformation, gestures towards the allegorical unions of the later Irish national tale, as popularised by Sydney Owenson's *The wild Irish girl* (1806) ('Conjugal fidelity', p. 184). By vilifying the prominent Protestant character in the story and by suggesting the possibility of a public resolution to sectarian violence in the private understanding reached between Pansfield and Elvina, 'Conjugal fidelity' counters Temple's 'imagology of horror' with a plot that both complicates Protestant narratives of victimhood and imagines an alternative future to continued religious factionalism.[14]

Griffith's story thus runs afoul of the virulent anti-Catholicism traditionally associated with the 'Irish Gothic', offering instead a message of toleration influenced by patriot politics of the 1770s and 1780s.[15] As it does so, it draws attention to the divergent uses and manifestations of the literary gothic in late eighteenth and early nineteenth-century Ireland. Not just an allegorical expression of its Anglo-Irish writers' fear of the repressed past and its people (the Catholic majority), the Irish literary gothic in this period proves a dynamic, cross-sectarian, and cross-cultural enterprise, as the following chapters demonstrate. This diversity has begun to be recognised in new research by Claire Connolly, Niall Gillespie, Richard Haslam, and Emer Nolan, who have initiated a recuperation of gothic works by Irish Catholic writers, tracing the ways in which gothic techniques could be harnessed to very different cultural and political ends in Romantic-era Ireland.[16] Like my reading of Griffith's 'Conjugal fidelity', such scholarship forcefully queries the normative limits of 'Irish Gothic', inviting us to engage in what Anne Williams calls '[a] thoughtful analysis of "Gothic"' that 'challenges the kind of literary history that organizes, delineates, and defines'.[17] To do so, this study proposes to widen and broaden the boundaries of Irish gothic literature within the remit of both Irish and gothic studies, taking its cue from Moretti's call 'to make the literary field longer, larger, and deeper'.[18] Its aim is to establish a 'historically longer, geographically larger, and morphologically deeper' conceptualisation of the Irish literary gothic that goes well beyond the comparatively few texts that now constitute our study of Irish writing and gothic literature alike.[19]

INTRODUCTION

How this is best accomplished is by a recovery of eighteenth- and nineteenth-century understandings of the term gothic and the literature associated with it. It cannot be stressed enough, but 'gothic' was not then a codified generic label. Instead, gothic – generally with a capital 'G' – referred to the past as well as to the chronological and social evolution that produced present-day Britain. To speak of the Gothic past was to conjure two apparently contradictory but no less linked ideas of, on the one hand, 'a distant, non-specific period of ignorance and superstition from which an increasingly civilized nation had triumphantly emerged',[20] and, on the other, an august political inheritance derived from a vaguely conceptualised set of Germanic and Teutonic tribes, including the Anglo-Saxons, who had given birth to modern British liberty, despite their inborn barbarity.[21] The latter usage functioned as a method of critiquing current governmental policies and political trends, with what William Molyneux termed the 'noble Gothick Constitution' coming to be understood as a far-removed 'fount of constitutional purity and political virtue from which the nation had become dangerously alienated'.[22]

It is with this sense of the term in mind that Walpole appended the subtitle 'a Gothic story' to the second edition of *Otranto*. In the historiography of 'the Gothic novel', his decision to do so has been hailed as the inaugural moment of the genre. But Walpole's use of his subtitle was not purposeful literary innovation, nor was it taken as such by contemporaries, who very rarely followed his example in naming their texts.[23] Instead, it acted as what Emma Clery calls 'a flippant paradox chiefly intended … to annoy stuffy critics. After all, how could a Gothic story have a modern author?'[24] As Clery's comments indicate, the pronounced negative critical response to *Otranto*, particularly in its second edition and its revelation that what Walpole had initially presented as a redaction of an ancient manuscript was actually a modern fiction, revolved around eighteenth-century conceptions of the past and its temporal and ideological relationship to the present. What caused concern was Walpole's perceived attempt to revive a savage past and its practices in an enlightened age, an act that clearly stirred fear in readers' hearts. As the *Monthly Review* declared, 'It is, indeed, more than strange that an Author, of a refined and polished genius, should be an advocate for re-establishing the barbarous superstitions of Gothic devilism!'[25]

The generic innovation Walpole himself laid claim to must be read in light of this attention to historical progress and cultural evolution. In the preface to the second edition of *Otranto*, Walpole famously declared his

5

work 'an attempt to blend the two kinds of romance, the ancient and the modern'.²⁶ His effort at generic fusion was driven by contempt for realism's 'damm[ing] up' of 'the great resources of fancy' with its 'strict adherence to common life' as well as an equal disdain for the 'unnatural' 'actions, sentiments, conversations, of the heroes and heroines of ancient days' (*Castle of Otranto*, p. 8). As a 'reconcil[iation]' of the two forms of romance, *Otranto* sought to place its characters in 'extraordinary positions' created by 'the powers of fancy at liberty' while still applying 'the rules of probability' to their behaviour (*Castle of Otranto*, p. 8).

In its focus on different types of prose fiction, Walpole's revival of romance emphasised the relationship between past and present evoked by his subtitle. The 'ancient' romance to which he refers in his preface conjures the medieval chivalric romances and seventeenth-century French prose fiction that Clara Reeve influentially identified as 'the polite literature of early ages' – 'fabulous Stor[ies] of such actions as are commonly ascribed to heroes, or men of extraordinary courage and abilities'.²⁷ For Reeve, romances were distinguished from the eighteenth-century British novel by way of the cultural stages that produced them; as Richard Maxwell observes, 'Romances are what precede novels, in a less modern, probably more warlike, state of society; once a polite and Augustan civilization is established, romance becomes novel, a process of metamorphosis and also of sublimation'.²⁸ '[T]he modern Novel', Reeve writes, 'sprung up out of its [the romance's] ruin'.²⁹ Reeve's comments coalesce with contemporary vindications of the developing novel as distinguished from romance and other forms of prose fiction by its didactic realism – that which made the novel modern and, thus, the appropriate literary production of an enlightened British nation. As discussed further in chapters 1 and 2, to suggest that 'a wild, extravagant, fabulous Story' such as that presented in *Otranto* could be accommodated within the new novel form and also appeal to educated readers underlined a discomfiting lack of social progression.³⁰ Walpole's mischievous subtitle, then, far from establishing a new literary genre, underscored cultural concerns over historical transition in the period.

Such anxieties are clearly evident in 'Conjugal fidelity', too. Griffith similarly frames her work as a reassertion of romance's place in modern society. Echoing Walpole's disdain for the manner in which 'Nature has cramped imagination' in eighteenth-century literature (*Castle of Otranto*, p. 9), Griffith applauds 'the romantic spirit' of the 'old-fashioned times' and decries the 'good-sense, politeness, and the true mode of *sçavoir vivre*' of the present day:

INTRODUCTION

> [I]f Madam Helen were alive at this day, and were to elope, as formerly she did, with Ensign Paris, her flight might, perhaps, furnish a paragraph for a Newspaper, but would not even rouse her Captain Menelaus to challenge her paramour to a single combat, or so much as inspire any of our ballad-mongers to bewail her mishap to the tune of *The Lady's Downfall*. ('Conjugal fidelity', p. 180)

With the values of the heroic age having given way to the politeness of genteel society in the 1780s, Griffith's tale suggests, romance has become obsolete. Without it, though, Griffith asserts, the most momentous occasions become simply a matter of dry reportage ('Conjugal fidelity', p. 180). Fittingly, therefore, Griffith offers her tale as proof of the existence of female heroism in a modern era: 'does not this fair Hibernian dame, in nobleness of soul, by far surpass your Arria's and your Portia's?' ('Conjugal fidelity', p. 191). Linking Elvina to the fabled figures and feats of Greek mythology, Griffith reasserts the modern-day relevance of romance and 'fancy', just as Walpole sought to do (*Castle of Otranto*, p. 9).

Partly an ironic commentary on polite society, Griffith's tale also more earnestly establishes the tacit contrast between past and present central to Walpole's labelling of his tale 'a Gothic story'. Its manipulation of its seventeenth-century setting to comment – however indirectly – on present-day politics further speaks to contemporary understandings of the Gothic past and the concerns raised over Walpole's evocation of it in *Otranto*. Although Griffith does not specifically label her tale Gothic, she nevertheless constructs the 1641 Rebellion as a period of antidiluvian religious and social strife from which modern Ireland had not yet significantly progressed. This uncomfortable conflation of past and present is precisely that which angered critics in the second edition of *Otranto*, and it positions Griffith's tale alongside Walpole's as part of a gothic literary output much larger and more diverse than is allowed by our current notions of 'Irish Gothic' and 'the Gothic novel'.

The striking connections between these two texts are worth noting for a number of reasons. First, they cast doubt on *Melmoth the Wanderer*'s primary status in the history of Irish gothic literature; second, they challenge the notion of the period between *The castle of Otranto* and the later works of Radcliffe and Lewis as a largely 'fallow' one in the production of 'the Gothic novel'.[31] Third, they open up a conversation about the terminological confusion produced when we start to scratch at the surface of the labels 'Irish Gothic' and 'the Gothic novel'. Such a discussion dovetails with recent critical attention to the classification of gothic literary production.

In the case of 'Irish Gothic', debate has been particularly heated, if inconclusive, as scholars propose and defend the application of various identifying labels, including 'canon', 'tradition', 'genre', 'mode', and 'register'.[32] Gothic Studies scholars have also begun to query the idea of gothic literature as a genre begun with *The castle of Otranto*, particularly in consideration of contemporary works. Confronted with a body of work that seems, at first glance, 'so clearly recognizable', but which 'has a habit of putting itself about, suddenly emerging in texts that appear to be playing by the rules of some quite different genre',[33] scholars have increasingly grappled with just how precisely to define Gothic.[34] Unsurprisingly, the answers reached are more often than not plural; as Alexandra Warwick observes, 'if there is any general consensus, it seems to be that Gothic is a mode rather than a genre, that it is a loose tradition, and even that its defining characteristics are its mobility and continued capacity for reinvention'.[35]

Many of the arguments for the use of the terms 'mode' and 'register' are compelling when speaking of Romantic-era gothic literature, but they also both miss the point and propose further retrospective tags that can only ever inadequately encompass the works in question. If eighteenth- and nineteenth-century authors did not themselves adopt the terminology of 'gothic', surely we should be asking in a historically specific manner *how* that term was understood and *why*, as a consequence, contemporary texts might usefully be described as such. Asking *why* and *how* rather than *what* allows us to account for the impact of changing and evolving temporal and cultural conditions in this period. It eliminates the single-minded focus on the novel as the principal gothic literary vehicle, accounting for the intrinsic generic instability of the Romantic period.[36] It takes into consideration both conservative and subversive viewpoints, both fear-inducing and farcical tones and moods, both overtly supernatural and more mundane characters and events. And it helps to integrate Irish writers into a wider British and European gothic literary production from which they are all too often excluded by nature of the derivative, secondary, or minor character of their publications. Not just 'a belated tradition coming out of English gothic', Irish gothic literature actively contributes to and informs a wider, cross-cultural gothic literary production in this period.[37]

This is not to suggest that the Irish literary gothic is indistinguishable from English or British gothic, or indeed, that gothic is everywhere and in everything, thus essentially nullifying the term. Instead, it is to argue that, despite inevitable variations and permutations, Irish writers participated in

INTRODUCTION

a widespread and inclusive literary phenomenon unrestricted by national boundaries and shaped by historically and culturally specific constructions of and reflections on the Gothic past. It thus works to overturn myopic critical attention to a core group of 'canonical', often specifically 'English', gothic texts that implies, as Terry Hale notes, that English authors were the only ones to adopt 'a popular aesthetic of horror in late eighteenth- and early nineteenth-century Europe'.[38] And, it evidences the folly of thinking about 'Irish Gothic' and 'the Gothic novel' as either separate bodies of literature or distinct genres, canons, or traditions in themselves. As the case of Griffith and Walpole suggests, Irish authors shared their cultural perception of the term gothic and the objects and activities associated with it not only with each other, regardless of religious, political, or ideological affinities, but also with their contemporaries in Britain, Europe, and further afield. The works discussed here thus construct a cosmopolitan conception of gothic literary production wherein questions of religious background, political affiliation, geographical location, and literary genre and form become less important than a mutual interrogation of the Gothic past.

RE-MAPPING IRISH GOTHIC LITERATURE

Replacing *what* with *how* and *why* also prompts further relevant queries, especially *who*, *where*, and *when*: who was writing gothic fiction in the Romantic period? Where and when were the stories set, published, and circulated? Who read and who decried them? Where do they fall formally, stylistically, and thematically within the wider literary production of the period? While these questions are not new in the study of gothic literature, this book approaches them with a fresh eye, considering them as part of the Moretti-inspired process of widening, deepening, and lengthening proposed earlier. Griffith's 'Conjugal fidelity' helps us to grasp the scope and significance of exploring these questions unhindered by traditional scholarly focus on definitions. Querying the many generic and thematic assumptions we have about both 'the Gothic novel' and 'Irish Gothic', as already discussed in this introduction, the tale further interrogates the usual chronological parameters of these bodies of literature and proposes a much earlier, more vital Irish gothic literary production than is usually recognised. By drawing attention to the eighteenth-century Irish writers and texts sometimes included in lists of Irish gothic texts but rarely afforded sustained critical attention, 'Conjugal fidelity' traces the limitations of current scholarly definitions and delimitations.[39] Thomas Leland's *Longsword, Earl of Salisbury* (1762) is a case in point. Recently identified as an earlier gothic novel than Walpole's *Otranto*, *Longsword* has yet to be fully integrated into the history of Irish and British gothic literature, principally because, as discussed in Chapter 1, the novel has been classed as 'historical' rather than 'gothic'.[40]

The chapters that follow consider a representative selection of texts, enumerated more fully in the Appendix, that evidence the cultural amnesia that continues to shape and inform our interpretations of Irish literary production in the latter half of the eighteenth and the beginning of the nineteenth century. These works were chosen for the manner in which they interrogate received notions of gothic literature in this period and sketch a much broader cultural practice centred on contemporary – rather than retrospective – conceptualisations of the term gothic and the literature that might be described as such. Their selection was guided by archival research in print and digital collections across Ireland and Britain as well as existing bibliographies of Irish and gothic literature. Early works such as Dorothy Blakey's *The Minerva Press 1790–1820* (1939) and Montague Summers' *A gothic bibliography* (1940) demonstrate the range of literature considered as part of a gothic literary tradition in the advent of scholarly attention to 'the Gothic novel'. Alongside Deborah McLeod's invaluable Ph.D. thesis on 'The Minerva Press' (1997), and Franz Potter's *The history of gothic publishing, 1800–1835* (2005), this scholarship uncovers many of the texts that have fallen victim both to Romantic-era disdain for gothic romances and the later canonisation processes effected by twentieth- and twenty-first-century literary studies. From a specifically Irish literature perspective, research by Rolf and Magda Loeber, in particular their indispensable *A guide to Irish fiction* (2006), has greatly expanded the limits of our literary consciousness, recovering to view a multitude of texts that now invite a re-consideration of the parameters of Irish literary production across the centuries.

Many of the lesser-known works included in these bibliographies and assessed in this book were dismissed by contemporaries as inconsequential, hack writing. Yet, they were often the most widely read fictions of their day and, as such, deserve much more careful consideration than they have generally been given in modern scholarship. Their value lies not just in their narratives, which are frequently much higher in quality than has been allowed, but also in their revelation of late eighteenth- and early nineteenth-century reading habits and trends. These works further provide useful insight into print culture and the emerging literary marketplace in the Romantic period. Equally, they position Irish authors at the centre of a new transatlantic literary world by which now little-known gothic texts came to be read and enjoyed by a truly global readership. Reading these works alongside those of more well-known contemporary authors such as Maria Edgeworth (1768–1849), Sydney Owenson, Lady Morgan (c. 1783–1859), Charles Robert Maturin (1780–1824), and the Banim brothers sheds new light on the rich diversity of Romantic-era Irish literary production. As it does so, it underscores the necessity of a study like this: the dismantling of restrictive, largely artificial, formal, and generic cateogorisations that have hindered a full comprehension of Irish and gothic literature of this period.

The virtual absence of a vast majority of the texts discussed here from the annals of literary history speaks to literary criticism's myopic focus on, in Moretti's terms, 'individual cases' rather than the 'collective'. As Moretti compellingly argues, critical emphasis on a selection of canonical texts in scholarly consideration of nineteenth-century British literary production excludes from view 99 per cent of the novels actually published in that period. Moretti proposes, in consequence, '[a] more rational literary history' via a quantitative, rather than a qualitative, approach.[41] In more recent work, as Ian Campbell Ross points out, Moretti has forcefully supported such an approach, arguing both for a global perspective on literature as well as one completely dependent on statistics and devoid of '*direct textual reading*'.[42] Moretti's globalising and quantifying perspective is in keeping with his recommendation that we study the 'collective' rather than 'individual cases', but, as Ross persuasively argues, the local and the individual still hold their place in literary analysis.[43] Moretti might contend that a study such as this – that is, one engaged in assessing a selection of Irish texts from a specific time period – amounts to a support of literary canons. Instead, in keeping with Ross's impassioned call for greater attention to the breadth and variety of early Irish fiction, this study aims 'not simply to enlarge … that "canonical fraction" of texts studied but to suggest that many, many books, that neither are, nor ever have formed, part of the canon, *do* matter'. Moreover, in recovering and re-evaluating such overlooked texts, this study is not just local or national but global in its concerns: in Ross's terms, it 'urges on readers the need for an enhanced understanding not only of the European literary system but of the idea of Europe itself which, in becoming more complex, necessarily becomes less monolithic'.[44]

Combining Moretti's quantitative methodology with a more traditional qualitative one, therefore, this study opens up Romantic literary history, both within the study of Irish literature and within gothic literary studies. It does so by broadening Moretti's concept of 'literary geography', though in different ways than Moretti himself has done in recent years.[45] In his 1998 study, *Atlas of the European novel, 1800–1900*, Moretti identified both '*space in literature*' and '*literature in space*' as crucial to a full understanding of the literary production of any given period. '*[E]ach space determines, or at least encourages, its own kind of story*', Moretti argues,

> There is no picaresque of the border, or *Bildungsroman* of the European in Africa: *this* specific form needs *that* specific space – the road, the metropolis. Space is not the "outside" of narrative, then, but an internal force, that shapes it from within. Or in other words: in modern European novels, *what* happens depends a lot on *where* it happens.[46]

Although Moretti refers specifically to geographical landscapes as the location(s) in and of literary texts, this study widens the notion of landscape to include temporal settings, formal/generic contexts, and ideological frameworks as well. It thus rephrases Moretti's compelling statement as follows: 'in modern European novels, *what* happens depends a lot on *where* and *when* it happens, literally and metaphorically'.

Paying attention to the where and when of Irish gothic literature forces us to think anew about current critical definitions of Irish Romantic literature and the literary gothic as a whole. By assessing Irish gothic works from the late eighteenth and early nineteenth centuries cartographically or, in other words, in terms of how they can be mapped alongside contemporary works by way of their geography, their chronology or approach to chronology, their formal and generic characteristics, and their ideological intent, we can begin to understand both the significant contribution made by these works to the development of the literary gothic and the reasons for their continued marginalisation in the twentieth and twenty-first centuries. In keeping with Moretti's emphasis on the visual representation of literature as a method of underlining the limitations of our current understandings, this study includes several tables, charts, and maps that provide a quantification of its central arguments.[47] These graphics unambiguously demonstrate the terms by which eighteenth- and nineteenth-century authors understood gothic literary production. The figures in Chapter 2, for instance, enumerate the many generic labels – none of them 'gothic' – with which writers described their publications. They further catalogue Irish use of what Robert Miles calls the 'marketing cues' used in titles to position texts as examples of what we now know as 'the Gothic novel'.[48] Chapter 3 includes a statistical illustration of the different geographic locations of the texts considered here, emphasising the global terrain mapped by Irish writers and their contemporaries in Britain throughout the eighteenth and nineteenth centuries. This figure decidedly overturns understandings of the dominance of Catholic Continental settings in 'the Gothic novel' while also shedding new light on the use by Irish and British writers alike of the 'Celtic periphery' as a gothic locale. Chapter 4's map highlights the worldwide reach of the gothic romances of Regina Maria Roche (c. 1764–1845), outlining the remarkable, if now little recognised, 'bibliographic everywhereness' of her works, as of those of many of her Irish contemporaries publishing with London's infamous Minerva Press, including Henrietta Rouvière Mosse (d. 1834), Sarah Green (fl. 1790–1825), and Mrs F.C. Patrick (fl. 1797).[49] The striking material dissemination and consequent expansive readership of Roche's novels and other Irish Minerva Press fictions underscores the necessity of re-assessing gothic works too often dismissed as inconsequential because of their popular – rather than elite – literary status.

As suggested by these 'graphs, maps, and trees', each of the chapters that follows represents an attempt to engage in the kind of 'radical remapping' of gothic 'territory' called for by Anne Williams in her assertion of the essential poetic nature of Romantic gothic literature.[50] Considering the formal, generic, geographical, temporal, and ideological 'settings' of Irish gothic literature, this book explores the 'place' of Irish gothic literature in relation to contemporary works. By so doing, each chapter, by necessity, considers the disparity between eighteenth- and early nineteenth-century conceptions of the term gothic and more modern definitions of gothic literature, 'Irish Gothic' and 'the Gothic novel' specifically. Chapter 1 begins with an investigation of what Montague Summers early identified as 'historical gothic' fiction.[51] In particular, it considers the naming of Walpole's *The castle of Otranto* and Leland's *Longsword* as 'historical novels', exploring these texts' shared interest in comparing and contrasting the past with the present. The first part of this chapter is especially concerned with re-locating the formal and generic origins of the body of literature we now define as gothic by examining the manipulation of the Gothic past in *The castle of Otranto*, *Longsword*, and several other early Irish gothic texts, including the works of James White (1759–99) and Anne Fuller's novel, *Alan Fitz-osborne; an historical tale* (1786). These works' concern with the Gothic past underlines the evident engagement with 'the medieval world' in the literary gothic, but, as the second section of this chapter demonstrates, such interest does not support the traditional characterisation of British gothic literature as both set in the medieval past and nostalgic for that past. Literary criticism's attention to the gothic's 'nostalgic medievalism' is, as Chris Baldick and Robert Mighall contend, fundamentally misguided: '[M]ost Gothic novels have little to do with "the medieval world", especially not an idealized one; [and] they represent that past not as paradisal but as "nasty" in its "possessive" curtailing of individual liberties'.[52]

The final part of Chapter 1 explores the manipulation of the relationship between past and present in Irish gothic fiction published after Walter Scott's *Waverley* (1814) and the putative inauguration of 'the historical novel'. It argues specifically that the gothic novel, on the one hand, and the historical novel, on the other, are not inherently distinct fictional forms, even in the age of Scott. Considering the enduring overlap of these forms in the early nineteenth century, this section emphasises the continuity between historical gothic fictions of the latter half of the eighteenth century and those of Scott and his Irish contemporaries. As it does so, it offers a reassessment of traditional paradigms of the development of the novel in early nineteenth-century Ireland. According to these, the historical novel as championed by Scott and, indeed, realist fiction as a whole, never properly succeeded in Ireland due to social, political, and historical conditions that transformed Scott's conservative narrative of progress into a laughable prospect. Thus, it is often argued, Irish writers imitating Scott were doomed to fail, producing narratives that resist, often through the use of gothic themes and imagery, the closure and reconciliation indicative of Scott's nostalgic, but deterministic, view of the past. This chapter argues against such assumptions, tracing instead the similarities between Scott's use of the Gothic past and that in several important, if overlooked, examples of early nineteenth-century Irish fiction, including Roche's *Trecothick bower; or, the lady of the west country* (1814).

Chapter 2 continues the formal and generic re-mapping of Chapter 1 with a particular focus on the terminology applied to literature now considered gothic. The first half of the chapter considers the use of the term 'romance' as the generic indicator favoured by authors of what we now call 'the Gothic novel'.[53] This terminological choice refers to contemporary discourse on the emergent novel as distinct from earlier romance traditions and suggests the ways in which authors who used it sought to

INTRODUCTION

free themselves from the constraints of didactic realism: that which the novel's early proponents had sought to establish as the defining characteristic of a form still largely considered suspect in the latter half of the eighteenth century. By describing their texts as 'romances', late eighteenth- and early nineteenth-century writers appealed to the imagination and to 'the characteristic historical and/or geographical otherness of romance' as, in part, a corrective to what Walpole understood as the realist novel's too keen attention to 'common life' at the expense of imagination (*Castle of Otranto*, p. 9).[54] Where we now expect a gothic text to include overt supernaturalism, whether explained or unexplained, the recourse to 'romance' for contemporaries, was much more widely understood. The supernatural as theatrically deployed by Walpole, therefore, was not necessarily a defining feature of texts concerned with the Gothic past. As Watt contends, 'While some form of supernatural agency was regarded as an essential component of terror-fiction by contemporary satirists, most critics who considered individual works at any length nonetheless understood that different treatments of the supernatural varied greatly in terms of their tone and register'.[55] The first three-quarters of this chapter therefore proposes a more nuanced understanding of the supernatural and romance more widely in several examples of early Irish gothic fiction.

In its final quarter, Chapter 2 considers more closely Irish gothic fiction in the context of Irish Romanticism. Much of the reason why Irish gothic literary production from the late eighteenth and early nineteenth centuries remains overlooked today, this section argues, has to do with current scholarly understanding of Irish Romanticism as dominated by regional, national, and historical literary forms that rose to prominence in the years surrounding Anglo-Irish Union (1801). Such is our concentration on the regional novel, the national tale, and the historical novel, that we very often forget that texts such as Edgeworth's *Castle Rackrent* (1800), Owenson's *The wild Irish girl* (1806), and Maturin's *The Milesian chief* (1812) emerged organically from the gothic fiction of the late eighteenth century.[56] Not only that, but these forms continued to deploy the themes, images, and tropes made familiar by earlier gothic works, such as Roche's *The children of the abbey* (1796), Fuller's *The convent; or, the history of Sophia Nelson* (1786), and White's *Earl Strongbow* (1789), amongst many others. Moreover, as is suggested by the continued publication in the early nineteenth century of Irish gothic fiction, including, for instance, *Plantagenet; or, secrets of the house of Anjou* (1802), *Villa Nova; or, the ruined castle* (1804), *The discarded son; or, haunt of the banditti* (1807), not to mention Maturin's celebrated

Melmoth the wanderer, national, regional, and historical literary forms vitally co-existed with, rather than replaced, the literary gothic in Ireland in the first three decades of the nineteenth century. Having previously considered the historical novel in detail in Chapter 1, Chapter 2 places Irish gothic fiction alongside the national tale in order to complicate our current tendencies to view the latter as both the dominant form of Irish Romantic literary production and inherently distinct from the literary gothic.

Chapter 3 moves on from formal and generic mappings of Irish gothic fiction to a consideration of its geographical settings. Within criticism of gothic literature of the late eighteenth and early nineteenth centuries, a Catholic Continental setting has come to be defined as a near necessity. Such settings are understood to underscore modern, rational Britishness by contrasting it with an atavistic Catholicism located safely outside English – if not British – national borders. Irish gothic literature often follows in this pattern, including the Catholic Continent in a geography of terror from which England is notably absent. Yet, it also frequently resists a related tendency manifest in English gothic literature of this period imaginatively to map Ireland and the 'Celtic Fringe' alongside France, Spain, and Italy, as a particularly gothic location.[57] This chapter therefore considers several Irish gothic texts that problematise the privileging of Catholic Continental and 'Celtic Fringe' settings as well as their use as a tool of British national vindication. It also, in its final section, assesses the privileging of travel in post-Anglo-Irish Union gothic romances concerned, like the contemporary national tale, with the geographical mapping and associated cultural vindication of Ireland. Rather than focus on the Anglo-Irish cultural encounters familiar from *The wild Irish girl*, *The absentee* (1812), and other widely known national tales, however, this chapter turns attention to texts that concentrate on Irish interactions with more far-flung communities in order to underline the role that tourism, exile, and military travel play in the assertion of Irish national significance in the early nineteenth century.

Expanding the notion of literary cartography addressed in Chapter 3, Chapter 4 considers the materiality of Irish gothic literature, taking its cue from Andrew Piper's convincing call to 'combin[e] an analysis of the movements and fixations *of* texts with the movements and fixations *within* texts'.[58] Such an approach enables a mapping of texts as 'interpretations of and interactions with the bibliographic environment[s] in which they appeared'.[59] Focusing on London's Minerva Press and, in particular, the novels of Regina Maria Roche, this chapter considers the textual

INTRODUCTION

placement of these works – their locations within specific material and print contexts – as indicative of the geographical and ideological reach and impact of Irish gothic literary production in the late eighteenth and early nineteenth centuries.

A FEW CAVEATS

In its attempt literally and metaphorically to place Irish gothic fiction back on the map of literary studies of the late eighteenth and early nineteenth centuries, this book cannot pretend, nor indeed would wish, to be either definitive or exhaustive. As Claire Connolly has perceptively observed, 'Our current sense of the quantity of Irish fiction has rather outstripped our interpretative procedures', meaning that, 'critical challenges outweigh bibliographical ones at present'.[60] In a study such as this, it would be easy, as Connolly wryly notes, to become 'lost in the sublime of literary history' and 'paralysed by dreams of a total literary history'.[61] While this monograph brings back to view a large quantity of Irish writing currently overlooked by literary criticism, its focus is on interpreting that literature rather than producing conclusive bibliographic quantifications of it. In this, it adopts the belief that detailed close readings of individual texts can productively lead back to the kind of distant reading advised by Moretti.[62]

As it does so, this book works within the confines of several boundaries and definitions, even as it remains ever aware of the need to deconstruct restrictions inherent to current categorisations of 'the Gothic novel', 'Irish Gothic', and Irish Romantic fiction. In particular, it includes only Irish works, where 'Irishness' is defined by reference to the author's birth in Ireland, the circumstance of the author having spent a significant portion of life in Ireland, or a given text's initial publication in Ireland. Irish content or subject matter is not a necessary component, but neither is it sufficient to include a work lacking any authorial link to Ireland. The concern here is specifically to sketch Irish gothic fiction as, in Moretti's terms, a 'geo-narrative system' produced by authors with a particular national loyalty to or affiliation with Ireland.[63]

The authorship make-up of the following study is also disproportionately female, in keeping with the novel's dominance by women writers in the Romantic period. Only 13 of the 114 works catalogued in the Appendix can be linked to identified male authors, thus speaking to what James Raven calls 'the march of the woman novelist (and of the more prolific individual woman novelist)' from the 1780s onwards.[64] Representative of a newly democratised print culture wherein the production and accessibility of books was dramatically widened, these works underscore the literary gothic's importance to a new era of female writing. In their frequent evocation of the fraught realities of women's existence in a patriarchal society at the very moment that women began to enter the literary marketplace in serious numbers, these works embody the 'female Gothic' influentially identified by Ellen Moers. In other words, they harness fear in order to explore the iniquities and everyday terror associated with being a woman in Romantic Britain and Ireland.[65] Their frequently sophisticated treatment of issues such as marriage, female imprisonment, and women's authorship, alongside matters of Irish, British, and European culture, politics, and history dramatically disproves contemporary critical perceptions of popular gothic romances as universally unskilled hack productions. Equally, the male-authored works considered here raise questions about the frequency with which men wrote, published, and indeed read gothic romances, interrogating the manner in which the literary gothic could align with apparently more serious and masculine genres such as historiography and the historical novel while also contributing to early nineteenth-century attempts to masculinise the novel.[66] Some of these issues are highlighted in the chapters that follow, particularly in Chapter 4, as well as in recent publications on Irish women writers publishing with the Minerva Press.[67] A detailed assessment of the gendered breakdown of Irish gothic authorship and an associated re-mapping of the conventional categories of 'male' and 'female' gothic – as of the subgenres of Romantic-era fiction more widely – is nevertheless the work of another monograph.

Chronologically, this study begins in the 1760s and ends in 1829, a period that provides an effective, if also misleadingly restrictive, time frame for gothic literary production in Ireland. The earliest work it considers is Leland's *Longsword*, a text that highlights contemporary understandings of the term gothic and an associated convergence of literary forms now considered distinctive. This is not to suggest that *Longsword* is the *first* Irish gothic novel; any attempt to locate such a text is, as Killeen argues, not only futile but unnecessarily reductive.[68] Nevertheless, this study follows Killeen's contention that the emergence of Irish gothic fiction begins to become visible in Ireland from the 1750s.[69] In drawing its consideration to a close in 1829, meanwhile, this study works from the belief, as asserted by Connolly, that Catholic Emancipation (1829) fundamentally transformed literary production in Ireland.[70] Again, this is not to deny the rich gothic *oeuvre* of later Irish authors such as Gerald Griffin (1803–40), James

INTRODUCTION

Clarence Mangan (1803–49), Le Fanu, Wilde, and Stoker. Instead, it is to focus on the foundational period of Irish gothic literary production in the context of what has often been understood as 'the rise' of 'the Gothic novel' in eighteenth- and early nineteenth-century Britain and Europe.

Further, as indicated by the title, this book focuses primarily on the novel, but it understands the novel in the loose terms of eighteenth- and nineteenth-century readers and writers. 'The "novel"' in the Romantic period, as Raven notes, 'has no rigid boundary – it can be pseudo-memoir, mock biography, short romance, children's tale, or fused with several other types of fiction (some not in prose, but partly or wholly in verse or written in dramatic parts).'[71] Accordingly, this study is fundamentally alert to the literary genres and forms – short fiction, nonfictional prose, poetry, and drama, that, as Connolly points out, 'surround and shape' the novel in this period.[72] Throughout, discussion of works recognised in modern terms as novels coincides with consideration of dramatic poems, historiographical works, short fiction, and a multitude of other genres and forms. This literature not only informed and often merged with the novel in the eighteenth and nineteenth centuries but also helped define a broader gothic literary production that went beyond the writing of novel-length fiction.

Relatedly, the work presented here is necessarily subdivided into chapters for the reading comfort of the reader, who might otherwise blanch at 200 pages of uninterrupted prose. These divisions are, in a fundamental way, artificial if unavoidable, with the unfortunate consequence of suggesting that the texts discussed in Chapter 1 have little to do with those analysed in Chapter 4. Nothing could be further from the truth. In fact, this study works from the central tenet that the texts examined within its pages form a collective that is, in turn, part of a larger collective or collectives of literature; they therefore necessarily and vitally overlap formally, generically, narratologically, and ideologically with each other, but also with other bodies of literature, defined nationally, generically, and formally, not considered here. For the sake of opening up Irish literature in the wider context of British and European Romanticism, however, it has been necessary, in a sense, to close it down by way of a particular focus on the texts and topics described above.

Finally, this study works from the understanding that plurality is an inescapable feature of gothic literary production. Accordingly, it very deliberately does not offer alternative definitions or labels to replace 'Irish Gothic' and 'the Gothic novel'. Moreover, while it works against the tendency to view gothic literature as a particular genre or canon, it does not advocate the systematic application of substitute ideas such as tradition, form, register, or mode, though it occasionally adopts the latter for ease of reference, particularly in Chapter 1. Otherwise, it uses what Suzanne Rintoul calls 'the [scholarly] inability to define the Gothic' to shape its own 'workable [mode] of interpretation' based on the Romantic period's own constructions of the term gothic and the cultural activity that might be associated with it.[73] Doing so helps us to get away from the restrictive and unrepresentative limitations signified by retrospective scholarly categorisations and allows us to appreciate the rich, historically and culturally specific plenitude of gothic literary production in the Romantic period.

With these considerations in mind, this book approaches its subject matter with the sense of humble elation described by Moretti, when he writes,

> graphs, maps, and trees place the literary field literally in front of our eyes – and show us how little we still know about it. It is a double lesson, of humility and euphoria at the same time: humility for what literary history has accomplished so far (not enough), and euphoria for what still remains to be done (a lot).[74]

Further, in its focus on Irish gothic fiction and, more particularly, Irish gothic novels, it acknowledges at one and the same time the sheer number of hitherto overlooked texts and the continued need for greater attention to such literature in all its forms. In this, it echoes the desire expressed by Rolf and Magda Loeber in their magisterial *Guide to Irish fiction*, that this work might 'fuel enthusiasm and energy' for future research. As with the Loebers, the hope is that this discussion will prompt readers to 'marvel at the richness of what constitutes Irish fiction', while they continue, in Moretti's terms, 'to widen the domain of the literary historian, and enrich its internal problematic' by further consideration of Irish gothic literature and its cross-formal, cross-generic nature.[75]

NOTES

1 Elizabeth Griffith, 'Conjugal fidelity: or, female fortitude', in Elizabeth Griffith and Oliver Goldsmith (eds), *Novellettes, selected for the use of young ladies and gentlemen* (London, 1780), p. 182. Subsequent references are to this edition and are given in parentheses in the text.
2 Siobhán Kilfeather, 'The gothic novel', in John Wilson Foster (ed.), *The Cambridge companion to the Irish novel* (Cambridge: Cambridge University Press, 2006), p. 80.

3 As discussed at greater length later in this introduction, this book avoids the use of the labels 'the Gothic novel' and 'Irish Gothic', except in inverted commas, as a method of highlighting the misleading and restrictive nature of these terms. It relies instead on largely undetermined forms: gothic and Irish gothic literature, Irish gothic literary production, the literary gothic, etc. Moreover, it capitalises the term gothic only when it is used to signify, as it did for eighteenth- and early nineteenth-century writers, an alternately barbarous and glorious past, as discussed in more detail on pp. 5–7.

4 For such readings, see, amongst others, Margot Gayle Backus, *The gothic family romance: heterosexuality, child sacrifice, and the Anglo-Irish colonial order* (Durham, NC: Duke University Press, 1999); William Patrick Day, *In the circles of fear and desire* (Chicago: University of Chicago Press, 1985); Roy Foster, *Paddy and Mr Punch: connections in Irish and English history* (London: Penguin, 1995); and Julian Moynahan, *Anglo-Irish: the literary imagination in a hyphenated culture* (Princeton, NJ: Princeton University Press, 1995).

5 Robert Miles, *Gothic writing, 1750–1820: a genealogy* (London: Routledge, 1993), p. 1.

6 David Punter, *The literature of terror*, 2 vols (2nd edn; London: Longman Group, 1996), vol. 1, p. 1.

7 James Watt, *Contesting the gothic: fiction, genre and cultural conflict, 1764–1832* (Cambridge: Cambridge University Press, 1999), p. 1; Richard Haslam, 'Irish gothic', in Catherine Spooner and Emma McEvoy (eds), *The Routledge companion to gothic* (London: Routledge, 2007), p. 86. See also E.J. Clery, 'The genesis of "Gothic" fiction', in Jerrold E. Hogle (ed.), *The Cambridge companion to gothic fiction* (Cambridge: Cambridge University Press, 2002), p. 21.

8 See Franco Moretti, 'The slaughterhouse of literature', *MLQ: modern language quarterly*, 61.1 (2000), 207–27.

9 Watt, *Contesting the gothic*, p. 1.

10 Jarlath Killeen, 'Making monsters: creating the Catholic Other in Sir John Temple's mythology of the 1641 rebellion', *Gothic Ireland: horror and the Irish imagination in the long eighteenth century* (Dublin: Four Courts Press, 2005), pp. 28–54.

11 Charlene Adair counts at least ten new editions of *The Irish rebellion* between 1646 and 1812, including 1713 (Dublin), 1716 (Dublin), 1724 (Dublin), 1746 (London), 1766 (Cork), and 1799 (Dublin), all designed to remind the Protestant population of Catholic untrustworthiness and to stir up anti-Catholic feelings, particularly at times of unrest; Adair, 'The trial of Lord Maguire and "print culture"', in Eamon Darcy, Annaleigh Margey, and Elaine Murphy (eds), *The 1641 depositions and the Irish Rebellion* (London: Pickering & Chatto, 2012), p. 180. On the similar function of sermons preached on 23 October, see Toby Barnard, 'The uses of 23 October 1641 and Irish Protestant celebrations', *English historical review*, 106 (1991), 889–920.

12 Adair, 'The trial of Lord Maguire', p. 180.
13 Martyn J. Powell, *Britain and Ireland in the eighteenth-century crisis of empire* (Basingstoke and New York: Palgrave Macmillan, 2003), p. 164.
14 Killeen, *Gothic Ireland*, p. 54.
15 On the diminution of 'the absolute, all-engrossing importance that the Protestant-Catholic conflicts had had throughout the seventeenth century' following the Jacobite Rebellion (1745) and under the influence of Irish Patriotism, see Joep Leerssen, *Mere Irish and Fíor-Ghael: studies in the idea of Irish nationality, its development and literary expression prior to the nineteenth century* (Cork: Cork University Press and Field Day, 1996), pp. 308–15. For the suggestion that this argument may not apply to the closing decades of the eighteenth century, see Sean Connolly, 'Patriotism and nationalism', in Alvin Jackson (ed.), *The Oxford handbook of modern Irish history* (Oxford: Oxford University Press, 2014), p. 33.
16 See Claire Connolly, *A cultural history of the Irish novel, 1790–1829* (Cambridge: Cambridge University Press, 2011); Niall Gillespie, 'Irish Jacobin gothic, c. 1796–1825', in Christina Morin and Niall Gillespie (eds), *Irish gothics: genres, forms, modes, and traditions, 1760–1890* (Basingstoke and New York: Palgrave Macmillan, 2014), pp. 58–73; Richard Haslam, 'Maturin's Catholic heirs: expanding the limits of Irish gothic', in Morin and Gillespie (eds), *Irish gothics*, pp. 113–29; and Emer Nolan, *Catholic emancipations: Irish fiction from Thomas Moore to James Joyce* (Syracuse, NY: Syracuse University Press, 2007).
17 Anne Williams, *Art of darkness: a poetics of gothic* (Chicago: University of Chicago Press, 1995), p. 13.
18 Franco Moretti, *The novel*, 2 vols (London: Verso, 2005), vol. 1, p. x.
19 Ian Campbell Ross, 'Mapping Ireland in early fiction', *Irish university review*, 41.1 (2011), 1.
20 Watt, *Contesting the gothic*, p. 14.
21 Clare O'Halloran, *Golden ages and barbarous nations: antiquarian debate and cultural politics in Ireland, c. 1750–1800* (Cork: Cork University Press and Field Day, 2004), pp. 41, 56.
22 William Molyneux, *The case of Ireland … stated* (Dublin, 1698); quoted in O'Halloran, *Golden ages and barbarous nations*, p. 57; Watt, *Contesting the gothic*, p. 14.
23 As Clery points out, only one 'significant work' to follow *Otranto* actually used the descriptor 'Gothic' in its title: Clara Reeve's *The old English baron: a gothic story* (1778), a revision of Reeve's earlier tale, *The champion of virtue* (1777); Clery, 'The genesis of "Gothic" fiction', p. 21.
24 Clery, 'The genesis of "Gothic" fiction', p. 21.
25 *Monthly Review*, 32 (May 1765), 394.
26 Horace Walpole, *The castle of Otranto*, ed. W.S. Lewis, introd. E.J. Clery (1764; Oxford: Oxford University Press, 2008), p. 8. Further references are to this edition and are given in parentheses in the text.

27 Clara Reeve, *The progress of romance, through times, countries, and manners; with remarks on the good and bad effects of it, on them respectively; in a course of evening conversations* (1785), in Gary Kelly (ed.), *Bluestocking feminism: writings of the Bluestocking Circle, 1738–1785, Volume 6: Sarah Scott and Clara Reeve* (London: Pickering & Chatto, 1999), pp. 163, 173.

28 Richard Maxwell, 'The historiography of fiction in the Romantic period', in Richard Maxwell and Katie Trumpener (eds), *The Cambridge companion to fiction in the Romantic period* (Cambridge: Cambridge University Press, 2008), p. 9.

29 Reeve, *The progress of romance*, p. 172.

30 *Ibid.*, p. 171.

31 Noting that 'the 1780s have been almost universally misrecognized as a fallow period before the boom of the 1790s', Clery argues that this is actually a period of 'escalating debate on the origins and character of romance', as manifest in both *The castle of Otranto* and 'Conjugal fidelity'. The resulting 'romance wars', Clery further contends, were directly relevant to the development of gothic literature; Clery, 'The genesis of "Gothic" fiction', p. 34.

32 For a succinct summation of the different arguments surrounding this terminological dispute, see Christina Morin and Niall Gillespie, 'Introduction: de-limiting the Irish gothic', in Morin and Gillespie (eds), *Irish gothics*, pp. 1–3.

33 Kilfeather, 'The gothic novel', p. 83.

34 Alexandra Warwick, 'Feeling gothicky?', *Gothic studies*, 9.1 (2007), 6–7.

35 *Ibid.*, 6.

36 See David Duff, *Romanticism and the uses of genre* (Oxford: Oxford University Press, 2009), pp. 161, 45.

37 Julia M. Wright, *Representing the national landscape in Irish Romanticism* (Syracuse, NY: Syracuse University Press, 2014), pp. 166, xxvi.

38 Terry Hale, 'French and German gothic: the beginnings', in Hogle (ed.), *The Cambridge companion to gothic fiction*, p. 63.

39 Siobhán Kilfeather, Jarlath Killeen, Rolf and Magda Loeber, and W.J. McCormack are among the handful of scholars to identify late eighteenth-century texts in their assessments of Irish gothic literary production. See, in particular, Kilfeather, 'The gothic novel'; Siobhán Kilfeather, 'Origins of the Irish female gothic', *Bullán*, 1.2 (1994), 34–45; Jarlath Killeen, *The emergence of Irish gothic fiction: history, origins, theories* (Edinburgh: Edinburgh University Press, 2014); Rolf Loeber and Magda Stouthamer-Loeber, 'The publication of Irish novels and novelettes, 1750–1829: a footnote on Irish gothic fiction', *Cardiff Corvey: reading the Romantic text*, 10 (2003), 17–44, www.romtext.org.uk/articles/cc10_n02, accessed 4 October 2016; and W.J. McCormack, 'Irish gothic and after (1820–1945)', in Seamus Deane (ed.), *The Field Day anthology of Irish writing*, vol. 2 (Derry: Field Day, 1991), pp. 831–949.

40 Loeber and Stouthamer-Loeber, 'The publication of Irish novels and novelettes', p. 28. Loeber and Stouthamer-Loeber also identify the anonymously published *The adventures of Miss Sophia Berkley* (Dublin, 1760) as another Irish precursor to *The castle of Otranto*. As it turns out, though, *Sophia Berkley* is actually a pirated edition of *The history of Amanda* (London, 1758); see Christina Morin and Jarlath Killeen, 'The new adventures of Miss Sophia Berkley: revisiting Ireland's "first" gothic novel', *Eighteenth-century Ireland*, 29 (2014), 155–63.

41 Franco Moretti, *Graphs, maps, trees: abstract models for literary history* (2005; London: Verso, 2007), p. 4.

42 Franco Moretti, 'Conjectures on world literature', *New left review*, 1 (2000), 57; quoted in Ross, 'Mapping Ireland in early fiction', p. 4. Original emphasis.

43 Ross, 'Mapping Ireland in early fiction', p. 4.

44 *Ibid.*, p. 16.

45 Franco Moretti, *Atlas of the European novel, 1800–1900* (London: Verso, 1998), p. 3.

46 *Ibid.*, pp. 3, 70. Original emphasis.

47 Moretti, *Graphs, maps, trees*, p. 2.

48 Robert Miles, 'The 1790s: the effulgence of gothic', in Hogle (ed.), *The Cambridge companion to gothic fiction*, p. 41.

49 Andrew Piper, *Dreaming in books: the making of the bibliographic imagination in the Romantic age* (Chicago: University of Chicago Press, 2009), p. 65. Piper uses this phrase in his discussion of the centrality of the novella collection in the Romantic period and its ability 'to address the problem of literary repetition and the bibliographic copy'. Here, it is repurposed to suggest the remarkable circulation of Roche's fiction and that of many of her contemporaries.

50 Williams, *Art of darkness*, p. 1.

51 See Montague Summers, 'Historical gothic', *The gothic quest: a history of the gothic novel* (1938; New York: Russell & Russell, 1964), pp. 153–201.

52 Chris Baldick and Robert Mighall, 'Gothic criticism', in David Punter (ed.), *A companion to the gothic* (London: Blackwell, 2001), p. 214.

53 Watt, *Contesting the gothic*, p. 3. Other common 'generic pointers' used by authors to signify gothic content, as Robert Miles has shown, include 'historical romance, legends, tales, memoir, [and] traditions'; Miles, 'The 1790s: the effulgence of gothic', p. 41.

54 Watt, *Contesting the gothic*, p. 5.

55 *Ibid.*

56 On the separation of regional and national fiction from gothic fiction in the literary history of Irish Romanticism, see Christina Morin, '"Gothic" and "national"? Challenging the formal distinctions of Irish Romantic fiction',

in Jim Kelly (ed.), *Ireland and Romanticism: publics, nations and scenes of cultural production* (Basingstoke and New York: Palgrave Macmillan, 2011), pp. 172–87.
57 Kilfeather, 'Origins of the Irish female gothic', 42.
58 Piper, *Dreaming in books*, p. 11. Original emphasis.
59 *Ibid.*, p. 12.
60 Connolly, *A cultural history of the Irish novel*, p. 18.
61 *Ibid.*
62 I am grateful to Orla Murphy for highlighting this possibility at a research seminar I was invited to give at University College Cork on 3 December 2014.
63 Moretti, *Atlas of the European novel*, p. 15.
64 James Raven has detailed the proportion of male to female authorship in the latter half of the eighteenth century, observing, 'Novels by identified male writers outnumber those by women writers by more than two to one in the 1770s'. By the 1780s, though, these figures begin to change, and the ratio of men to women starts to balance out and, indeed, reverse; 'Historical introduction: the novel comes of age', in James Raven and Antonia Forster (eds), *The English novel 1770–1829: a bibliographical survey of prose fiction published in the British Isles. Volume 1: 1770–1799* (Oxford: Oxford University Press, 2000), pp. 48, 49.
65 See Ellen Moers, 'Female gothic', *Literary women* (1963; London: The Women's Press, 1978), pp. 90–110.
66 On the masculinisation of the novel in Romantic-era fiction, see, in particular, Ina Ferris, *The achievement of literary authority: gender, history, and the Waverley Novels* (Ithaca, NY: Cornell University Press, 1991) and Jacqueline Pearson, 'Masculinizing the novel: women writers and intertextuality in Charles Robert Maturin's *The wild Irish boy*', *Studies in Romanticism*, 36.4 (1997), 635–50.
67 See Christina Morin, '"At a distance from [my] country": Henrietta Rouvière Mosse, the Minerva Press, and the negotiation of Irishness in the Romantic literary marketplace', *European Romantic review*, 28.4 (2017), 447–60; and 'Irish gothic goes abroad: cultural migration, materiality, and the Minerva Press', in Marguérite Corporaal and Christina Morin (eds), *Traveling Irishness in the long nineteenth century* (Basingstoke and New York: Palgrave Macmillan, 2017), pp. 185–203.
68 Killeen, *The emergence of Irish gothic fiction*, p. 71.
69 *Ibid.*, p. 12.
70 Connolly argues that Catholic Emancipation 'ended a formative phase of the history of the Irish novel'; Connolly, *A cultural history of the Irish novel*, p. 196.
71 James Raven, 'The anonymous novel in Britain and Ireland, 1750–1830', in Robert J. Griffin (ed.), *The faces of anonymity: anonymous and pseudonymous*

publication from the sixteenth to the twentieth century (Basingstoke and New York: Palgrave Macmillan, 2003), p. 142.
72 Connolly, *A cultural history of the Irish novel*, p. 14.
73 Suzanne Rintoul, 'Gothic anxieties: struggling with a definition', *Eighteenth-century fiction*, 17.4 (2005), 709.
74 Moretti, *Graphs, maps, trees*, p. 2.
75 Rolf and Magda Loeber, with Anne Mullin Burnham, *A guide to Irish fiction, 1650-1900* (Dublin: Four Courts Press, 2006), p. cv; Moretti, *Graphs, maps, trees*, p. 2.

I

Gothic temporalities: 'Gothicism', 'historicism', and the overlap of fictional modes from Thomas Leland to Walter Scott

∾

In 1762, Thomas Leland, a Church of Ireland clergyman, historian, and Professor of Oratory at Trinity College Dublin, published his only novel, *Longsword, Earl of Salisbury*. Praised by *The Critical Review* as 'a new and agreeable species of writing, in which the beauties of poetry, and the advantages of history are happily united', *Longsword* enjoyed both favourable reviews and popular acclaim.[1] It was reprinted in 1763, 1766, 1775, and 1790, and twice adapted for the stage as *The Countess of Salisbury*.[2] Yet, the novel remains little read today. In its twinned contemporary approbation and current neglect, *Longsword* stands in direct contrast to Walpole's *The castle of Otranto* (1764), which famously provoked controversy, especially on the publication of its revised second edition, and now enjoys the relatively uncontested reputation as the *first* British gothic novel. However, it is worth remembering that Walpole's tale and its self-description as 'a Gothic story' appeared in a context in which several, often competing connotations of the term gothic held wide sway in the British popular imagination. It also bears repeating that, in Walpole's wake, very few writers adopted the terminology 'gothic' to describe their fiction, defying the common critical assumption that Walpole began a new literary craze with *Otranto* and, thus, gave birth to 'the Gothic novel' as we now know it. Such thinking fosters a neat and compartmentalised notion of the literary gothic and late eighteenth-century fiction as a whole that is at odds with the reality. The unfortunate effect is the marginalisation of texts such as *Longsword* that eschewed Walpole's overt supernaturalism while pursuing a similar critical exploration of the fraught transition from pre-modernity to modernity.

Compellingly identified by Montague Summers as an important example of 'historical gothic' fiction, *Longsword* unsettles many of the expectations we now have for 'the Gothic novel': the tale is primarily set in England, during the reign of Henry III (r. 1216–72); there are no ghosts, goblins, or witches, and the anti-Catholic element of the story focuses not so much on the abuses of the Church but on a kind of institutional corruption that is seen to plague even the highest realms of the nation.[3] In fact, much of the narrative appears to function as a veiled political commentary, lamenting the weakness of a monarch who has allowed himself to be governed completely by an evil minion and urging the return to 'a wise and virtuous rule' rooted in England's long history of liberty.[4] The restitution of such a rule and the king's regained sovereignty by the novel's conclusion indicates Leland's concern with the past as providing essential lessons for the present, particularly in terms of governmental rule and the security of individual rights and liberties.

With its central interest in British history's relevance to contemporary society, *Longsword* has readily lent itself to analysis as an early example of the historical novel more commonly associated with Sir Walter Scott.[5] The gothic elements of the text indicated by Summers' terminology have less frequently garnered attention. Rolf and Magda Loeber describe *Longsword* as a pre-*Otranto* gothic novel owing to its inclusion of 'the odious monk, Reginald, the sire of an unholy brood of monastic fiends and baronial tyrants, who appears in scenes of suspense and terror.'[6] A more convincing argument for *Longsword*'s 'gothicism' lies precisely in the novel's 'historicism'. *Longsword*'s use of history compellingly speaks to contemporary perceptions of Gothic as evocative of the past, its people, and its traditions. In this, Leland's tale underlines the cross-formal and cross-generic nature of gothic literature as it developed in the latter half of the eighteenth century. Investigating *Longsword* as an early example of either historical *or* gothic fiction, not both, does an injustice to the text. It also effectively misunderstands the overlap of historical and gothic literary modes in the late eighteenth and early nineteenth centuries.[7]

The same is arguably true for *The castle of Otranto*. Condemned for its excesses and overt supernaturalism, the second edition of *Otranto* was associated with a misleading depiction of the past and its relationship to the present. This was the primary source of concern for critics, as noted in this book's introduction: that *Otranto*'s depiction of history might yield misconceptions about Walpole's contemporary England. Even in its first edition, *Otranto* was understood primarily by way of its relationship to the past and viewed as a kind of antiquarian curio that could reveal much about a bygone society and culture. Tellingly, Scott spoke of *Otranto* with particular reference to its 'accurate display of human character' and its faithful depiction of 'domestic life and manners, during the feudal times, as might actually have existed'.[8] As Maxwell contends, Scott understood *Otranto* as 'a landmark experiment in the practice of antiquarian historical fiction'. In turn, Maxwell argues, *Otranto* became a crucial influence in the construction of history in Scott's own novels.[9]

Thanks to Scott's pronounced hesitancy to acknowledge his literary influences, the significance of the gothic historicism of texts such as *Longsword* and *Otranto* goes relatively unnoticed.[10] Critical attention to Scott has encouraged the perception of him as the uncontested progenitor of a new genre – the historical novel – notwithstanding the fact that, as Katie Trumpener observes, 'most of the conceptual innovations att[r]ibuted to Scott were in 1814 already established commonplaces of the British novel'.[11] Georg Lukács simultaneously termed *The castle of Otranto* 'the most famous "historical novel" of the eighteenth century' and dismissed Walpole's treatment of history as 'mere costumery' brooking no comparison with the depiction of historical character in Scott's novels.[12] Subsequent scholarship has generally followed suit, proclaiming Scott the creator, *ex nihilo*, of the historical novel with the publication of *Waverley* (1814). In this scenario, the historicism of Walpole's text is categorised as different in kind from that of Scott's historical novel. Correspondingly, any gothic elements evident in Scott's fiction are accidental, rather than symptomatic of the convergence of historical and gothic modes in the late eighteenth and early nineteenth centuries.

Against the abjuration of influence enacted by Scott and modern scholarship alike, this chapter traces the vital inherence of gothic and historical modes from roughly 1762 to 1825. The first section of the chapter focuses on *Otranto* and *Longsword* as specific interventions into contemporary discourse concerning history, historiography, and the transition to modernity. Rather than view such engagement with the past as confined to a later historical fiction tradition more commonly associated with Scott, this section insists that the largely retrospective distinction between late eighteenth-century historical and gothic fiction is misleading. Both *Longsword* and *Otranto*, it argues, demonstrate how inherently intertwined these terms and the literary forms they have come to connote were for their authors and contemporary society. Both texts similarly underline the very different notions of the term gothic late eighteenth-century writers had in comparison to twentieth- and twenty-first-century constructions. Comparative analysis of these texts as at once gothic and historical thus provides a fresh perspective on the origins of British gothic literature. This is true not just in its re-integration of Leland's tale into the literary history of the gothic, but also in its suggestion of a more nuanced understanding of the formal, generic, and ideological fluidity that produced the literary gothic.

The second section of this chapter further examines the intersection of historical and gothic modes in the eighteenth century, evaluating several texts that might be seen as the direct inheritors of the historical gothicism of *Longsword* and *The castle of Otranto*. Published primarily in the period between *The castle of Otranto* and what has been called 'the effulgence of Gothic' that occurred in the 1790s,[13] these texts defy the prevalent belief that the literary gothic lay relatively dormant in the 1770s and 1780s.[14] Fully engaged in negotiating the relationship between the present and the Gothic past – social, cultural, and political – these texts, including Anne Fuller's *Alan Fitz-Osborne* (1789) and the works of James White (1759–99), beginning with *Earl Strongbow* (1789), demonstrate that Irish authors in the wake of Leland and Walpole routinely queried the meaning of a Gothic heritage to eighteenth-century Britain.

The final section of the chapter considers the mutable boundaries between gothic and historical modes in fiction produced from 1814 and the ostensible introduction of 'the historical novel' onwards. Anne H. Stevens argues that gothic and historical fiction began markedly to differentiate themselves by the 1790s, when 'two separate traditions with two different and recognizable sets of features' had emerged. As a result of this process of distinction, Stevens contends, what Scott really develops with his Waverley novels is a discrete 'novelistic subgenre', identifiable, despite variations and experimentation, by a specific set of characteristics that helps distinguish it from other forms of prose fiction.[15] Nevertheless, Stevens admits, the 'generic features' associated with historical and gothic fiction continue to 'overlap', even after the two forms had become unique in the late eighteenth century.[16] This sustained formal intersection emphasises the continuity between historical gothic fictions of the latter half of the eighteenth century and those of Scott and his contemporaries. It also encourages a reassessment of traditional paradigms of the development of the novel in contemporary Ireland. Conventional arguments insist that the historical novel as exemplified by the Waverley novels never found a successful Irish expression thanks to historical, political, and cultural circumstances that rendered Scott's conservative narrative of progress abortive. However, as this chapter demonstrates, Scott's fictions reveal a similar take on the Gothic past as that found in several important, if overlooked, examples of early nineteenth-century Irish fiction.

HORACE WALPOLE, THOMAS LELAND, AND THE GOTHIC PAST

By the time he published *Longsword* in 1762, Thomas Leland had already established himself as a serious man of letters, editing, with John Stoke, *The Philipic Orations of Demosthenes* (1754), translating Demosthenes's *Orations* (1756–60), and publishing *A history of the life and reign of Philip, King of Macedon* (1758). In this context, Leland's only novel is often presented as generically closer to historiography than fiction, an assessment in keeping with Leland's own advertisement of *Longsword* as a kind of history-writing. The preface to the novel, in fact, claims that '[t]he out-lines of the following story; and some of the incidents and more minute circumstances, are to be found in the antient English historians' (*Longsword*, vol. 1, [p. iv]). Contemporary criticism of the novel eagerly adopted Leland's own emphasis on historical truths, praising the novel's foundation 'on real facts' and dismissing its reference to itself as a 'romance' as generically inappropriate and far too 'modest'.[17] Although Leland refrained from detailing his source material, his use of 'identifiable historical sources' is clear, as Maxwell observes.[18] The resulting 'sense of chronology' evident in *Longsword* bears comparison with that of preceding historical prose fiction by writers such as Madame de Lafayette (1634–93), Courtilz de Sandras (1644–1712), and the abbé Prévost (1697–1763).[19] It also seemed to invite reviews that focused on the novel's historical content and praised it for its edifying recourse to the past. Naming *Longsword* 'a new and agreeable species of writing', *The Critical Review* underlined the novel's informative and instructive historicism: 'The story of this romance (as he modestly entitles it) is founded on real facts, and without doing any great violence to truth, pleases the imagination, at the same time that it improves the heart'.[20] Similarly, the *Monthly Review* recommended *Longsword* as a tale in which '[t]he truth of history is artfully interwoven with agreeable fictions, and interesting episodes' in such a way 'that no species of writing could *amuse* with less injury to the morals, and *virtuous manners* of the Reader'.[21]

The terms by which *Longsword* was assessed are also intriguingly present in the reviews of *The castle of Otranto*. Even before Walpole appended the subtitle 'a Gothic story' to the second edition of his tale, *Otranto* was concerned with exploring and representing the Gothic past, both as a barbaric, pre-modern era, and as an important phase in the conception of political liberty and virtue. Accordingly, the novel's reception, in its first and second editions, revolved largely around its conceptualisation of the past and, in particular, its representation of that past's relationship to the present. As has been well rehearsed by critics of the literary gothic and of eighteenth-century British literature, the first edition of Walpole's tale, presented as 'an ancient Italian manuscript' written by 'Onuphrio Muralto, Canon of the Church of St. Nicholas at Otranto' and later discovered, translated, and printed by 'William Marshal', appealed to critics, who understood it as an intriguing historical artefact (*Castle of Otranto*, p. 1). Referring to the savagery of the time period that supposedly produced the tale, the *Monthly Review* praised *Otranto* as a relic of the past able to reveal much about the past to modern readers willing to endure 'the absurdities of Gothic fiction'.[22] The critical about-face performed by the *Monthly Review* upon the publication of the second edition of *Otranto* was a direct response to Walpole's revelation that his tale was not, in fact, an authentic historical object, but instead a modern production masquerading as one. The problem, for critics, was the conflation of past and present enacted by this revelation. As the *Monthly Review* contemptuously declared, viewing *Otranto* as a truly 'Gothic' text, 'we could readily excuse its preposterous phenomena, and consider them as sacrifices to a gross and unenlightened age'. When, however, the tale is pronounced 'a modern performance, the indulgence we offered to the foibles of a supposed antiquity, we can by no means extend to the singularity of a false tale in a cultivated period of learning'. The *Monthly Review* concluded by excoriating Walpole for debasing himself and, implicitly, society as a whole, by his reification of a brutal past.[23]

The critical uproar caused by the second edition of *Otranto* pointed to the ways in which Walpole's tale, however glib, was seen subversively to question Enlightenment views of the present's relationship to the past.[24] Against the Enlightenment 'narrative of progress', *Otranto* posited a troubling historical continuity instead.[25] In this, according to the *Monthly Review*, *Otranto*'s use of the supernatural was of particular concern, precisely because it emphasised the disturbing lack of temporal distance between past and present. As Clery observes, 'Rationally speaking, ghosts and goblins are not *true*, but when they appear in the literary artifacts of past ages, they are *true to history* ... For the enlightened reader, ancient romances are at once fictions *and* historical documents'. By this thinking, Clery adds, that which 'allows for the depiction of irrational impossibilities in works from the distant past' is also that which 'must ... disallow it in modern fictions'.[26] What made the second edition of *Otranto* so threatening, then, was its suggestion that superstitious beliefs lived on in the eighteenth century, defying the period's view of itself as an enlightened age: 'Description gives rise to prescription', Clery writes, 'a nation guided by reason, in an age of reason, will not produce modern literary works which could be mistaken for the products of the age of superstition; if such a work does appear, it must not be countenanced'.[27]

Yet, while the *Monthly Review* represented *Otranto* as an anachronistic production at odds with eighteenth-century rationality, it did so by way of a curious appeal to the language of superstition: '*Incredulus odi*, is, or ought to be a charm against all such infatuation'.[28] 'To disbelieve is to dislike', the *Monthly Review* asserted.[29] It thus drew a definitive line between the first edition of *Otranto* as an historical artefact to be wondered at and empirically assessed and the second edition as a false and therefore more threatening representation of history and, perhaps more importantly, its relationship to the present. At the same time, the review linked rational disbelief to the same irrational and superstitious ideas for which it condemned *Otranto*: enlightenment understanding, it proposed, necessarily acts as 'a charm' to ward off 'infatuation'. The *Monthly Review*'s striking combination of superstition and empirical scepticism in this instance evidences, in Diane Long Hoeveler's phrase, 'the rise of ambivalent secularization' in the latter half of the eighteenth century.[30] The literary gothic, for Hoeveler, is the product of the shift between religion-dominated early modern European society to more secular, less religiously inflected social models under the pressure of various socio-political and socio-cultural changes in the mid-eighteenth century. Despite the emphasis in the latter half of the eighteenth century on an Enlightenment understanding of rational historical and social progress, Hoeveler asserted, popular gothic productions such as operas, melodramas, chapbooks, and ballads, not to mention novels, continually referred back to 'the realms of the supernatural, the sacred, the maternal, the primitive, the numinous, and [the uncanny]' even as they sought to confine such elements rigidly to the past.[31] What we see in gothic literature, Hoeveler contended, 'is not a simple forward-moving trajectory that we would recognize as the Enlightenment project', but, instead, 'an oscillation in which the transcendent and traditional religious beliefs and tropes are alternately preserved and reanimated and then blasted and condemned' – a wavering strikingly present in the *Monthly Review*'s appraisal of *Otranto* as well.[32]

As is clear from the contrasting critical reception of the first and second editions of *Otranto*, the tale's overt supernaturalism presented a simultaneous flirtation with and condemnation of atavistic superstition, a movement that is intrinsically linked throughout to competing notions of historical progression. In this sense, *Otranto*'s debt to preceding historical fiction is clear. Prévost's fiction, for example, has been understood as 'pre-Gothic' in its charting of a widespread contemporary 'fear of violent change and its effects on what had been a stable class system'.[33] In other words, it anticipates the anxieties about social transformation evidenced in *Otranto*, as in *Longsword* before it. Where Prévost's works fearfully depict 'violent change', Leland and Walpole instead suggest what was perhaps more threatening still: that there had been essentially no change or progress from past to present. As with eighteenth-century antiquarian research, in fact, *Otranto* highlighted, in Rosemary Sweet's phrase, 'the constant interaction between past and present'.[34] In so doing, Walpole's text constructed eighteenth-century society as not only indebted to, but essentially a mirror of, the Gothic past it affected to portray.

What set Leland's *Longsword* apart from *Otranto* was its lack of supernatural content. Without *Otranto*'s explicit depictions of the paranormal, Leland's tale could be seen to deny any unsettling link between past and present in support of Enlightenment ideals of historical progression. This is suggested by *Longsword*'s critical reception. From its publication, Leland's novel was reviewed favourably and, as Watt points out, 'widely praised'.[35] This was so, Clery maintains, because the novel 'was presented unequivocally as a work of the present which depicted the medieval age in the manner approved by the present'. *Longsword* was thus seen '[to offer] "the advantages of history" – an informative picture of the past which illustrated progress while stimulating through its strangeness – but without corrupting the faculty of judgement with fantastic improbabilities'.[36] For Clery, the popularity of Leland's novel, as well as its 'universally favourable and unproblematic' reception, owed primarily to the author's 'exclu[sion of] any hint of the supernatural or marvellous'. In resisting the lure of the numinous, Leland was able to appeal to and satisfy contemporary taste for 'images of the gothic past as [already evident in the works of] Macpherson, Walpole and Chatterton' while simultaneously avoiding the threatening suggestion of the present age's regression to or lack of progression from former unenlightened superstitions or religious dominance.[37]

As *Longsword* is so little read today, a brief summary of the tale is useful. The narrative recounts the Ulyssean wanderings of its hero, William, Earl of Longsword, as he travels from France to England after having victoriously prevented French usurpation of English-held lands in France. Like Odysseus, William finds his homecoming both protracted and problematic, not simply because of the misadventures he meets in trying to reach that home but also because his native country offers very little welcome to the returned hero. In fact, William's homeland spectacularly scorns its defender's earlier longing and disproves his belief in his country's essential difference – one based on notions of liberty and governmental justice – from France. Rather than triumphant processions and tears of joy, William returns to a continuation of the struggles he experienced in France. In his absence, his castle has been invaded by Raymond, nephew of the King of England's corrupt and controlling chief counsel, Hubert; William's wife has been informed of his death, and his young son has been sent away to a secret destination. As William struggles to reach his home, his wife, Ela, is subjected to Raymond's lascivious advances and eventually forcefully dragged to the altar in a sham marriage ceremony interrupted at the fateful moment by a messenger bearing the news that William is actually alive. His return to his castle instigates a righting of the private and public wrongs committed in his absence – Raymond hangs himself rather than face justice; Ela and William are re-united; their son is returned to them, and, further afield, the king ousts his evil right hand man and regains authority and control over himself and his kingdom.

With such a conclusion, *Longsword* seems clearly to invite allegorical political readings such as those advanced by Fiona Price and James Watt.[38] These will be discussed later in this chapter. Here, it is worth pausing on the manner in which *Longsword* envisions a telling overlap of past and present, pre-modern and modern, which, owing to the novel's apparent lack of unearthly events, becomes inherently more terrifying, precisely because more rational and plausible, than anything in *Otranto*. Just as with Walpole's later text, in fact, nothing is as it seems in *Longsword*, and, while critics applauded the novel's lack of 'marvellous' events, Leland's tale retains striking – if subtle – remnants of the supernaturalism for which the second edition of *Otranto* was later harshly condemned. A case in point: after having vanquished his French foe, William envisions a triumphant return to England 'loaded with the sports of Gascoigne', but his journey is impeded by a vengeful Nature: 'winds and seas conspired together, and united their unrelenting fury against the bands of England: when the roaring hurricane deafened us with its horrid menaces, and the frequent lightning served to disclose all the terrors of the gloomy deep' (*Longsword*, vol. 1, pp. 11–12). When the storm abates, William and his men find themselves beset by nature still, in a kind of elemental punishment for unidentified crimes: their battered ship approaches 'a coast utterly unknown' and 'the rock which lay in ambush to destroy us, assailed our vessel; the waves rushed impetuously through the breach'. 'Death', William says, 'stood with open arms to receive his prey!' (*Longsword*, vol. 1, p. 13).

Later, having been captured by his French enemy, Mal-leon, as he attempts to free a friendly Frenchman who had earlier saved his life, William overhears his captors debating his murder in appropriately eerie circumstances: 'It was now the dead midnight hour: on that side where my chamber looked down upon the troubled river, I plainly heard my two guards in dreadful conference encouraging each other to the horrid purpose of murder'. When eventually rescued from this fate, William is described as 'issu[ing] forth as if restored from the grave' (*Longsword*, vol. 1, pp. 27, 28). Such language and its connotation of an inherently porous boundary between life and death as well as the numinous and the rational continues with William's description of D'Aumont, one of Mal-leon's spies. Taken in by D'Aumont's lies, William 'resign[s] [him]self entirely to the influence of this new friend, whose power was like that of those infernal imps who, they say, command the winds to roar or be still, and the waves to swell or to subside, as their wicked purposes require' (*Longsword*, vol. 1, p. 43). Explaining himself further, William suggests that he had been bewitched:

> Hast thou never heard that the enemy of mankind oftentimes presents shocking and frightful phantoms before the eyes of the holy hermit, in order to distract his thoughts and to confound his purposes? Such were the arts by which this Frenchman practiced upon my soul. (*Longsword*, vol. 1, p. 44)

William's usurper, Raymond, also implies that his actions have been the result of a strange enchantment. Determining to leave the home he has invaded before forcefully compelled to do so, Raymond laments, 'Cursed castle! ... cursed be the hour in which I first entered these fatal walls! And for ever cursed be the slaves who forced me, against my better reason, to persevere in cruelty!' (*Longsword*, vol. 2, p. 59).

The novel's conclusion envisions the overthrow of such mystical enthrallment. The king is said to exert himself, breaking the spell held over him by Hubert, and 'ignominiously banish[ing]' his former 'wicked favourite' (*Longsword*, vol. 2, p. 80). The ending thus encourages allegorical interpretations of Leland's tale, published as it was during the Seven Years' War (1756–63). Henry's re-establishment of his rightful rule and the concomitant defeat of enemies both foreign and domestic have frequently been read as a symbolic assertion of (eventual) English triumph over the tyranny and absolutism represented by mid-eighteenth-century France. As Price suggests, Leland's novel urges England not to fall into the trap of 'corrupted values' epitomised by Mal-leon.[39] As if such a warning were too veiled by the fictional nature of the tale, Leland includes what Toni Wein calls a 'eulog[y]' of George III as a 'glorious Monarch' (*Longsword*, vol. 2, p. 71).[40] Against Price's understanding of Leland's caution to eighteenth-century England, Wein reads this praise of George III as a glorification of present British governance, 'a chauvinistic tribute to the homeland', and an attendant understanding of 'the past as debased in comparison with the glorious future that awaits'.[41] However, such readings ignore the manner in which the past – in the form of superstition and enchantment – continues to impinge upon the present and the future, hindering any unproblematic understanding of the novel's optimistic ending. Indeed, while William's apparent resurrection leads to the restoration of his usurped castle and the new ordering of public and private 'homes', the memory of past disruption continues to haunt William's castle in the form of Ela's ongoing insanity. William's triumphant, if long awaited, homecoming is undermined by the blank stare, dejected 'sigh[s]', and 'weeping' with which his senseless wife greets him (*Longsword*, vol. 2, p. 76). Not expecting to find Ela in this state, William gives in, at least momentarily, to despair: 'No word of congratulation! No look of joy! Is this the happiness which my busy fancy formed! Is this my reception!' (*Longsword*, vol. 2, p. 76). Ela is said gradually to recover under William's devoted care, but a suggestive mar on the novel's sanguine conclusion remains.

The novel's ending, then, leaves the reader, like the characters themselves, with an upsetting indication of ongoing disruption – one implicitly upheld by an intriguing textual variant. In the first Dublin edition of the novel, William frames his return home and the incomplete recuperation of his wife in terms that evoke the uncanny, haunting nature of the past and its ability to turn the familiar suddenly strange: 'He now reflected on his wrongs with emotion', we are told (*Longsword*, vol. 2, p. 80). Both the first and second editions of the novel published in London, however, qualify the 'emotion' described with the word 'less': 'He now reflected on his wrongs with less emotion.'[42] The indication is that the passage of time has reconciled William both to what has happened and to the changes past events have wrought in his life. These textual variants produce an ambiguity that underscores the novel's liminality – both comforting and upsetting, both historical and gothic, both pre-modern and modern. As they do so, they undermine any straightforward attempt to read the novel as vindicating present over past, either in fictional or extra-diegetical terms. This indeterminacy is of vital importance in the consideration of the text as a kind of political allegory – an issue to which this chapter now turns.

LELAND'S HEIRS: ANNE FULLER AND JAMES WHITE

In suggesting an ongoing link between past and present, both *Longsword* and *Otranto* posited a threatening proximity between pre-modern and modern, calling upon contemporary understandings of the Gothic past to construct Enlightenment Britain as prey to superstitions and fears putatively consigned to history. At the same time, referencing the apparently contradictory understanding of Gothic as indicative of Britain's noble political roots, Leland and Walpole implied that the nation had become degraded from its august political past. Such a complaint was not new in the 1760s, as suggested by Jonathan Swift's belief, expressed in his correspondence in the 1720s and 1730s, that upon the recovery of 'the Gothic system' relied the present and future liberty of British, as well as European, society as a whole.[43] Swift's views on present politics make it clear that the idea of the Gothic political past as something from which Britain had become far too ideologically removed held wide sway from early in the century. The anxiety with which *Otranto* was met points to a latent fear of acknowledging the kind of social and political regression outlined by Swift. Walpole's self-professed attempt at generic blending intimated 'that there must be something awry in contemporary social order', as W.S. Lewis writes: 'If the conventions of ancient romance can be revived with success by modern authors, then what does that say about the present?'[44] Such thinking clearly feeds into allegorical readings of *Otranto* as exploring questions of rightful inheritance and proper rule. More particularly, *Otranto* is often understood to imagine the (supernatural) overthrow of tyranny and the restoration of legitimate governance at a time when Walpole himself was seriously disaffected with British politics. Over the course of

1763 and 1764, Walpole and his much loved cousin, Henry Seymour Conway, found themselves at odds with the majority feeling in the Commons over a debate centred on the arrest of John Wilkes for seditious libel – a charge related to statements Wilkes had made about the King in the *North Briton*. Severe repercussions fell on Conway, who, in April 1764, was deprived of the civil and military posts he held; so enraged was Walpole at this turn of events that he resolved to overthrow a government that he understood as speedily bringing about 'a return to absolutism'.[45]

In the well-rehearsed arguments about the connection between Walpole's immersion in this tense political affair and *Otranto*, the author is said to channel his discontent with the tyrannical authority of George III and his Tory supporters into an allegory about an equally despotic ruler – Prince Manfred – and his replacement by the legitimate heir to Otranto – Theodore. With the latter representing a wrongfully usurped 'ancient political order', and the former political corruption and degeneration, *Otranto* explores, in Price's terms, 'the opposition between ancient virtue and modern vice'.[46] Price locates a similar investigation in *Longsword*. In that novel, she argues, Leland's self-professed reliance on the truth of history masks his real intent: to comment upon present politics by way of an implicit process of comparison and contrast with the Gothic past.[47] Leland himself cagily disavows any kind of moral lesson along the lines of that applauded by the *Monthly Review*:

> It is generally expected that pieces of this kind should convey some useful moral: which moral, not always, perhaps, the most valuable or refined, is sometimes made to float to the surface of the narrative; or is plucked up at proper intervals, and presented to the view of the reader, with great solemnity. But the author of these sheets hath too high an opinion of the judgment and penetration of his readers, to pursue this method. Although he cannot pretend to be very *deep*, yet he hopes he is *clear*. And if anything lies at bottom, worth the picking up, it will be discovered without his direction. (*Longsword*, vol. 1, unpaginated advertisement)

As Price argues, Leland here 'implies that the language that describes history is not only invisible but ideologically neutral. Any moral lesson issues from the substance of history itself'. Correspondingly, Price contends, *Longsword* becomes an allegory, 'us[ing] the reign of Henry III, when territories had just been won in Gascony, to warn George III about the dangers of favouritism and absolutism'.[48]

Price thus views *Longsword* as an allegorical critique, however 'politically cautious', of existing political structures in Britain.[49] Watt, meanwhile, understands the text as foundational in the establishment of what he calls 'the Loyalist Gothic romance'.[50] Such fiction, Watt explains, concerns itself with 'an unambiguous moral and patriotic agenda' in the wake of the Revolutionary War in America and in the face of ongoing concerns about France. In this scenario, Leland's novel is undeniably conservative, not subversive, and is aimed, like Clara Reeve's later novel, *The old English baron* (1778), at 'provid[ing] a reassuring moral and patriotic fable during a period of national crisis'.[51] It is to this end that France is negatively epitomised in the aptly named Count Mal-leon, who is described as 'impetuous' and 'env[ious] of [the] superior worth and greatness [of his English enemy, William, Earl of Salisbury]' (*Longsword*, vol. 1, p. 18).[52] Tellingly, after Mal-leon imprisons Les Roches, the sympathetic Frenchman who had helped William escape, William violently exclaims, '[I]s charity so great a crime? Is tyranny suffered to rage thus without control in France?' (*Longsword*, vol. 1, p. 20). In contrast, William envisions his native land as a 'seat of honour and security' (*Longsword*, vol. 1, p. 53).

William's later return home proves disenchanting, largely because of the effects of misrule in the land. As the elderly knight, Sir Randolph, laments, England is suffering under a tyrannical rule by proxy: 'We all know with what uncontrouled power Hubert rules in the court of England: how his subtle arts of insinuation have penetrated into the inmost heart of our Henry; and now direct all it's [sic] notions and designs' (*Longsword*, vol. 1, p. 59). The disparity between the England of William's longing and that of reality leads Jacqueline, Les Roches' daughter, who has accompanied William to England in the hope of saving her father from Mal-leon, to remonstrate: 'Where is that power and influence … in the court of England which Lord William boasted? If his own wrongs cannot there find redress, if he must have recourse to the precarious chance of arms, in vain have I sought relief in this strange land' (*Longsword*, vol. 2, p. 29). William, in his turn, laments England's political fall from grace: 'When shall our distracted country feel the blessings of a wise and virtuous rule? Shall faction and tumult for ever disturb the land, and sordid avarice and slavish adulation for ever surround the throne?' (*Longsword*, vol. 2, p. 32).

Despite his concerns about the present health of his native country, William continues to believe in the righteousness of English political and judicial systems. Determined to free his castle and his family from Raymond's tyranny, William throws himself on 'the justice of [his] liege Lord' (*Longsword*, vol. 2, p. 36). The king's response, authorising William to reclaim his estates and his wife, suggests that all is not lost and augurs a return to a more just rule, a movement apparently, if not definitively, heralded by the novel's conclusion. With the restoration of private and public order, Leland's tale implies that the much wished-for overthrow of 'absolute and violent power' has occurred, replacing 'lawless oppression' with 'that inestimable blessing, a wise, righteous, and well attempered rule' (*Longsword*, vol. 2, p. 78).

The interest shared by Leland and Walpole in the political past and present of the British nation is one similarly professed by their 'heirs'. If, in 1778, Clara Reeve was advertising her novel, *The old English baron*, as 'the literary offspring of the Castle of Otranto',[53] another text, only a year later, prided itself on being '*The Literary Offspring of Longsword, Earl Of Salisbury*'.[54] In describing themselves in this way, both texts proclaimed their interest in what Watt calls 'the non-specific rhetoric of Gothic liberty and vigour'.[55] They also signalled their intentions 'to explore the mythology of English national identity', as Scott would later do in his revision of his novels' 'Gothic ancestry'.[56] Reeve's 'picture of Gothic times and manners' refers to the understanding of the Gothic past as a foreign and bizarre epoch temporally and ideologically removed from modern-day England (*Old English baron*, p. 2). Although specifically recalling the second edition of *Otranto* with her subtitle, 'a gothic story', Reeve tones down the supernatural excess of Walpole's tale in order to concentrate on the political and moral virtue of an idealised past. Reeve's recourse to the past thus suggests, as Maxwell compellingly contends, that 'virtue is more comfortable, more at home, in a distant period … Morally, at least, the past was better than the present'.[57] Price similarly claims that *The old English baron* 'argues for the need to return to a gothic origin [of national governance] supposedly connected with liberty'.[58]

Several Irish texts from this period might equally claim to be the literary offspring of both *The castle of Otranto* and *Longsword*, underlining as they do the varying and often ambiguous ways in which the Gothic past was envisioned as an important point of political reference for contemporary Britain.[59] Set, like *Longsword*, during the reign of Henry III, Anne Fuller's *Alan Fitz-Osborne* (1786) pictures its eponymous hero taking part in the Second Barons' War (1264–67) against a sovereign despised by his people for giving preference to the non-English counsel of William de Valence, a figure apparently representative of the French-born Peter des Roches, bishop of Winchester.[60] Because of Henry's dependence on de Valence as well as his injustice as a monarch, the English populace is described as looking to Simon Montford, Earl of Leicester – an obvious (anglicised) reference to the historical figure, Simon de Montfort, who led the opposition against Henry III in the Second Barons' War – 'as the only person who could save the state, and render the people happy'.[61] Yet, Montford himself proves a tyrant, and just three years after his successful coup, the people begin to call for Henry's eldest son, Edward, 'to interpose his authority and save the sinking nation' (*Alan Fitz-Osborne*, vol. 2, p. 122).

Joining with Edward in his attempt to regain proper control of the nation is Alan Fitz-Osborne, Jr., along with his uncle and guardian, Walter Fitz-Osborne, and Walter's son, William. While Alan is serious about his loyalty to Edward, his uncle is an ambitious political chameleon paying lip service to Edward while slyly currying favour with each contesting faction. Walter detests Alan both because of his obvious friendship with and attachment to Edward and because Alan serves as a constant reminder of the sins of Walter's past, namely his lust-driven murder of Alan's mother, Matilda, and his subsequent dispossession of Alan of his rightful inheritance. Alan's increasing resemblance to his wronged father – dispatched to the Crusades in order to allow Walter to court the scornful Matilda – prompts Walter's determination to kill Alan. But his efforts are repeatedly undermined by the appearance of a 'phantom' Matilda, whose 'pale, ghastly, and bloody' form conjures him not to kill Alan and demands justice for her murder (*Alan Fitz-Osborne*, vol. 1, p. 83).

The novel's conclusion sees Walter punished for his crimes after Alan discovers his father alive in the Holy Land. Together, the wronged Fitz-Osbornes journey back to England to confront their villainous family members. In the ensuing scuffle, Walter is fatally wounded by his resurrected brother. His death is fittingly couched in terms of supernatural revenge: as he lays dying, Walter sees a spectral Matilda ushering him to Hell: 'Oh horror! – horror! … She holds the dagger o'er my head – Ha! – that crimson stream – it drops – it covers – it stifles me!' (*Alan Fitz-Osborne*, vol. 2, p. 340). Matilda thereafter returns to her rightful home, so to speak, when her son exhumes her body from the unconsecrated ground in which Walter buried her and re-inters her in the family's ancestral vault.

Matilda's vindication and attendant homecoming are paralleled by the voyage of the newly installed King Edward, as he travels to England from the Holy Land, where he has been engaged in the Crusades. Together, these returns represent the righting of public and private wrongs that have plagued England under the reign of Henry III. In contrast to his father, Edward is portrayed as a compassionate and just ruler, not easily swayed by insinuating men like Walter. Indicatively, while leading the campaign against Montford in a bid to restore his father to rule, Edward refuses to humiliate his enemies. Instead, he 'command[s] his soldiers to desist from pursuing the vanquished – "They are Englishmen", said he, "they are my children. He who has misled them is no more, and they will return to their duty!"' (*Alan Fitz-Osborne*, vol. 2, p. 134). However, Edward's mercy and faith in the loyalty of the English people are traits not shared by his father, who eventually begins to suspect Edward himself of treason and sends him on Crusade. Henry soon regrets this decision and calls for Edward's return, but he dies before Edward can reach England. Edward, in his turn, decides to prolong his travels, not feeling any urgency to return now that his father is gone. The novel thus concludes with the suggestion, but not, by any means, the surety of Edward's triumphant homecoming. As with *Longsword*, a significant shadow is cast over England's national future, despite the death of the problematic and unpopular Henry III. With the new king absent in France, misrule and unrest threaten from the margins.

J.M.S. Tompkins summarily dismissed *Alan Fitz-Osborne* as evidencing only 'a little disconnected information about the Barons' War' in order to lavish attention on 'such attractions as the bleeding spectre of Matilda'.[62] Tompkins's negative assessment is voiced as part of an argument centred on the unjust neglect of one of Fuller's contemporaries, James White, a Dublin-born, Trinity College Dublin-educated man, who garnered attention first as a relatively successful translator and novelist, and then as a man with a 'freakish personality' that eventually led him into full-blown insanity and death by starvation.[63] Although White's novels – *Earl Strongbow* (1789), *The adventures of John of Gaunt, Duke of Lancaster* (1790), and *The adventures of King Richard Coeur de Lion* (1791) – are notable for the tone of levity they frequently reveal, they also clearly reflect the political concerns of White's other works, including *Hints for a specific plan for an abolition of the slave trade and for the relief of the negroes in the British West Indies* (1788), *Speeches of M. de Mirabeau* (1792), and *The history of the revolution of France* (1792).[64] Moreover, they channel the same elegiac tone evident in White's poem *Conway Castle* (1789), which White himself compared directly to Gray's *Elegy written in a country churchyard* (1751). Tompkins considered *Conway Castle* 'pleasant romantic stuff, slight but graceful, showing the influence of Gray and Collins', but White's poem is also strongly indicative of the manner in which its author viewed the relationship between past, present, and future.[65] Much more than 'an experimental surrender to mere feeling', as Tompkins has it, *Conway Castle* refers directly to Britain's Gothic political and architectural history in order to compare past and present.[66] Describing the castle as it stands in contemporary North Wales,

White outlines its construction in the reign of Edward I and posits that, '[e]ven in their present state [of ruin], the walls and Castle of Conway afford the most complete example to be met with in this island, of the strength and grandeur of fortified places in the days of chivalry'.[67]

The Gothic ruins of Conway Castle in White's poem serve as, in Ina Ferris's terms, 'vestiges of antiquity [that] allow for a nostalgic turn to a heroic national past away from the mean-minded and utilitarian present'.[68] The idealised heroism of the past is represented by Edward I, who is praised in the course of the poem as an ideal ruler:

> Blest Chief! that could reject a regal station,
> To loose a fetter'd land, Ambition's rage controul,
> And rouse to grandeur an afflicted nation. (*Conway Castle*, p. 7)

Not simply wistful for an aggrandised past, the poem also looks hopefully forward. Speaking to a despairing water-sprite who laments the loss of past days, the narrator asserts: 'These halls, unhonour'd now, with revelry shall ring, / These oak-crown'd hills return the note of gladness' (*Conway Castle*, p. 11). The poem ends on the optimistic prediction that Britain, like Conway Castle itself, will eventually regain its former glory:

> Ev'n to the misty cliffs that shade the *Cambrian* plains
> Shall commerce, child of Peace, grim want disarming,
> Extend her jocund sway; Where lonesome Echo reigns,
> Shall Plenty tune her voice, the village charming. (*Conway Castle*, p. 11)

With a similar optimism, White's 1789 novel, *Earl Strongbow*, engages in a superficial longing for the past that is very quickly overshadowed by a depiction of the necessity of pre-rational epistemes giving way to British modernity, a fictional trajectory long associated with Scott in the early nineteenth century. White's novel narrates a progressive chronological journey into history, beginning with the visit of an eighteenth-century traveller to Strongbow's near-ruined castle in the Welsh town of Chepstow. Residing there for some time, owing to his fondness for '[the] monuments of ancient grandeur, particularly of the gothic kind', this unnamed visitor begins reading a manuscript that tells of a series of midnight encounters between a prisoner in the castle during 'the reign of Charles the second' and the ghost of Strongbow himself.[69] During the course of this interpolated narration, Strongbow frequently laments the strange customs of the eighteenth century and contrasts the present negatively with his own times. Although Strongbow says that he is 'sensible' of the manner in which the 'system of life' to which he was accustomed might be considered 'objectionable', he nevertheless paints the excesses of the present as significantly more problematic:

> We handled the battle-ax, you wield the dice-box. We ran at the ring, you play at ombre. Our breakfast was beef and ale, yours is toast and chocolate. Instead of wigs we wore helmets, and were oftener clad in a suit of steel, than in one of cut velvet. We were a stately and robust race, you are an enervated and unmajestic generation! (*Strongbow*, vol. 1, p. 66)

Despite Strongbow's evident longing for his own age, the novel elsewhere shows a confirmed resignation to the passage of time. In particular, Strongbow's invasion of Ireland is depicted as a necessary and beneficial step that benefited both Ireland and Britain as a whole: 'Accompanying Strongbow's polemic against [modern] luxury and corruption', Watt argues, 'is a myth of manifest destiny which promotes Ireland's role as "an invaluable portion of the British Empire!"'[70]

White ultimately refrains from denouncing Strongbow's invasion of Ireland as a colonial endeavour like that he derided by his involvement in the impeachment of the East India Company's Warren Hastings. He nevertheless differentiates between the Ireland of the past and the Ireland of the present. Much as Maria Edgeworth would later insist that the Rackrent landlords are a historical – not contemporary – reality in *Castle Rackrent* (1800), White asserts that the Ireland invaded by Strongbow was in a serious state of degradation, from which it had, phoenix-like, triumphantly arisen by the eighteenth century. Musing on his arrival in Ireland and subsequent role as the first Lord Lieutenant, Strongbow wonders at the changes wrought by passing centuries:

> How different were we who invaded Ireland, in language, custom, manners, sentiments, knowledge of navigation and the art of war ... from you of the present days! how different too that nation which submitted to our yoke, from that which now forms an invaluable portion of the British empire! Dublin, how changed from what it was when I held the rod of power! (*Earl Strongbow*, vol. 2, p. 35)

To elucidate the differences between twelfth- and eighteenth-century Ireland, Strongbow describes arriving at the town of Wexford, which he finds in a near ruinous state. The walls surrounding the city and 'which the Danes had erected with care and cost' are 'neglected' and crumbling; 'weeds and brambles' have overtaken the battlements, and, in many places, 'huge pieces of the wall had given way, the stones having been picked out to construct adjacent cabins, the possessors of which were too slothful to supply themselves from a quarry'. Worse still, the Irish people seem to regard the walls – the emblems of a past described as glorious and triumphant, if only for the Danes – as a convenient outhouse: 'The platforms, where the Danes had strode in warlike shew, or sate and discoursed upon the deeds of heroic times, had been long appropriated to the easement of nature' (*Earl Strongbow*, vol. 2, pp. 60–1).

Faced with such barbarians, Strongbow unsurprisingly takes control of Wexford with ease. He and his men actually conquer the town unresisted, as their opponents lay sunk in a drunken stupor produced from the overindulgence of a festive saint's day. Despite this overtly negative – near parodic – image of the Irish people, Strongbow declares eighteenth-century Wexford 'an ingenious and polite town' (*Earl Strongbow*, vol. 2, p. 63). The modern Irish people are also described in glowing terms: 'brave, hospitable, generous: in activity of body, in hilarity of mind, unrivalled by any of the northern Europeans'. Their future, the narrative indicates, promises to be bright: 'When enlightened by science, and refined by the labours of the poet and Philosopher (blessings that are stealing fast upon them) they display an intellectual ability, which few nations can equal, and none excel' (*Earl Strongbow*, vol. 2, p. 64). Following this encomium, White seems to arrive at the true crux of his political argument: 'Peradventure, the time may come, when the senate of Britain shall owe its brightest ornament, her theatre its wittiest pieces, her armies their wisest generals, to the nation she now despises' (*Earl Strongbow*, vol. 2, p. 65).

When paired with a critique of contemporary British society effected by, in Watt's terms, 'an idealizing appeal to the … past', Strongbow's assertion of the value, worth, and hitherto unrecognised potential of the Irish people is striking.[71] It suggests that the key to future glory and restored national virtue lies in Ireland's recognition as an integral contributor to the British nation. Rather than dwell on what White admits was a barbaric, if only momentarily degraded, Irish society and culture, *Earl Strongbow* insists that the re-assertion of British greatness represented by Strongbow himself may well result from the workings of Irish individuals. Yet, as with *Longsword*, the novel's conclusion leaves all such optimism in doubt, casting the rehabilitation of both Irish culture and the British nation itself in terms of potentiality. Indicatively, the novel's twice removed narration of Strongbow's tale – told first to a seventeenth-century prisoner kept in Chepstow Castle and then read, in manuscript form, by an eighteenth-century tourist – implies that the cause of Strongbow's continued haunting of his former home remains unresolved. Strongbow had first appeared to the Chepstow inmate conjuring him to erect a monument to Otho, a faithful servant, who Strongbow had accidentally killed during a momentary rage occasioned by the news that his beloved Geralda had retired to a convent believing Strongbow to be married. Once this memorial is raised, Strongbow vowed, he 'shall … desert these ancient towers, and rest in the regions of unembodied beings, till we shall finally be summoned into the presence of our Redeemer' (*Earl Strongbow*, vol. 2, p. 130).

Whether Strongbow's request has been fulfilled remains finally unclear at the end of the novel. The entreaty itself concludes White's tale, which never returns to the frame narrative involving the eighteenth-century antiquarian enthusiast. That we finally should remain in the seventeenth-century manuscript suggests the foreshortening of distance between the two narrative spaces, creating an ongoing immersion in a tale equated by the more modern narrator to romance. There is no re-emergence from romance to realism, or as Northrop Frye might suggest, from a 'dream'/'night' world of chaos and disruption to restored and invigorated normality.[72] Instead, White leaves us in the past, refusing to return to the contemporary period and thereby foretelling a future in which Strongbow's tale is continuously repeated and Strongbow himself forced perpetually to haunt his own home seeking resolution and rest. The lingering doubt about the result of Strongbow's appeal casts a peculiar shade of ambivalence over the tale's at times whimsical and imaginative take on historical events. Correspondingly, a similar uncertainty is thrown over the future rehabilitation of Ireland and the British nation envisioned by Strongbow as he recounts his past exploits.

With its layered narratives and considered comparisons of seventeenth- and eighteenth-century society, *Earl Strongbow* attests to Irish gothic literature's keen interrogation of the Gothic past and its bearing on the present. Whether they use overtly supernatural effects, as in *Alan Fitz-Osborne*, or confine themselves to more subtle indications of a hauntingly recurring past that can be simultaneously endowed with positive and negative attributes, as in *Longsword* and *Earl Strongbow*, the works discussed here clearly evidence an ongoing overlap of the formal, generic, and ideological characteristics of what we now refer to, separately, as gothic and historical fiction. As such, they urge a reconsideration of our current understanding of gothic literary production and its active engagement with the fraught notions of Enlightenment progress and modernity. Moreover, they prompt a re-evaluation of the nineteenth-century development of the historical novel later associated with Scott, an issue considered in the final section of this chapter.

IRISH GOTHIC IN THE AGE OF WALTER SCOTT

Published in the same year as Scott's *Waverley*, Regina Maria Roche's *Trecothick bower; or, the lady of the west country* (1814) provides an instructive example of the continued intersection of historical and gothic literary modes in early nineteenth-century Irish fiction. Centred on the treachery of Morcar, the Earl of Sebergham and a great favourite of his monarch, Edward IV (1442–83), the novel combines a historical setting with repeated descriptions of sublime scenery, explained and unexplained supernatural events, and a series of disastrous shipwrecks, imprisonments, duels, and attempted rapes. Determined to marry Lady Emmeline, the daughter and heiress of the Baron of Trecothick, Morcar betrays her lover, Edmund, by sending him on a fool's errand to France on the pretext of furnishing him with the means of regaining his reputation – tarnished due to his family's unsuccessful support of the house of Lancaster at the Battle of Barnet (14 April 1471). In the meantime, Morcar prevails on Emmeline's parents to allow him to marry her instead, whisking them away from their family seat in Cornwall to Grey Cliff Tower, his ancestral home in 'the north'.[73] En route, Emmeline is captivated by 'the rude fells of those northern regions' and echoes Burkean ideas of the natural sublime in finding her 'imagination' 'exalted' and her 'thoughts' 'entertain[ed]' by the 'stupendous waterfall[s]', 'distant mountains', and 'majestic promontor[ies]' that everywhere meet her eye (*Trecothick bower*, vol. 1, pp. 148, 150).

Emmeline's sublime experience of the north is further enhanced by 'the traces of antiquity every where discernible' (*Trecothick bower*, vol. 1, p. 148). These take the form of edifices such as Morcar's 'ancient fortress', 'the ancient intrenchments lying contiguous' to Pendragon Castle, and 'the remains' of 'the temple in which the greatest of the divinities of the Pagan Saxons was worshipped' at Kirby Thore (*Trecothick bower*, vol. 1, pp. 154, 152, 149). As suggested by the latter example, the 'ancient grandeur' Emmeline locates in the ruined temple relates not just to its natural and architectural appearance but also to its association with popular traditions (*Trecothick bower*, vol. 1, p. 149). This attention to folk beliefs and customs recurs throughout Emmeline's trip to the north, as when, for instance, she and her travelling companions 'visit the curious grottoes on the banks of the Emont here [near Penrith]' which are supposed, 'according to the traditions of the vulgar', to have provided a home for 'a giant named Isis, who unmercifully devoured every thing living that came his way' (*Trecothick bower*, vol. 1, pp. 153–4). At Pendragon Castle, Emmeline is intrigued by the 'tradition' surrounding 'the prince' said both to have given his name to the castle and to have 'died by poison put into a well, early in the sixth century' (*Trecothick bower*, vol. 1, p. 149). Later, upon reaching Grey Cliff Tower, Emmeline is enchanted by the tradition of St Herbert, 'the remains of whose romantic heritage, in a beautiful island of the lake' form part of Morcar's estate (*Trecothick bower*, vol. 1, p. 157).

The vestiges of ancient architecture that Emmeline encounters, along with their associated legends and traditions, function in much the same manner as do the ruins of Conway Castle in White's poem of that name. In other words, they allow Emmeline and us, as readers, to escape into a heroic, semi-mythologised past distant from the base realities of the present. This is, in effect, the whole reason behind Emmeline's willingness to embark on the trip in the first place: escape from Morcar's persistent demands for an immediate marriage. While the north thus appears to represent a romanticised if still backward, pre-modern chronotopic and geographical space, Emmeline's return to the more modern realm of her own home is accompanied by a sense of dread attached to her impending marriage to Morcar: 'At length the day for setting out on this [their return to Trecothick Castle] arrived; fancying herself, in the preceding journey, escaping from something dreaded, very different were the feelings of Emmeline on that and the present one' (*Trecothick bower*, vol. 1, p. 202). The journey south soon becomes even more upsetting than anticipated when Emmeline's mother falls ill and dies, temporarily postponing her marriage but also pointing to a more general sense of illness plaguing the nation at large.

In fact, from the start of the novel, Edward IV has been presented as unfit to rule: 'dissipated', unable to command his people's 'heartfelt homage', and far too heavily swayed by the conniving Earl of Gloucester, who is himself ambitious, calculating, and unprincipled (*Trecothick bower*, vol. 1, p. 4; vol. 3, p. 10). Edward's eventual death, followed by Gloucester's defeat, and his replacement by Henry VII, augur a return to political stability as well as the eventual righting of private wrongs that have seen Trecothick dispossessed of his estate and title, Edmund convinced of Emmeline's infidelity and married to another woman, and Emmeline freed from her secret marriage to Morcar but tricked into believing Edmund no longer cares for her. Petitioned to reinstate the Baron of Trecothick to his former position, Henry VII immediately grants the request and punishes the man behind the deception that had originally caused it. Unlike Edward IV, Henry VII, we are told, 'was not impervious to the voice of truth'; more than that, he appears intent on 'acquir[ing] a reputation for equity and justice' (*Trecothick bower*, vol. 3, p. 241). He also ensures Edmund's restoration to favour after Edmund distinguishes himself fighting for Henry in the battle against Gloucester.

Henry's new reign signals the restitution of just rule and the righting of both public and private wrongs that have plagued the novel. Yet, as in *Longsword*, jarring reminders of the past continue to emerge in the present. The most striking instance of this occurs in the apparent mirroring of Emmeline's fate with that of the heroine featured in the interpolated tale of St Herbert, narrated to her by Morcar at his family home in Keswick. At surface level, the narrative operates analogously to earlier patriotic 'celebration[s] of actual, if mythologized, historical figures and/or events' and is intended, like them, 'to connect with or tap into … a living past' in order to engage with national history and identity.[74] Historically, St Herbert was an ascetic hermit known for living in seclusion on the island of Derwent Water and dying on the same day – 20 March 687 – as his close friend and spiritual adviser, St Cuthbert, to whom he paid a yearly visit.[75] In Roche's hands, he becomes a once powerful Saxon chief who contributed to the conquest of 'the northern part of the island [of Britain]' and helped form the Anglo-Saxon Heptarchy that would eventually become a unified kingdom in the ninth century (*Trecothick bower*, vol. 1, p. 159). Despite his final renunciation of the world, the military force he is seen to exert, particularly over the neighbouring Cumbrians, lives on when his enemy's ancestral inheritance is won by 'the chance of war' by another 'noble Saxon', from whom Morcar is descended (*Trecothick bower*, vol. 1, p. 195).

Morcar recites this narrative to Emmeline with pride, suggesting that he intends her to interpret it as evidence of his impressive lineage. Its obvious connection to Emmeline's own experience in Herbert's betrayal of Cathol over desire for Morna clarifies Roche's concern: to align this Germanic Gothic heritage not just with Morcar's own treachery but also with the political instability and misrule with which he is linked. Indeed, Morcar's favour with Edward rests on his acquiescence to his monarch's whims; Edward prefers him over his other advisers because Morcar is 'ever ready, without rebuke or animadversion, to assist him in any bold emprise or licentious frolic' (*Trecothick bower*, vol. 1, p. 4). As Edward's rule comes to a disastrous end, so, too, does Morcar, but not without lingering effects on Emmeline, who receives several mystifying visits from cloaked strangers suggesting that Morcar still retains his power over her. She must therefore relinquish her opportunity to marry Edmund when he returns to Trecothick after being restored to royal favour. More than that, the continued, if briefly interrupted, internecine warfare depicted in Herbert's narrative is one that, despite Henry's accession to the throne, continues to characterise Emmeline's England. Tellingly, Henry's reign is never fully established by the end of the novel, nor do we receive confirmation that his 'principal [aim]' of proving an equitable and just ruler is fulfilled (*Trecothick bower*, vol. 3, p. 241).

Clearly evocative of earlier historical gothic fictions such as *Longsword* and *Alan Fitz-Osborne*, *Trecothick bower* conceals in its quasi-authentic historical details a cautionary, if superficially optimistic, political commentary on the rule of the Prince Regent, and future king of England, George IV (r. 1820–30).[76] Much like *Longsword* before it, *Trecothick bower* appears to call upon George IV to secure national and international peace at the conclusion of the Napoleonic Wars, against all the odds presented by his infamous personal and political exploits.[77] Yet, its frequent recourse to supernatural figures and events, and its hesitancy fully to ratify a narrative of progress signalled by Henry's accession to the throne casts significant doubts on the present and future security of the British nation. For this, the novel might easily be dismissed as indicative of the general failure of the historical novel in Ireland. As the traditional argument goes, Irish writers were unable successfully to mimic Scott's promotion of union with Britain as both the inevitable and the desired end to historical rebellion and unrest in Scotland. This was due, it is often said, to the very recent nature of the Anglo-Irish Union and the violence surrounding it, not to mention the history of dispossession it seemed to revive. Thomas Flanagan influentially argued that, when nineteenth-century Irish authors attempted to reproduce Scott's historical novel, they inevitably 'brought with them the old, sullen grudges and the old delusive lies', rendering them incapable of 'transcend[ing] hatred, accusation, and guilt'.[78] The most they succeeded in doing was producing 'a slavish conformity to the kinds of plot and character which [Scott] developed'.[79] James Cahalan similarly contends that Scott's famous 'moderation' was 'impossible … for Irish historical novelists faced with a present that was nearly as nightmarish as the past'.[80] More recently, Emer Nolan has summed up the conventional arguments concerning the Irish historical novel as a powerlessness '[to depict] historical change in what Georg Lukács calls a "felt relationship" to the present' because 'Irish history did not lend itself very readily to plots about enlightened reconciliation, or gradual but steady progress'.[81]

Such assessments are connected, as Nolan points out, to wider arguments about the development of Irish Romantic fiction and the oft-repeated claim that the realist novel was 'almost impossible to write in nineteenth-century Ireland'.[82] In Terry Eagleton's memorable phrasing, Ireland lacked the 'settlement and stability' necessary to the realist novel.[83] If Irish writers continued to eschew realism in the nineteenth century, Jacqueline Belanger counters, it suggests not an Irish literary or cultural failure but the need to reconsider 'the critical prominence we have given to realism itself'.[84] Such questioning is integral to nineteenth-century Irish fiction in its particular deployment of non-realist genres, such as sensation fiction, as Siobhán Kilfeather persuasively argued.[85] These genres 'offered writers the opportunity to interrogate the mechanisms by which grand historical narratives invade and evacuate individual subjectivities in what are conventionally presented as the private spaces of home, family, and sexuality'.[86]

To suggest, however, that non-realist genres were a particular marker of nineteenth-century Irish literary production is tacitly to reify traditional accounts of Scott as having rejected romance and the gothic literary mode in order to triumph realism and the historical novel. Thus, while Scott was an avid reader of terror literature and confessed a youthful inclination for 'the wonderful and terrible, – the common taste of children, but in which I have remained a child even unto this day',[87] his Waverley novels are seen to shun the gothic and 'the clichés of extravagant romance' for the ideals of 'historical realism'.[88] What made Scott's historicism different from that of preceding gothic fictions such as *Longsword* and *The castle of Otranto* was the detail he bestowed on his depiction of the past and the manner in which he presented it. According to Lukács and those that have followed him, Scott's historicism 'reproduced a coherent, credible, and consistent image of a specific historical era'; that of earlier writers such as Fuller, Leland, Walpole, and White, created, in contrast, a 'vague impression of the past acceptable in fictions which concentrated upon situations of terror'.[89] Moreover, as Price points out, the key to Scott's 'new' perspective on history, as postulated by Lukács, was the manner in which he transformed violent and rapid political change into 'inevitable development'.[90]

For Lukács and indeed, many of Scott's contemporaries, the historical verisimilitude characteristic of the Waverley novels relied upon a rejection of the trappings of earlier gothic fiction. Yet, 'Gothic modes of history', Fiona Robertson writes, 'were not preparations for the real thing but ways of presenting the past and imaginative responses to the past which survive in the Waverley Novels'. This gothic practice, Robertson continues, fundamentally 'intrude[s] into, complicate[s], and fashion[s]' the Waverley novels.[91] Scott may have distanced himself from the influence of gothic literary production in order to promote the view of his novels as original and groundbreaking, but his works repeatedly reveal a continued engagement with the Gothic past in its many guises.

An earlier monograph by the present author looked at the manner in which the past in Scott's Waverley novels frequently threatens to break free from the containment imposed upon it by the author's celebrated commitment to progress and the concomitant relegation of the past to ancient history.[92] Like that study, this book aims not to provide a detailed analysis of Scott's fiction but instead to call attention to Scott's enduring, if conflicted, depictions of the Gothic past, particularly in the form of superstition, legends, and popular folklore. Cahalan positions Scott's use of such material in his works as confirmation of his commitment to historical verisimilitude; as a fundamental component of Scottish history, such tales provide an important element of accuracy and authenticity to Scott's depiction of the past.[93] Certainly, this was how Scott represented his engagement with the supernatural, leading several contemporary readers to deride, as James Hogg called it, Scott's 'half-an-half' perspective: 'Even Sir Walter Scott is turned renegade and with his stories made up of half-an-half like Nathaniel Gow's toddy is trying to throw cold water on the most certain though most impalpable phenomena of human nature'.[94] Samuel Taylor Coleridge similarly complained that Scott 'relates ghost stories, prophecies, presentiments, all praeter-supernaturally fulfilled' only 'most anxious[ly] to let his readers know, that he himself is far too enlightened not to be assured of the folly and falsehood of all that he yet relates as truth, and for the purpose of exciting the interest and emotions attached to the belief of their truth'.[95]

Coleridge's assessment of Scott's engagement with the supernatural and other elements of folkloric belief supports Ian Duncan's recent identification of 'two valences of romance' in Scott's works. On the one hand, Duncan asserts, 'romance signifies an individualist estrangement from real life, a puerile narcissism and egotistical delusion' that must be corrected, 'outgrown or cured'. On the other hand, 'romance signifies the heritage of a cultural identity that is lost but ethically true, an historically alienated ancestral patriarchy recalled in vision or legend'.[96] Contemporary reviews of Scott's works evidence warring accounts of 'the heritage of a cultural identity' evident in the use of, for instance, witches, soothsayers, prophecies, spirits, and grey ghosts.[97] Thus, as *The Critical Review*'s assessment of *Waverley* indicates, the description of superstitions and supernatural beliefs is inevitable in an authentic depiction of Scottish historical reality: 'Our tale (and where is there a Scottish tale without them) has its superstitions, its witcheries, and its second sight'.[98] But, the illustration of such beliefs should be condemned, as the use of the supernatural in the second edition of *Otranto* was, precisely because it indicates the continued existence of atavistic and irrational perspectives in the present day. This is why *The Critical Review* censured *Guy Mannering* (1815), refusing 'exclusively [to] compliment the morality of the piece' on account of its encouragement of ongoing belief in 'marvellous' ideas such as second sight.[99] The second sight may be an authentic historical and, indeed, present reality in Scotland, *The Critical Review* suggested, but the representation of it as such in a modern work of fiction aimed at English readers was not to be applauded.[100] The *Monthly Review* similarly condemned the use of second sight in the novel as a 'gross improbability' and an 'absolute moral impossibility'.[101] While it could be countenanced in 'the regions of romance', Scott's celebrated realism forbade it entering here:

> [I]n a species of writing which founds its only claim to our favour on the reality of its pictures and images, the introduction of any thing that is diametrically contrary to all our ordinary principles of belief and action is as gross a violation of every rule of composition as the appendage of a fish's tail to a woman's head and shoulders.[102]

As indicated by these reviews, Scott's fiction was often implicated in the problematic transition from pre-modernity to modernity at the heart of gothic literary production. Despite the association of the Waverley novels with realism and historical truths – one central to the differentiation of 'novel' and 'romance', as Chapter 2 will discuss in more detail – they frequently introduced an ambiguity about the relationship of the past and present, as did Scott's poetic works before them. Francis Jeffrey was particularly scathing about Scott's version of history in *Marmion* (1808). Considering that work in the *Edinburgh Review*, Jeffrey dismissed its reliance on romance, suggesting that its 'images borrowed from the novels of Mrs. Ratcliffe [sic] and her imitators' promised not to amuse but to bore its readers.[103] In particular, Jeffrey objected to 'the insufferable number, and length, and minuteness of those descriptions of antient dresses; and manners, and buildings; and ceremonies, and local superstitions; with which the whole poem is overrun'; such details were, according to Jeffrey, fundamentally out of place in a 'modern' text:

> We object to these, and to all such details, because they are, for the most part, without dignity or interest in themselves; because, in a modern author, they are evidently unnatural; and because they must always be strange, and, in a good degree, obscure and unintelligible to ordinary readers.[104]

Later, echoing the language of earlier reviews of Walpole's *Otranto*, Jeffrey argued that the kind of details Scott provided are very welcome when found 'in *old* books ... because they are there authentic and valuable documents of the usages and modes of life of our ancestors'. 'In a *modern* romance, however', Jeffrey declared, 'these details being no longer authentic are of no value in point of information' and, therefore, threaten to fatigue readers.[105]

Tedium was not Jeffrey's principal concern, as is evident in the caution with which he concluded his review. Writing that he believed it his 'duty to make one strong effort to bring back the great apostle of the heresy to the wholesome creed of his instructors', Jeffrey claimed to want 'to stop the insurrection before it becomes desperate and senseless, by persuading the leader to return to his duty and allegiance'. Scott's 'duty', as Jeffrey saw it, was the abandonment of 'the wicked tales of knight-errantry and enchantment'.[106] Central to Jeffrey's review, then, is the suggestion that the repeated representation and re-presentation of history in the form of 'stupid monkish legends ... ludicrous description[s] of Lord Gifford's habiliments of divination ... and ... various scraps and fragments of antiquarian history and baronial biography' threatened to confuse the distance between past and present in readers' minds.[107] The danger here, as with the second edition of *Otranto*, was the collapse of the distinction between history and present-day reality, one that, in the context of Scott's popularity, had potentially serious consequences, both for the course of English literature and for the wellbeing of its readers.[108] Accordingly, while Jeffrey 'ostentatiously object[s] on aesthetic grounds that Scott's historical details are unauthentic and therefore tedious', as Michael Gamer argues, he 'nevertheless asserts that Scott's work are indeed ... calculated recastings of history ... capable of achieving political effects'.[109]

Jeffrey's negativity – though not repeated in his future assessments of Scott's poetry – evidences the way in which Scott's 'recourse to the "rudeness" of the distant past' was often linked ominously to gothic romance.[110] Murray Pittock argues that 'the supernatural Gothic in Scott is almost always associated with the infantilized, credulous Scotland of the Jacobite and Catholic past', but Scott frequently reveals a rather more equivocal attitude to the 'marvellous' historical details to which Jeffrey objected.[111] In *Waverley*, tellingly, the hero's attempt to reason with Fergus Mac Ivor over the appearance of the fateful Bodach Glas, or 'grey ghost' – a folkloric figure supposed to presage death – is ultimately abortive, as the destiny it foretells is fulfilled, if in a slightly different way than Fergus assumed it would be, by the end of the novel. On the one hand, Waverley's resolute rationality, even at the moment of Fergus's execution, coupled with Fergus's death signals the containment of a superstitious belief associated with Catholicism and traditional Highland culture. On the other hand, Fergus's execution proves the essential truth of the Bodach Glas's prediction, suggesting the ongoing import and relevance of such beliefs.[112] Similarly, in *The bride of Lammermoor* (1819), the cryptic Ravenswood family prophecy is satisfied, despite Edgar Ravenswood's initial, sceptically modern take on its forecast.[113] As he is swallowed by quicksand, becoming 'invisible, as if [he] had melted into the air', Ravenswood transforms into legend himself, underlining its continued power and potency.[114]

Similar inconsistencies about superstition, legend, and folkloric belief might be traced in a majority of the Waverley novels, emphasising a striking line of continuity between Scott's historical novels and those of his Irish contemporaries. Chief among his imitators in Ireland were Charles Robert Maturin and the Banim brothers. Scott maintained a lengthy correspondence with the former and was heavily influenced in the composition of *The bride of Lammermoor* by Maturin's hybrid tale, *The Milesian chief* (1812).[115] Typically, Scott never acknowledged this influence, and his relationship with Maturin is generally seen as an unbalanced one, with Maturin gaining immeasurably more from it than Scott.[116] Certainly, Maturin remained grateful for the financial assistance and literary patronage Scott provided over the years, and he was also very ready to admit the inspiration he found in Scott's works. In composing his final novel, *The Albigenses* (1824), for instance, Maturin confessed that he had purposely followed the example of Scott's *Ivanhoe* (1820):

> [T]he work ... has been flattered by some literary men to whom I have read it, with a strong resemblance to 'Ivanhoe' which I admit was my model, – I have studiously avoided the faults so justly charged on Melmoth, and tried to form myself on the style of my friend Sir Walter Scott.[117]

Conventionally read as a paltry imitation of Scott's model, *The Albigenses* is not, in fact, Maturin's first or only fictional engagement with the issues of historicity, authenticity, and the translation of popular culture into print central to the Waverley novels.[118] But, it is often held up as proof of the failure of the historical novel to thrive in Ireland, an assessment linked to the obvious overlap of gothic and historical modes of fiction in *The Albigenses*.[119] The novel is a fascinating example of the cross-formal nature of early nineteenth-century literature, combining an investigation of the Catholic Church and the Albigensian sect of the thirteenth century and identifiable, if anachronistically deployed, historical figures with lycanthropes, power-hungry abbots, mad crones, cross-dressing women, and a Black Knight that recalls the expunged Satan in Maturin's earlier play, *Bertram; or, the castle of St Aldobrand* (1816).[120] More than that, in its particular linkage of past and present, the novel insists on the kind of qualified historiographical accuracy associated with Scott's historical novel while using historical fact urgently to locate the past's intrusion into the present.[121]

A similarly doubled use of history is also present in Maturin's lesser known, posthumous short story, 'Leixlip Castle: an Irish family legend' (1825).[122] As in *The Albigenses*, Maturin here carefully constructs a specific historical context, beginning the narrative proper with a description of '[t]he tranquillity of the Catholics of Ireland during the disturbed periods of 1715 and 1745'.[123] He also notes the widespread if 'secret disgust' felt by many Irish Jacobite sympathisers 'at the existing state of affairs', observing that, in response, many 'quitt[ed] their family residences and wandere[d] about like persons who were uncertain of their homes, or possibly expecting better from some near and fortunate contingency' ('Leixlip Castle', p. 1). Maturin's brief sketch of this period in Ireland is, as Trumpener suggests, based in fact, as many Irish Catholics did experience the quiet despair to which Maturin refers.[124] Not trusting his readers to realise the accuracy of his fictional report, however, Maturin appends a brief preface to the tale intended to emphasise the narrative's factual basis: 'The incidents of the following tale are not merely *founded* on fact, they are facts themselves' ('Leixlip Castle', p. 1). All the principal incidents related are, Maturin insists, '*facts*', derived from his own family history ('Leixlip Castle', p. 1).

Despite this heavy emphasis on verifiable fact, Maturin classifies the tale in his preface as 'a fine specimen of Gothic horrors' ('Leixlip Castle', p. 1), emphatically highlighting the strange and unnatural events characterising his narrative. Indeed, as suggested by the tale's subtitle, the narrative revolves around not just a 'story, history, [or] account' of the Blaney family passed down through the generations, but also the less verifiable beliefs 'handed down by tradition from early times and popularly regarded as historical'.[125] Here, Maturin both draws on Scott's use of such material and anticipates the revival of interest in Irish legendary material signalled by the publication of Thomas Crofton Croker's *Fairy legends and traditions of the south of Ireland* (1825–28). Moreover, like Scott, Maturin displays a contradictory attitude to the supernaturalism at the heart of his tale. As Trumpener argues, Maturin 'evokes the supernatural to demonstrate what needs to be rooted out of a culture if it is to advance' only 'to suggest the impossibility of such suppressions and to stage the inevitable return of the repressed'.[126]

The tale is set in the titular castle, rented in 1720 by a disaffected Catholic baronet, Sir Redmond Blaney, who removes to Leixlip with his three daughters in disgruntlement over the victorious boastings of his Whig neighbours 'in the north' ('Leixlip Castle', p. 1). While Blaney himself undergoes a process of 'tranquiliz[ation]' at Leixlip castle, 'los[ing] his tenacity in political matters', his daughters begin to register in fatally supernatural ways the continued hold of the past on the present ('Leixlip Castle', p. 3). First, the youngest daughter disappears with 'an old woman, in the *Fingallian* dress (a red petticoat and a long green jacket)', to be seen fleetingly over the next ten years, 'as diminutive in form, as though she had not grown an inch since she was ten years of age, and always crouching over a fire, … complaining of cold and hunger, and apparently covered with rags' ('Leixlip Castle', pp. 3, 4). Then, the eldest daughter is murdered on her wedding night by her suddenly deranged bridegroom – hitherto recognised as 'a [Catholic] gentleman of competent fortune and unexceptional character' ('Leixlip Castle', p. 4) – in a scene reminiscent of Scott's *The bride of Lammermoor*. Finally, the middle daughter, left largely to her own devices, imbibes from the servants a 'taste for superstitious and supernatural horrors' that eventually has 'a most disastrous effect on her future life' ('Leixlip Castle', p. 5). One 'withered crone', in particular, promises to show the susceptible Anne her future husband on Halloween eve ('Leixlip Castle', p. 5). Predictably, the affair ends badly for Anne: soon after her divination, she marries the Scottish Jacobite Baronet, Sir Richard Maxwell, and lives happily together with him for years until they become suddenly and irreconcilably estranged. The cause of their separation is Maxwell's discovery in Anne's possession of 'an iron weapon … encrusted with blood', the dark reminder of that long ago Halloween eve, when

Anne saw not her future husband, but '[a] vision of indescribable horror' ('Leixlip Castle', p. 12). It turns out that this blade was the weapon used by Maxwell to kill his younger brother at a feast meant to 'harmoniz[e]' the 'deadly feud' between them, and thrown by him from the deck of the ship in which he escaped from Scotland to Ireland '*on the night of the 30th of October*' ('Leixlip Castle', pp. 12, 13).[127]

Eventually, Maxwell is terrifyingly confronted by the past he had attempted to forget each year, 'retiring to his own chamber, and remaining invisible to his family on the anniversary of the 30th of October' ('Leixlip Castle', p. 11). Similarly, while Blaney seeks to flee the continued memory of political defeat and dispossession in Kildare, the power of the past dramatically transforms Leixlip Castle into 'a living tomb' for Blaney and his daughters.[128] Indeed, as Pittock contends, the very fact that Blaney rents, rather than purchases, Leixlip Castle is a compelling reminder of Irish Catholic dispossession: 'the displaced Catholic aristocracy can only hire the history they once owned'.[129] The fates of all characters involved are what Trumpener identifies as a sign of 'suspension or regression' associated with '[t]he failure of the Jacobite cause'.[130] While Blaney and Redmond equally attempt 'to flee the political fallout from the '15 and the bellicosity of clan society', escape is ultimately impossible.[131] Instead, the past continues to intrude upon the present with devastating personal, familial, and, it is suggested, socio-political effects. In Maturin's narrative, Pittock argues, the Catholic aristocracy represented by Blaney and Maxwell has 'no future';[132] like Edgar Ravenswood in *The bride of Lammermoor*, Blaney and his family simply become part of the legends that have been so fatally a part of their history. As such, they remain a potent symbol of the convergence of past and present.

Published the same year as 'Leixlip Castle', John and Michael Banim's *The fetches* also comments perceptively on the adjoining, sometimes overlapping, nature of past and present.[133] One of the novels included in the Banim brothers' *Tales by the O'Hara family* (1825), *The fetches* generally has been eclipsed in studies of the Irish historical novel by John Banim's *The Boyne water* (1826), which is itself frequently dismissed as a servile and ineffective imitation of Scott.[134] The many arguments about *The Boyne water* and its inability accurately to reproduce Scott's model in Ireland need no rehearsal here. Contemporary reviews of *The Boyne water* and Banim's *The Nowlans* (1826), however, warrant a brief consideration. These reviews are worth noting because they highlight the apparent distinction between Scott's use of history and Banim's – a difference that forms the basis for most modern analyses of the Irish historical novel – while also underlining another element of Banim's imitation: his use of the supernatural. Take, for example, the *Monthly Review*, which condemned Banim for 'awakening' in *The Boyne water* 'the memory of all that fierce spirit of religious dissention, which near a century and a half, and the gradual influence of more tolerant and charitable principles, have scarcely had power to soothe and to put to rest'. It then identified Banim's 'worst fault' as his 'palpable and servile imitation of Scott', one that was 'almost always unskilful'. This ersatz reproduction of Scott's model was particularly offensive in its use of the supernatural, indicated in Banim's presentation of the sibyl, Onagh. '[I]n the highest degree ridiculous', Onagh evidenced the author's 'depraved taste for the preternatural', one that 'violates all reason and probability, by the introduction of unreal visions of witchcraft, in the very midst of authenticated scenes of real life'.[135] In a similar vein, the *Monthly Review* likened *The Nowlans* to debased popular fiction such as gothic romance: 'The coarse delineation of such utter depravity, is the ordinary and stock resource of inferior fiction-mongers; who labour to make up, by thickening and deepening the naked horrors of their plots, for the want of interest with which they otherwise lack the ingenuity to invest their narratives'. Despite Scott's distancing of himself from such unoriginal authorship, the *Monthly Review* nevertheless linked him to it as well in noting that many of the 'wonderful' and 'strange' accidents and coincidences to be found in *The Nowlans* owe directly to Banim's 'broad imitation of Sir Walter Scott'.[136]

In its carefully constructed historical context and its exploration of the folkloric belief in a banshee-like figure, *The fetches* anticipates both the attention to historical detail and the threatening evocation of the supernatural found in *The Boyne water* and *The Nowlans*. As Connolly observes, its introduction, entailing an epistolary exchange between Abel and Barnes O'Hara detailing the production of the ensuing tale, 'marks the passage of everyday time within which novels are written, published and read'.[137] At the same time, in its focus on 'the superstition of "The Fetch"', the novel 'acknowledg[es] the endurance of "primitive times" in the present, chiefly in the shape of a living tradition of wonders and superstitions'.[138] As in Scott's conflicted attitude towards romance, we might detect in *The fetches* an interest in relaying the superstition authentically – an issue discussed at length in the novel's 'Introduction' – annexed to an apparent commitment to dispelling its power.[139] Constructing the narrative as incontrovertible, the introduction informs us that it is an edited version of the 'notes of a true and real Fetch history' written by 'the celebrated Doctor Butler' (*The fetches*, pp. 133, 132). Butler is himself a central character in the tale, the medical attendant of the young Kilkenny College student, Tresham. He and Tresham represent apparently divergent perspectives on 'national superstitions', as Richard Haslam has argued (*The fetches*, p. 114).[140] While Tresham gives in to a passionate but academic interest in the fetch – a spectral impersonation of a living individual whose appearance in the morning or the evening augurs long life or certain death, respectively – Dr Butler 'is hostile to all forms of superstition'.[141]

It soon becomes apparent that Dr Butler is not simply intended to cure Tresham of his consumptive illness but also of his dangerous fascination with the fetch. Like Edward Waverley, Tresham is presented as seriously misguided by his education. '[A] deep reader, and an exceeding visionary', Tresham is 'superstitious, moping, and melancholy', and is known by his fellow students as 'a Rosycrucian, ... a soothsayer and ghost-seeker' (*The fetches*, pp. 149, 150). Thanks to the advantages of education and travel afforded to 'a young gentleman ... the descendant of an English family, settled in the south of Ireland', Tresham presents himself as less obviously mired in superstition than his dwarfish servant, Larry (*The fetches*, p. 143). Tresham's 'supernaturals', unlike Larry's, are said to be 'systematized so as to suit his intellect and education' (*The fetches*, p. 196). In contrast, Larry remains attached to the confused 'primitiveness of raw material' (*The fetches*, p. 196). While 'Tresham is more scholarly than Larry', Haslam writes, 'their metaphysics differ in degree rather than kind'.[142]

Faced with the superstitious beliefs of both men, Dr Butler determines to lead them out of their backward understanding, using fear and deception as his weapons. Ultimately, though, he begins to doubt his own rational commitment to disproving the fetch:[143]

> Rejecting from the first, with laughter and scorn, every thought of supernatural omen, and crushing it under a load of manly indifference, there now and then stirred, however, in the bottom of the doctor's soul, and under all that philosophical pressure, a something, that like an incipient earthquake at the base of a real mountain, slightly disturbed the mass. (*The fetches*, pp. 358–9)

By the end of the novel, Dr Butler's rationality has turned against him, for, when Tresham sees his lover, Anna, for a final time, the lies Dr Butler has told him for the sake of his health convince him that he is seeing her fetch. Anna, too, believes that what she sees – 'so dreadfully like' Tresham (*The fetches*, p. 385) – is his fetch. She conjures him to speak to her and convince her that he is Tresham in the flesh, but as he does so, he falls to the ground in a deadly swoon. Anna now realises that Tresham has been slowly dying for months, becoming confirmed in the opinion that 'the Fetch does not come in vain' (*The fetches*, p. 387). Now even more convinced than ever that Tresham's fetch had earlier appeared to her, Anna catches the body of her lover in her arms and throws herself over the precipitous cliff on which they are sitting. She is impelled to do so, in part, by the image of 'two figures, the counter parts of her lover and herself, standing, hand in hand, together' under the nearby waterfall (*The fetches*, p. 391). Her family and friends witness her last act and 'her fearful scream, as if of joy, not terror' (*The fetches*, p. 392).

There is, in this conclusion, an implied verification of the fetch and its prophetic powers.[144] As with Roche's *Trecothick bower* and Maturin's 'Leixlip Castle', then, *The fetches* might be seen to confirm the prevailing belief that Scott's historical novel simply did not suit nineteenth-century Irish reality. As Connolly contends, 'Characterised by beliefs that were supposed to belong to the past or to the infancy of culture, the literature of early nineteenth-century Ireland might be said to fail to produce uncanny effects because of the vitality of certain cultural practices – including the culture of supernatural belief'.[145] Yet, Scott's works themselves endow the mystical and eerie with a similar enduring strength. What these works help to highlight, therefore, is not the failure of Scott's model in Ireland, but instead the inadequacy of current conceptualisations of Scott's historical novel. Critically influenced and informed by gothic literary production, the historical novel was never a complete or irrevocable departure from it. Instead, the historical and the gothic converge throughout the early nineteenth century, producing a hybrid literary form that relies heavily on an evocation of the Gothic past and a continued interrogation of the meaning of history to present reality. To attempt to understand these forms as separate and distinct entities is both unwittingly to endorse Scott's self-interested endeavour to construct his 'original' genius and to misunderstand the cross-generic nature of Romantic literary production.

CONCLUSION

The issue of formal and generic overlap is one not solely confined to the categories of gothic and historical fiction, as shown in the next chapter. Instead, just as the texts discussed here threatened to dismantle eighteenth- and early nineteenth-century notions of social, cultural, and political progress and modernity, so too did their cross-formal and cross-generic nature present problems to literary notions of evolution and improvement. This is most readily apparent in the literary gothic's continued refusal to adhere to the terminological distinctions by which we now order late eighteenth- and early nineteenth-century literature. In particular, although literary scholars often make a distinction between 'romance' and 'novel' in this period, early Irish gothic fiction, like much of the British fiction we now know of as 'gothic novels', flirted with both terms. In so doing, this literature complicates both late eighteenth-century and more recent views of the novel's triumph over earlier forms of prose fiction and suggests the many layers of formal and generic overlap denied by retrospective constructions of 'the gothic novel'.

NOTES

1 *The Critical Review*, 13 (March 1762), 252.
2 *The Countess of Salisbury* was performed in Dublin and London in 1765 and 1767, respectively; Loeber and Loeber, *A guide to Irish fiction*, p. 748.
3 Summers, *The gothic quest*, pp. 153–201.
4 Thomas Leland, *Longsword, Earl of Salisbury: an historical romance*, 2 vols (Dublin, 1762), vol. 2, p. 32. Further references are to this edition and are given in parentheses in the text.
5 Richard Maxwell, 'The historical novel', in Richard Maxwell and Katie Trumpener (eds), *The Cambridge companion to fiction in the Romantic period* (Cambridge: Cambridge University Press, 2008), p. 67; Fiona Price, 'Ancient liberties? Rewriting the historical novel: Thomas Leland, Horace Walpole and Clara Reeve', *Journal for eighteenth-century studies*, 34.1 (2011), 20. See also Summers, *The gothic quest*, p. 158, and Anne H. Stevens, *British historical fiction before Scott* (Basingstoke and New York: Palgrave Macmillan, 2010), particularly Chapter 2, 'Historical novels, 1762–1783', pp. 21–50.
6 Loeber and Stouthamer-Loeber, 'The publication of Irish novels and novelettes', p. 28.
7 Ian Campbell Ross highlights this formal crossover, arguing that 'historical, sentimental and Gothic fiction [frequently] overlap' in eighteenth-century Irish prose fiction. The examples he notes include Leland's *Longsword*, Anne Fuller's *Alan Fitz-Osborne* (1787) and *The son of Ethelwolf* (1789), and Regina Maria Roche's *The children of the abbey* (1796), all of which are discussed in more detail later in this chapter; Ian Campbell Ross, 'Prose in English, 1690–1800: from the Williamite Wars to the Act of Union', in Margaret Kelleher and Philip O'Leary (eds), *The Cambridge history of Irish literature*, 2 vols (Cambridge: Cambridge University Press, 2006), vol. 1, p. 273.

8 Walter Scott, *Lives of the novelists*, 2 vols (Philadelphia, PA, 1825), vol. 2, pp. 120, 128; see also Ruth Mack, 'Horace Walpole and the objects of literary history', *ELH*, 75:2 (2008), 371.
9 Maxwell, 'The historical novel', p. 76.
10 Scott was often slow to acknowledge the debt his fiction owed to the works produced by his peers and to cultural phenomena such as the gothic, as was infamously made clear in the first chapter of *Waverley*. See Sir Walter Scott, *Waverley; or, 'tis sixty years since*, ed. Claire Lamont (1814; Oxford: Clarendon Press, 1981), p. 3; Katie Trumpener, *Bardic nationalism: the Romantic novel and the British Empire* (Princeton: Princeton University Press, 1997), p. 139; and Nicola J. Watson, *Revolution and the form of the British novel, 1790–1825: intercepted letters, interrupted seductions* (Oxford: Clarendon Press, 1994), p. 126. On Scott's influences, including the literary gothic, see Peter Garside, 'Popular fiction and national tale: hidden origins of Scott's *Waverley*', *Nineteenth-century literature*, 46.1 (1991), 30–53; Ian Duncan, *Modern romance and transformations of the novel: the gothic, Scott, Dickens* (Cambridge: Cambridge University Press, 1992); Fiona Robertson, *Legitimate histories: Scott, gothic, and the authorities of fiction* (Oxford: Clarendon Press, 1994); and Michael Gamer, *Romanticism and the gothic: genre, reception, and canon formation* (Cambridge: Cambridge University Press, 2000), particularly Chapter 5, '"To foist thy stale romance": Scott, antiquarianism, and authorship', pp. 163–200.
11 Trumpener, *Bardic nationalism*, p. 130.
12 Georg Lukács, *The historical novel*, trans. Hannah and Stanley Mitchell (1937; Lincoln, NE: University of Nebraska Press, 1983), p. 19.
13 See Miles, 'The 1790s: the effulgence of gothic'.
14 Punter argues that although '*Otranto* originated a genre, it was another thirteen years before a successor appeared' in the form of Reeve's *The old English baron*; Punter, *The literature of terror*, vol. 1, p. 47. See also note 31 above, p. 23.
15 Stevens, *British historical fiction before Scott*, pp. 49, 121.
16 *Ibid.*, p. 49.
17 *The Critical Review*, 13 (March 1762), 252. For a more detailed discussion of the overlap of Leland's historical writings and *Longsword*, see Christina Morin, 'Theorizing "Gothic" in eighteenth-century Ireland', in Morin and Gillespie (eds), *Irish gothics*, pp. 13–33. See also Killeen, 'Remembering history: public memory, commemoration, and necrophilia', *The emergence of Irish Gothic fiction*, pp. 157–90.
18 Maxwell, 'The historical novel', p. 67.
19 *Ibid.*
20 *The Critical Review*, 13 (March 1762), 252.
21 *Monthly Review*, 26 (March 1762), 236–7. Original emphasis.
22 *Monthly Review*, 32 (February 1765), 97–9.
23 *Monthly Review*, 32 (May 1765), 394.

24 Elizabeth Fay, *Romantic medievalism: history and the Romantic literary ideal* (Basingstoke and New York: Palgrave Macmillan, 2002), p. 10.
25 Price, 'Ancient liberties?', p. 20.
26 E.J. Clery, *The rise of supernatural fiction, 1762–1800* (Cambridge: Cambridge University Press, 1995), p. 54.
27 *Ibid.*, p. 55.
28 *Monthly Review*, 32 (May 1765), 394.
29 Clery translates '*incredulus odi*' as 'to believe is to dislike'; *The rise of supernatural fiction*, p. 54.
30 Diane Long Hoeveler, *Gothic riffs: secularizing the uncanny in the European imaginary, 1780–1820* (Columbus, OH: Ohio State University Press, 2010), p. 6.
31 *Ibid.*, p. xv.
32 *Ibid.*, p. xvi. For a similar argument about the secularising tendency in eighteenth-century literature, see Carol Stewart, *The eighteenth-century novel and the secularization of ethics* (Farnham: Ashgate, 2010).
33 Hoeveler, *Gothic riffs*, pp. 47, 41.
34 Rosemary Sweet, *Antiquaries: the discovery of the past in eighteenth-century Britain* (London: Hambledon and London, 2004), p. xiv.
35 Watt, *Contesting the gothic*, p. 47.
36 Clery, *The rise of supernatural fiction*, p. 60.
37 *Ibid.*
38 See Price, 'Ancient liberties?', and Watt, *Contesting the gothic*.
39 Price, 'Ancient liberties?', p. 23.
40 Toni Wein, *British identities, heroic nationalisms, and the gothic novel, 1764–1824* (Basingstoke and New York: Palgrave Macmillan, 2002), p. 5.
41 *Ibid.*; Price, 'Ancient liberties?', p. 25.
42 See Thomas Leland, *Longsword, Earl of Salisbury* (London, 1762), vol. 2, p. 204, and Thomas Leland, *Longsword, Earl of Salisbury* (2nd edn; London, 1763), vol. 2, p. 204.
43 Writing to Alexander Pope in 1721, Jonathan Swift expressed his admiration for 'the wisdom of that Gothic Institution, which made [Parliaments] Annual' and connected the absence of that same institution in present-day England with an inherent lack of liberty: 'I was confident our Liberty could never be placed upon a firm foundation till that ancient law were restored among us'. Later, Swift bitterly complained, 'We see the Gothic system of limited monarchy is extinguished in all the nations of Europe. It is utterly extirpated in this wretched kingdom, and yours must be the next'. See Jonathan Swift to Alexander Pope, 10 January 1721, and Jonathan Swift to William Pulteney, Earl of Bath, 8 March 1734[–35]; in David Woolley (ed.), *The correspondence of Jonathan Swift, D.D.*, 4 vols (Frankfurt am Main: Peter Lang, 1999–2007), vol. 2, p. 360, vol. 4, p. 66.

44 W.S. Lewis, Introduction, in Horace Walpole, *The castle of Otranto*, ed. W.S. Lewis (London: Oxford University Press, 1964), p. xxv.
45 Price, 'Ancient liberties?', p. 26. On the political events of 1763 and 1764, as well as the involvement of Walpole and Conway, see, for instance, Lewis, 'Introduction', pp. xxvii–xxviv, and Price, 'Ancient liberties?', p. 26.
46 Price, 'Ancient liberties?', p. 27.
47 *Ibid.*, p. 22.
48 *Ibid.*, pp. 22–3.
49 *Ibid.*, p. 23.
50 Watt, *Contesting the gothic*, p. 47.
51 *Ibid.*, p. 49.
52 For a contrasting view of Leland's depiction of Mal-leon, see Price, 'Ancient liberties?', p. 23.
53 Clara Reeve, *The old English baron*, ed. James Trainer, introd. James Watt (1778; Oxford: Oxford University Press, 2008), p. 2. Further references are to this edition and are given in parentheses in the text.
54 *Reginald Du Bray: an historick tale. By a late lord, greatly admired in the literary world* (Dublin, 1779), p. 1. *Reginald Du Bray*'s anonymous Dublin printing, coupled with its reference to *Longsword*, may have been intended to mislead readers into believing it was an original Irish publication. In fact, it is a reprint of the second volume of *The rival friends; or, the noble recluse: a novel* (London: T. Vernor, 1776). See James Raven and Antonia Forster, with Stephen Bending, *The English novel 1770–1829: a bibliographical survey of prose fiction in the British Isles. Vol. 1, 1770–1799* (Oxford: Oxford University Press, 2000), p. 247, and Dorothy Blakey, *The Minerva Press 1790–1820* (London: The Bibliographical Society at the University Press, Oxford, 1939), p. 140. A second Dublin edition appeared in 1784 under the title *Reginald Du Bray: an historic tale. By a late nobleman*; reference to *Longsword* is here omitted.
55 Watt, *Contesting the gothic*, p. 51.
56 Ian Duncan, 'Walter Scott, James Hogg and Scottish gothic', in Punter (ed.), *A companion to the gothic*, p. 75.
57 Maxwell, 'The historical novel', pp. 69–70.
58 Price, 'Ancient liberties?', p. 31.
59 Another Irish text that follows the example set by Leland and might be classed, like it, as a loyalist gothic romance as identified by Watt is Stephen Cullen's *The castle of Inchvally: a tale – alas! too true* (1796), discussed in more detail below, p. 100. See Watt, *Contesting the Gothic*, p. 65.
60 A central character in both *Longsword* and *Alan Fitz-Osborne*, the historical des Roches was complicit in de Burgh's fall from royal favour in 1232 but himself fell from favour by 1234, when he was banned from the court and unceremoniously told 'to meddle no more in political affairs'. Despite his lack of official court position through much of the 1220s and 1230s, de Burgh was

viewed with distrust because of the influence he held over Henry III, who had spent much of his childhood in the bishop's household and care. This hostility was compounded by de Burgh's birth and upbringing in France, which, it seems, laid him open to suspicion from the native English baronage, members of whom accused him of, among other things, displaying favouritism towards fellow emigrés and plotting a French takeover of England; Nicholas Vincent, 'Roches, Peter des (*d.* 1238)', *Oxford dictionary of national biography* (Oxford, 2004; online edn, 2008), www.oxforddnb.com, accessed 17 July 2013.

61 Anne Fuller, *Alan Fitz-Osborne, an historical tale*, 2 vols (London [1787]), vol. 2, p. 11. Further references are to this edition and are given in parentheses in the text.
62 J.M.S. Tompkins, 'James White, Esq. a forgotten humourist', *Review of English studies*, 3 (1927), 149.
63 *Ibid.*, p. 145. Tompkins (p. 156) notes that White's death was recorded in the register for the Church of St James, Abson: '1799, James White, Esq.: (he ended his existence by Famine – supposed to be insane) his name not learnt for sometime. March 15th.'
64 The latter two are translations from the works of Rabaut Saint-Étienne (1743–93).
65 Tompkins, 'James White', p. 148.
66 *Ibid.*
67 James White, *Conway Castle; a poem* (London, 1789), unpaginated advertisement. Further references are to this edition and are given in parentheses in the text.
68 Ina Ferris, *The Romantic national tale and the question of Ireland* (Cambridge: Cambridge University Press, 2002), p. 104.
69 James White, *Earl Strongbow: or, the history of Richard de Clare and the beautiful Geralda*, 2 vols (Dublin, 1789), vol. 1, pp. 4, 10. Further references are to this edition and are given in parentheses in the text.
70 Watt, *Contesting the gothic*, p. 43.
71 *Ibid.*
72 See Northrop Frye, *The secular scripture: a study of the structure of romance* (Cambridge, MA: Harvard University Press, 1976), particularly Chapter 3, 'Our Lady of Pain: heroes and heroines of romance', pp. 63–93 and Chapter 4, 'The bottomless dream: themes of descent', pp. 95–126.
73 Regina Maria Roche, *Trecothick bower; or, the lady of the west country*, 3 vols (London: A.K. Newman, 1814), vol. 1, p. 147. Further references are to this edition and are given in parentheses in the text.
74 Watt, *Contesting the gothic*, p. 51.
75 C.L. Kingsford, 'Hereberht (*d.* 687)', rev. Marios Costambeys, *Oxford dictionary of national biography* (Oxford, 2004; online edn, 2004), www.oxforddnb.com, accessed 29 April 2015.

76 By 1814, the Prince Regent was acting effectively in place of his ailing father, George III.
77 That Roche believed he had done so is clear in her dedication to *Contrast* (1828), where, in committing the novel to Princess Augusta, Roche praised her brother, George IV, as '[having] signally advanced the glory of this country, by every means in his power, and who, by his humane and liberal patronage, has encouraged and called into action the various energies and talents of a free people'; *Contrast*, 3 vols (London: A.K. Newman & Co., 1828), vol. 1, p. xi.
78 Thomas Flanagan, *The Irish novelists, 1800–1850* (New York: Columbia University Press, 1958), pp. 188–9.
79 *Ibid.*, p. 189.
80 James Cahalan, *Great hatred, little room: the Irish historical novel* (Dublin: Gill and Macmillan, 1983), p. 15.
81 Emer Nolan, 'Banim and the historical novel', in Jacqueline Belanger (ed.), *The Irish novel in the nineteenth century: facts and fictions* (Dublin: Four Courts Press, 2005), p. 80.
82 *Ibid.*; Jacqueline Belanger, 'Introduction', in Belanger (ed.), *The Irish novel in the nineteenth century*, p. 15.
83 Terry Eagleton, *Heathcliff and the great hunger: studies in Irish culture* (London: Verso, 1995), p. 147.
84 Belanger, 'Introduction', p. 16.
85 See Siobhán Kilfeather, 'Sex and sensation in the nineteenth-century Irish novel', in Margaret Kelleher and James Murphy (eds), *Gender perspectives in nineteenth-century Ireland: public and private spheres* (Dublin: Irish Academic Press, 1997), pp. 83–92.
86 *Ibid.*, p. 86.
87 John Gibson Lockhart, *Memoirs of the life of Sir Walter Scott, Bart.*, 10 vols (2nd edn; Edinburgh, 1839), vol. 1, p. 37; quoted in Robertson, *Legitimate histories*, p. 52.
88 Robertson, *Legitimate histories*, p. 6.
89 *Ibid.*, p. 48.
90 Price, 'Ancient liberties', p. 20.
91 Robertson, *Legitimate histories*, pp. 7–8.
92 Christina Morin, *Charles Robert Maturin and the haunting of Irish Romantic fiction* (Manchester: Manchester University Press, 2011), pp. 154–7.
93 Cahalan, *Great hatred, little room*, p. 7.
94 Douglas S. Mack (ed.), *James Hogg: selected stories and sketches* (Edinburgh, 1982), p. 145; quoted in Robertson, *Legitimate histories*, p. 13.
95 Thomas Middleton Raysor (ed.), *Coleridge's miscellaneous criticism* (London, 1936), p. 332; quoted in Robertson, *Legitimate histories*, p. 13.
96 Duncan, *Modern romance and transformations of the novel*, p. 59.

97 Watt, *Contesting the gothic*, pp. 151–2.
98 *The Critical Review*, 5th ser., 1 (March 1815), 294.
99 *The Critical Review*, 5th ser., 1 (June 1815), 600, 603.
100 *Ibid.*, p. 601. A negative contrast between the pre-modern Scottish people and the modern English reader is established when the reviewer writes, 'Possibly all this may be true to nature, as the Scotch have not yet thrown off their belief in witchcraft, and continue bigots to the influence of second sight' (p. 601).
101 *Monthly Review*, 2nd ser., 77 (May 1815), 86.
102 *Ibid.*
103 [Francis Jeffrey], Review of *Marmion; a tale of Flodden Field*, *Edinburgh Review*, 12 (1808), 9.
104 *Ibid.*, 28.
105 *Ibid.*, 30–1. Original emphasis.
106 *Ibid.*, 35.
107 *Ibid.*, 32.
108 Jeffrey suggests that Scott's particular use of history in *Marmion*, combined with his popular appeal, promised to create 'an indiscriminate taste for chivalrous legends and romances in irregular rhime'. In this, Scott was bound to attract 'as many copyists as Mrs. Radcliffe or Schiller' at the same time that he became 'the founder of a new schism in the catholic poetical church, for which, in spite of all our exertions, there will probably be no cure, but in the extravagance of the last and lowest of its followers'; *ibid.*, 34.
109 Gamer, *Romanticism and the gothic*, p. 189.
110 Watt, *Contesting the gothic*, p. 134. Gamer notes that Scott, offended by Jeffrey's review, invited Jeffrey to Abbotsford for a conciliatory dinner; afterwards, 'Jeffrey never wrote another negative review of Scott's poetry'; Gamer, *Romanticism and the gothic*, p. 189.
111 Murray Pittock, *Scottish and Irish Romanticism* (Oxford: Oxford University Press, 2008), p. 213; Jeffrey, Review of *Marmion*, 9.
112 See Scott, *Waverley*, pp. 276–7, 325–6.
113 Robertson, *Legitimate histories*, pp. 214–25. For the exchange between Ravenswood and his credulous servant, Caleb Balderstone, regarding the family prophecy, see Sir Walter Scott, *The bride of Lammermoor*, ed. Fiona Robertson (1819; Oxford: Oxford University Press, 1991), p. 186.
114 Scott, *The bride of Lammermoor*, p. 268; Morin, *Charles Robert Maturin*, p. 156.
115 On the similarities between the two novels, see Robertson, *Legitimate histories*, pp. 214–25.
116 For the correspondence between Maturin and Scott, see Fannie E. Ratchford and Wm. H. McCarthy, Jr. (eds), *The correspondence of Sir Walter Scott and Charles Robert Maturin, with a few other allied letters* (Austin, TX: University of Texas Press, 1937).

117 British Library 41996/27, letter from Maturin to Hurst, Robinson & Co., 25 June 1821.
118 Morin, *Charles Robert Maturin*, p. 155.
119 See Dale Kramer, *Charles Robert Maturin* (New York: Twayne, 1973), pp. 133–6 and Robert E. Lougy, *Charles Robert Maturin* (Lewisburg, PA: Bucknell University Press, 1975), pp. 75–81. Both Kramer and Lougy advance a defence – not a denunciation – of Maturin's work as a text inspired by, but intrinsically different from, Scott's historical novel due both to Maturin's continued interest in the gothic and to his perception of contemporary Ireland's social, cultural, religious, and political situation.
120 On Scott's recommendation, Maturin omitted the bodily representation of the devil – referred to as the Black Knight – from *Bertram* before the play was successfully performed at Drury Lane Theatre in May 1816. Scott later came to regret his advice, reprinting, with some inaccuracies, the excised sections in his review of Maturin's later novel, *Women; or, pour et contre* (1818). See Ratchford and McCarthy (eds), *The correspondence of Sir Walter Scott and Charles Robert Maturin*, and Sir Walter Scott, Review of *Women; or, pour et contre* by Charles Robert Maturin, *Edinburgh Review*, 30.59 (1818), 234–57. For a useful comparison of the three principal texts of the play, including the manuscript Maturin sent to Scott, the Larpent copy, and the performance text, see Jeffrey Cox, *Seven gothic dramas, 1789–1825* (Ohio: Ohio University Press, 1992), pp. 315–83.
121 Morin, *Charles Robert Maturin*, p. 157.
122 The tale was originally published in *The literary souvenir; or, cabinet of poetry and romance* (London: Hurst, Robinson, & Co., 1825), pp. 211–32.
123 Charles Robert Maturin, 'Leixlip Castle; an Irish family legend', in Richard Dalby (ed.), *Twelve gothic tales* (Oxford: Oxford University Press, 1998), p. 1. Further references are to this edition and are given in parentheses in the text.
124 Trumpener, *Bardic nationalism*, p. 223.
125 See 'legend, n.', *OED online* (Oxford University Press, March 2015), www.oed.com, accessed 14 May 2015.
126 Trumpener, *Bardic nationalism*, p. 225.
127 Original emphasis.
128 *Ibid.*, p. 223.
129 Pittock, *Scottish and Irish Romanticism*, p. 232.
130 Trumpener, *Bardic nationalism*, p. 224.
131 *Ibid.*
132 Pittock, *Scottish and Irish Romanticism*, p. 232.
133 Connolly, *A cultural history of the Irish novel*, p. 178.
134 See, amongst others, Cahalan, *Great hatred, little room*, p. 49; Flanagan, *The Irish novelists*, p. 189; Derek Hand, *A history of the Irish novel* (Cambridge: Cambridge University Press, 2011), pp. 83–4.

135 *Monthly Review*, 3rd ser., 2 (August 1826), 355, 364.
136 *Monthly Review*, 3rd ser., 4 (February 1827), 129–30, 130–1.
137 Connolly, *A cultural history of the Irish novel*, p. 178.
138 John and Michael Banim, *The fetches*, in John and Michael Banim, *Tales by the O'Hara family*, vol. 2 (London: W. Simpkin and R. Marshall, 1825), p. 113. Further references are to this edition and are given in parentheses in the text; Connolly, *A cultural history of the Irish novel*, p. 178.
139 On the discussion between Abel and Barnes O'Hara about the representation, in print, of orally transmitted legends and superstitions, see Connolly, *A cultural history of the Irish novel*, pp. 178–82. For the argument that the fictional creation of the O'Hara brothers 'reinforces the air of authenticity that infuses their work', see Hand, *A history of the Irish novel*, p. 83.
140 Haslam, 'Maturin's Catholic heirs', p. 114.
141 *Ibid.*
142 *Ibid.*
143 *Ibid.*, p. 116.
144 *Ibid.*, p. 117. Contemporary reviewers equally detected a confirmation, rather than deflation, of the myth of the fetch; see *La belle Assemblée*, 3rd ser., 1 (May 1825), 217–18.
145 Connolly, *A cultural history of the Irish novel*, p. 187.

2

Gothic genres: romances, novels, and the classifications of Irish Romantic fiction

In his *Revelations of the dead-alive* (1824), John Banim depicts his time-travelling narrator encountering future interpretations of the fiction of Walter Scott. In twenty-first-century London, Banim's narrator realises, Scott is little read; when he is, he is understood, as James Kelly points out, 'not as the progenitor of the historical novel but rather as the last in line of an earlier Gothic style'.¹ According to the readers encountered in his travels, Scott is actually the 'last and most successful adaptor or modifier' of a gothic literary mode introduced by Walpole and practised by Lewis and Radcliffe.² Commenting slyly on the question of Scott's originality while also denying lasting fame to the period's most financially and popularly successful novelist, Banim's *Revelations of the dead-alive* perceptively reveals the formal and generic slippages of historical and gothic fiction in the late eighteenth and early nineteenth centuries. As it does so, it underscores the formal and generic fluidity of Romantic-era literature. While modern-day readers frequently view gothic and historical fictions of this period as distinctly different types of writing, especially in the period following the publication of *Waverley* (1814), contemporary accounts of these fictions are much more equivocal in their categorisations of works that were unquestioningly understood as cross-formal and cross-generic.

Looking back to the novels of James White, considered in Chapter 1, we see the manner in which late eighteenth-century critics struggled with the formal classifications that are often accepted without question today. Reviews of White's *Earl Strongbow* (1789) oscillated in their classifications of the tale as either historical or romantic in nature. *The Critical Review* briefly dismissed White's use of the ghost of Strongbow to narrate the tale as 'trite and hackneyed' before offering a 'minute' dissection of the novel's many historical anachronisms.³ Despite highlighting the 'inconsistency' of a language unsuitable to the time of Charles II and various other anachronistic misdemeanours, *The Critical Review* ultimately commended *Earl Strongbow* as an amusing publication able to teach its readers much about the past: 'we have been entertained with the tale. It is not an eventful story to please general readers; but we think many will be instructed in some points of history by it, and particularly in the manners of their ancestors.'[4] The *Gentleman's Magazine*, in contrast, emphasised the novel's romantic quality, introducing *Earl Strongbow* as an 'imitation of Gothic romance possess[ing] a degree of merit which ought not to pass unnoticed.'[5] And, where *The Critical Review* had found the ghost of Strongbow tired and stale, the *Gentleman's Magazine* praised White for his originality: 'The ghost of an antient baron, who stands high in the chronicles of military renown, rehearsing his adventures, in a narration continued through several progressive nights, each of which forms a chapter, is an idea that has not been started by any other writer.'[6]

White's next novel, *The adventures of John of Gaunt, Duke of Lancaster* (1790), also met a mixed reception owing to its striking combination of quasi-factual historical detail and imaginative fictional narrative. The tale recounts the various escapades of the eponymous John of Gaunt (1340–99), the younger brother of Edward, the Black Prince, as he accompanies his sovereign brother, first to Wales, and then to Scotland, where they become embroiled in a war between that nation and England over the ransom of the imprisoned King of Scotland, David II. Describing the battle in which the English triumph over the Scottish as well as the hasty war council that precedes it, White inserts a footnote containing a barbed observation on the accuracy of historiography: 'Strange that none of the annalists or chroniclers have taken the least notice of this battle, or of the parliamentary debate which preceded it, or of any of the circumstances here related. Culpable negligence!'[7] White's footnote forces the reader into a peculiar position of ambivalence: until the battle, the tale has been presented as unequivocally fanciful in nature, a kind of chivalric *Gulliver's travels* (1726). As war is introduced, White asks his reader to accept his fantastical narration as more accurate and truthful than history writing. In so doing, White effects a deliberate blurring of the boundaries between fact and fiction, suggesting his particular interest in ongoing debates over the value and appeal of prose fiction.

Unimpressed with White's construction of a close proximity between fiction and historiography, *The Critical Review* scathingly condemned *John of Gaunt* as not only uninteresting but also alarmingly deceptive for readers:

> [W]hat purpose do these antique-modern tales answer? They are less entertaining ..., less interesting, and less instructive than even the modern ones; for the evident fiction destroys the interest, and the mixture of ancient and modern customs, which cannot be discriminated by general readers, will mislead.[8]

With the tale's fictionality ruining any claim to historical value, *John of Gaunt* threatened, according to *The Critical Review*, to merge fact and fiction in the minds of susceptible readers. To be both interesting and instructive, *The Critical Review* suggested, involved a less fantastical approach to prose fiction; the review therefore concluded with the advice that White 'meet us again like a man of this world'.[9]

What White needed, *The Critical Review* proposed, was the kind of didactic realism that had come to represent by the latter half of the eighteenth century that which distinguished the novel from earlier forms of prose fiction, the romance in particular. For writers such as Samuel Richardson and Henry Fielding, didactic realism crucially differentiated the novel from preceding prose fictions, including the mid- to late seventeenth-century French chivalric works by La Calprenède (1609?–63) and Madeleine de Scudéry (1607–1701), among others. Against the improbabilities and excesses of texts such as *Cassandre* (1644–50) and *Artamène; ou le grand Cyrus* (1649–53), the novel offered edifying and entertaining realism. As Fielding wrote in the preface to *Joseph Andrews* (1742), 'those voluminous Works commonly called *Romances*, namely *Clelia, Cleopatra, Astræa, Cassandra*, the *Grand Cyrus*, and innumerable others ... contain, as I apprehend, very little Instruction or Entertainment'. Fielding saw *Joseph Andrews*, in contrast, as akin to history writing and championed his novel as a work in which '[d]elight is mixed with Instruction, and the Reader is almost as much improved as entertained'.[10] Ten years later, the dangers of over-indulgence in romances would be humorously portrayed in Charlotte Lennox's *The female Quixote* (1752), in which the heroine is depicted as requiring a 'cure' from the delusions produced by her romance reading. In this, both Fielding and Lennox foretell the opinion put forth by James Beattie in his *Dissertations moral and critical* (1783):

> Romances are a dangerous recreation. A few, no doubt, of the best may be friendly to good taste and good morals; but far the greater part are unskillfully written, and tend to corrupt the heart, and stimulate the passions. A habit of reading them breeds a dislike to history, and all the substantial parts of knowledge; withdraws the attention from nature, and truth; and fills the mind with extravagant thoughts, and too often with criminal propensities.[11]

Within this context of condemnation of the romance as socially and morally destructive, Leland's advertisement of *Longsword* as 'an historical romance' is notable, suggesting what E.J. Clery calls '[t]he return of romance to eighteenth-century fiction'.[12] Similarly, Walpole's stated desire 'to blend the two kinds of romance, the ancient and the modern' marked a turning point in the history of the novel as well as in the development of the literary gothic, as Clery observes (*Castle of Otranto*, p. 9). What makes *Otranto* so important, Clery contends, is its combination of the realism of the novel and the fantasy of the romance: 'The credible emotions of the characters connect us to incredible phenomena and events and allow terror to circulate via a process of identification and projection'.[13] David Punter similarly argues that it is *Otranto*'s merging of realism and romance in the form of the supernatural that establishes the novel as the originating moment of eighteenth-century gothic fiction.[14] What *Otranto* managed to do, according to both Clery and Punter, was to merge the improbabilities and interest in the past of earlier romance traditions with the realism of the novel that had apparently replaced them. Correspondingly, Punter contends, *Otranto* is 'the earliest and most important manifestation of the late eighteenth-century revival of romance'.[15]

Indicative of the critical tendency to distinguish prose fiction as either romance or novel by way of didactic realism, such arguments elide the continued overlap of these generic categorisations and the texts to which they are applied. Moreover, the idea of romance's 're-emergence' suggests that, with the 'origin' and 'rise' of the novel, the romance – and its associated fantastical elements – fell out of favour and was largely replaced by or, at the very least, subjugated to the novel. In fact, as Brean Hammond and Shaun Regan compellingly claim, 'it is entirely possible to argue that the novel never did distinguish itself from romance in such a neat and wholesale manner'.[16] The late eighteenth-century literary gothic's oscillation between terms – 'romance', 'novel', 'historical romance', 'tale', 'story', 'history', etc. – makes clear the essential indeterminacy of formal and generic borders in this period. As a form of self-identification in an atmosphere of ongoing, often heated discussion about the worth of prose fiction, these terms held an importance often overlooked in current references to texts by shortened titles that exclude meaningful generic categorisations contained in subtitles. It is not insignificant, for instance, that of the five fictional works published by Ann Radcliffe between 1790 and 1797, not one advertises itself as a 'novel', and four refer to themselves as 'romances' in their titles.[17] That the choice of terminology could determine, positively or negatively, the way in which a text was read and reviewed is clear from *The Critical Review*'s reference to Leland's decision to call *Longsword* a romance: 'The story of this romance (*as he modestly entitles it*) is founded on real facts'.[18] The implication is that, as a work containing the truth of history, *Longsword* is superior to a mere romance.

The notable lack of the term gothic in the self-identification of prose fiction of the late eighteenth and early nineteenth centuries makes attention to the generic affiliations of the works discussed here of crucial importance. Although we tend to follow the term 'gothic' with 'novel' when speaking of the literary gothic, as Williams points out, doing so overlooks both the comparative absence of 'gothic' as a generic descriptor and the natural hybridity of the categories variously referred to as 'romance', 'novel', 'tale', and 'history'.[19] The first part of this chapter explores the ongoing debate over these generic borders and classifications, focusing on Irish gothic literature's frequent uncovering of the porousness of boundaries between fact and fiction, novel and romance – an indeterminacy as socially threatening as the overlap of past and present made manifest in Walpole's *Otranto* and Leland's *Longsword*. The second part looks more particularly at examples of late eighteenth- and early nineteenth-century Irish gothic fiction that function as commentaries on, or, indeed, parodies of romance and the literary gothic. These texts might be read, like Lennox's *The female Quixote* and Austen's *Northanger Abbey* (1818), as containing romance, in the doubled sense of including and restraining or controlling it. Yet, closer inspection reveals that these works – Anne Fuller's *The convent; or, the history of Sophia Nelson* (1786), Mrs F.C. Patrick's *The Irish heiress* (1797) and *More ghosts!* (1798), Eaton Stannard Barrett's *The heroine, or, adventures of a fair romance reader* (1813), and Alicia Le Fanu's *Strathallan* (1816) – self-consciously highlight their textuality in a bid to underline the manufactured nature of all prose fiction as well as the taxonomies used to differentiate one text from another.[20] Accordingly, they are most accurately described as 'book[s] about other kinds of writing'.[21] Moreover, while they frequently register, like *The female Quixote* and *Northanger Abbey*, a cautionary note about the delusory potential of romance, they also accompany such lessons with a broader critique of undiscriminating or misguided reading – a practice that more often than not turns all forms of literature, factual or fictional, into latent threats.

The final section of this chapter turns attention to one of the leading formal classifications of Romantic-era fiction that has led to the continued neglect of Irish gothic literature in this period: the recognition of the 'national tale' as distinct from 'the Gothic novel'. Pioneered by Sydney Owenson, Lady Morgan in 1806, the national tale has become a major focal point in scholarship of Irish Romantic fiction, designated as a new literary form that emerged in response to the debate over and introduction of Anglo-Irish Union (1801). As with Scott's historical novel, the national tale's predominance has frequently effected an erasure of the lines of continuity between 'national' texts such as *Castle Rackrent* (1800), *The wild Irish girl* (1806), and *The Milesian chief* (1812) and the gothic fiction of the late eighteenth century. It is worth remembering, though, that the term 'a national tale' is as slippery as 'the Gothic novel'. First introduced in the subtitle of *The wild Irish girl*, the phrase has become synonymous with a literary novelty and originality founded on a desire to make the 'real' Ireland known to an English reading public. However, it was very rarely adopted by authors in Owenson's wake, suggesting that 'the national tale', like 'the Gothic novel', is a retrospective construction that inadequately addresses the formal and generic hybridity of the literature it attempts to describe.[22] Considering the continued emergence of gothic themes, tropes, and ideas – specifically a concern with investigating and negotiating the past's relation to the present as well as a related interest in the revival of romance – in several texts now considered 'national tales', this section interrogates the relationship of 'gothic' and 'national' fiction. To do so, it looks in particular at Owenson's *O'Donnel: a national tale* (1814), a key text in the renegotiation of prevailing understandings of the national tale and its relationship to contemporary Irish gothic literary production.

THE LITERARY GOTHIC AND THE REVIVAL OF ROMANCE

In Eaton Stannard Barrett's *The heroine, or, adventures of a fair romance reader* (1813), the well-read, rational hero, Robert Stuart, gently admonishes the heroine of the novel's title for over-indulging her love of romances. Stuart indicates that it is not the reading of works such as *The mysteries of Udolpho* (1794) and *The Italian* (1797) that is dangerous, but the wholesale submission to their fantasies. 'I do not protest against the perusal of fictitious biography altogether', Stuart says, 'for many works of this kind may be read without injury, and some with profit'. Examples of these, Stuart suggests, include '[n]ovels such as the Vicar of Wakefield, The Fashionable Tale, and Coelebs, which draw man as he is, imperfect, instead of man as he cannot be, superhuman'. Such works 'are both instructive and entertaining', Stuart reasons. Even '[r]omances such as the Mysteries of Udolpho, the Italian, and the Bravo of Venice, which address themselves to the imagination alone', can be 'often captivating, and seldom detrimental', Stuart admits. But they are also 'so seductive ... that one is apt to neglect more useful books for them; besides, when indulged in extreme, they tend to incapacitate us from encountering the turmoils of active life'.[23] In separating texts such as Goldsmith's *The vicar of Wakefield* (1766), More's *Coelebs in search of a wife* (1808), and Edgeworth's *Tales of fashionable life* (1809–12) from *The mysteries of Udolpho*, *The Italian*, and Lewis's *The bravo of Venice* (1805), Stuart establishes a generic distinction between 'novel' and 'romance' akin to that advanced by Richardson and Fielding. Where novels are 'instructive and entertaining' because they focus on 'man, as he is', 'romances' are 'captivating' and 'seductive' in their presentation of 'man, as he cannot be'. At the same time, Stuart makes it clear that there is nothing suspicious about romances in and of themselves; they are, as Stuart argues, 'seldom detrimental'. What is worrying is the way in which romances are read: 'indulged in extreme', romances have the potential to blur the line between reality and fantasy, thus unfitting their readers for real life, as is the case with Barrett's heroine, Cherry Wilkinson.

There is much of interest in Stuart's advice, including a significant echoing of Austen's *Northanger Abbey* and its self-reflexive commentary on the dangers of prose fiction and 'horrid' works such as *The mysteries of Udolpho*.[24] Most notable in terms of this chapter's discussion is Stuart's classification of all prose fiction – novels and romances – as 'fictitious biography'. This is an important act of generic conflation; by considering novels and romances together as essentially the same thing, Stuart underlines the slipperiness of generic boundaries we now tend to accept unquestioningly. His description of the novel as based on realism and 'both instructive and entertaining' versus the romance as fantastical, 'captivating', and potentially 'detrimental' references contemporary concerns with the regulation of prose fiction. Yet, his blanket term to describe both novel and romance – 'fictitious biography' – points to the continued intersection of these forms, as it does to the merging of factual and fictional prose styles in this period. Tellingly, Cherry's re-education revolves not around a shift from 'romance' to 'novel', but instead from prose fiction to '[m]orality, history, languages, and music' (*The heroine*, p. 288).

Mrs F.C. Patrick's earlier novel, *The Irish heiress* (1797), condemns the overconsumption of prose fiction in comparable terms to those used by Stuart in *The heroine*. Nevertheless, the text makes no distinction – implicit or explicit – between 'romance' and 'novel'. Instead, it categorises all prose fiction as potentially misleading when consumed in excess. Speaking of her natural social awkwardness as a young woman, the narrator speculates that 'a few well chosen Novels might have been of service to me, in informing me a little of manners and polite conversation; what warnings I might have drawn from Evelina without any danger as to morals'. The didactic potential of Fanny Burney's *Evelina* (1778) notwithstanding, the narrator is barred from reading novels as a child, even though her unaffectionate mother and sister 'read nothing else'. While a 'few' novels might be a good thing, *The Irish heiress* makes it clear that too many can certainly be a bad thing. Commenting on the excessive novel-reading of her mother and sister, the narrator condemns the habit as responsible for 'enervat[ing] the mind, and mak[ing] one seek for nothing but amusement, whereas that should be only as a relaxation from more fatiguing, and … more interesting subjects'.[25]

Despite its conservative view of novel-reading, *The Irish heiress* was criticised in *The Critical Review* for straying too far from the dictates of instructive realism: 'While the Irish heiress remained in her own country, the narrative bore many marks of reality. It was a plain tale, in which the writer and heroine appeared to be one and the same; but her departure for France destroyed the illusion, and we afterwards find the grossest fictions blended with real events'.[26] The review referred to *The Irish heiress* by its own terminology – as a 'novel'. Still it highlighted the novel's romantic, unrealistic features as precisely those deserving condemnation, noting with disgust the introduction of '[c]haracters connected with the French revolution', not because of their association with the revolution but because of the author's inaccurate depiction of them: 'The duke of Orleans is represented as being enamoured of the heiress, then a married woman; and Robespierre is an agent employed to solicit her favours'.[27] The work in question appears to be a novel, the review suggests, but lacking the genre's edifying realism, it becomes nothing more than mere romance: 'There are certainly parts of this novel which claim approbation: but the misfortune of the writer seems to have been, the adjustment of a plan, which he (or perhaps she) had not skill or patience to execute'.[28]

Its condemnation aside, *The Critical Review*'s complicity with *The Irish heiress*'s self-identification as a novel points to the terminological flexibility of late eighteenth- and early nineteenth-century prose fiction. Indeed, despite the strenuous arguments advanced by proponents of the novel about its value over the romance, journals continued to group novels and romances together. They also used the terms 'romance' and 'novel' largely interchangeably. An instance of this occurs in the *Monthly Review*'s assessment of *Earl Strongbow*, which it initially classified as a 'romance' characterised by a dangerous blend of '[h]istory and fable'. Later in the same review, *Earl Strongbow* is identified as a 'novel' with some evident merit: 'if we add that the novel is neatly written, and that the characters are well drawn and supported, we imagine these qualifications are as much as the readers of works of entertainment, generally, require'.[29] Indicatively, the *Edinburgh Review* regularly noted the publication of works such as *The heroine*, Roche's *Trecothick bower*, and Alicia Le Fanu's *Strathallan* under the combined heading, 'Novels and Romances'.[30]

Contemporary critical accounts of Romantic-era prose fiction emphasise its cross-generic nature and reflect a wider understanding of literary classifications in this period.[31] In his *Essay on light reading, as it may be supposed to influence moral conduct on literary taste* (1808), Edward Mangin argued that '[t]he word novel is a generical term; of which romances, histories, memoirs, letters, tales, lives, and adventures, are the species'.[32] Amanda Gilroy and Wil Verhoeven elaborate upon Mangin's list to account for further 'subspecies': 'the romance of real life', for example, and 'philosophical histories', the 'philosophical romance', the various permutations of 'tale', including 'national', 'moral', and 'fashionable', as well as those of 'novel', like 'horrid', 'terrific', 'gothic', 'Jacobin', 'Anti-Jacobin', and 'silver fork', and John Galt's 'theoretical histories'.[33] The importance of this generic hybridity in the assessment of late eighteenth- and early nineteenth-century prose fiction should not be underestimated, especially when speaking of the literary gothic. While we frequently refer to 'the Gothic novel' as a recognisable generic categorisation, what we are actually talking about is a varied body of prose fiction that very rarely identified itself as gothic. Instead, according to contemporary modes of literary nomenclature, works with what we would now identify as gothic content described themselves with reference to a diverse range of terms including, but certainly not limited to, 'novel' and 'romance'. Of the 114 Irish works catalogued in the Appendix here, not one specifically identifies itself as gothic along the lines of the second edition of *The castle of Otranto* or *The old English baron*.

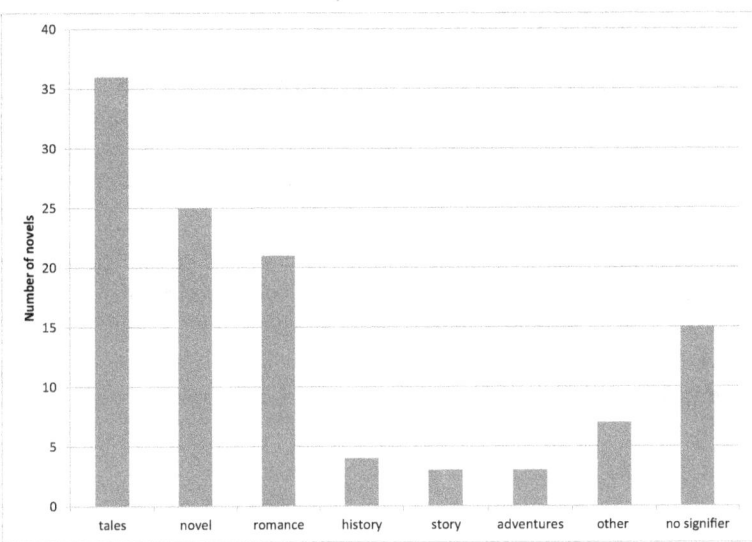

Figure 1 Irish gothic texts and their generic identifiers

The principal terms used to describe the works enumerated here are 'tale', 'novel', and 'romance', in that order.[34] (See Figure 1.)

Even here, generic and formal boundaries are not as clear-cut as we might wish, as evidenced by the many works documented in the Appendix that display combined variants of the terms listed here, including Elizabeth Griffith's *The history of Lady Barton, a novel, in letters* (1771) and *The story of Lady Juliana Harley, a novel* (1776). Strikingly, the largest number of combinations and variants occurs with 'history' and its referents: Anne Fuller's *Alan Fitz-Osborne; an historical tale* (1787) and *The son of Ethelwolf; an historical tale* (1789), for example, and Anna Milliken's *Corfe Castle; or, historic tracts. A novel* (1793), Mrs Sarah Green's *The royal exile; or, victims of human passions. An historical romance of the sixteenth century* (1810), and the Reverend George Croly's *Salathiel; a story of the past, the present, and the future* (1828). Many of these terms, whether combinations or not, belong to the category of 'generic pointers (historical romance, legends, tales, memoir, traditions)' identified by Robert Miles as the 'marketing cues' British authors used in the latter half of the eighteenth and the beginning of the nineteenth century to position their texts as examples of 'terror fiction'.[35] Other indicators, as Miles outlines, include geographical features (the recess, ruins, the rock, Alps, black valley, black tower, haunted cavern); architectural features (priory, castle, abbey, convent, nunnery, ancient house, cloister); … ghost and its cognates (apparition, specter, phantom, the ghost-seer, sorcerer, magician, necromancer, weird sisters); exotic names (Manfredi, Edward de Courcy, Wolfenbach); and generic or historical figures (the monk, the genius, the minstrel, knights, the royal captives, Duke of Clarence, Lady Jane Grey, John of Gaunt).[36]

Incorporating these categories into the assessment of the Irish works considered here shows that the use of generic or historical figures outweighs that of other identifying features. (See Figure 2.)

Here again significant overlap occurs, with a number of works deploying terminology from more than one category in their titles. Roche's novels,

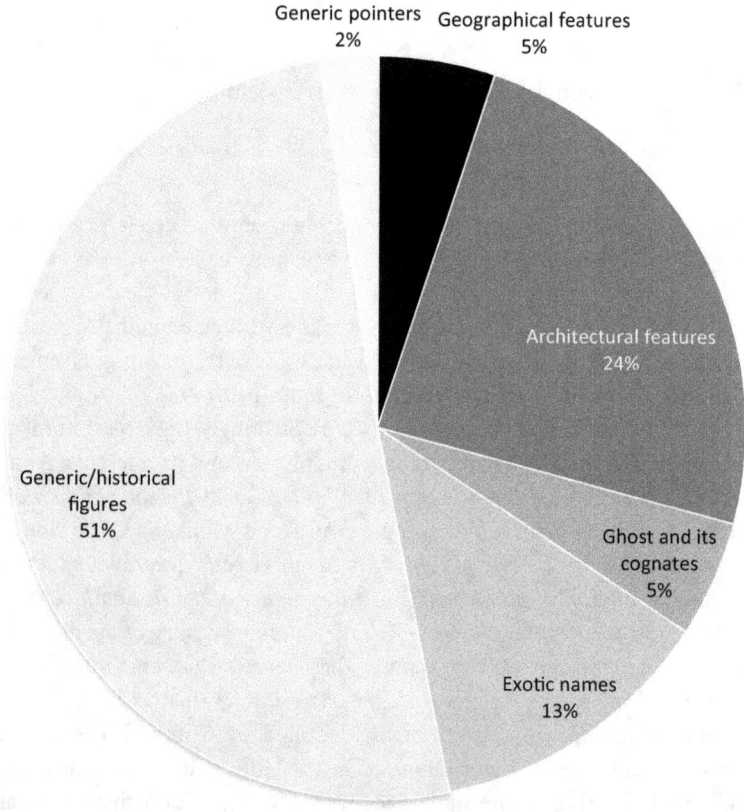

Figure 2 The marketing cues of Irish gothic fiction

for example, frequently combine generic pointers, architectural features, and generic or historical figures, as in *The children of the abbey; a tale* (1796), *The houses of Osma and Almeria; or, the convent of St Ildefonso. A tale* (1810), and *Trecothick bower; or, the lady of the west country. A tale* (1814). The same might be said of Anna Milliken's *Plantagenet: or, secrets of the house of Anjou. A tale of the twelfth century* (1802). Similarly, Charles Phillips's *The loves of Celestine and St Aubert; a romantic tale* (1811) calls upon both generic pointers and exotic names, and Catharine Selden's *Villa Nova; or, the ruined castle. A romance* (1805) on architectural features and generic pointers, to situate themselves in the literary marketplace.

These charts make conspicuous both the centrality and continued imprecision of literary labels in this period. On the one hand, the extensive use of particular formal and generic signifiers indicates a keen authorial awareness of the manner in which books were judged by their covers or, more accurately, their titles, by readers and reviewers. On the other hand, the multiplication of terminological variants and combinations highlights the sheer indeterminacy of such signifiers. While certain authors and critics, especially those concerned with a project of masculinising the novel as a genre, insisted on clear demarcations between various forms of prose fiction, especially 'romance' and 'novel', the fact is that such categorisations were tentative and fluid at best.[37] As evidenced by the varied use of terminology in the late eighteenth and early nineteenth centuries, prose fiction was very much the 'dialogic' arena envisioned by Mikhail Bakhtin.[38] More modern understandings of the emergence or rise of the novel out of previous forms of prose fiction, including the romance, misleadingly repeat contemporary, ideologically inflected differentiations of the novel like that voiced by Clara Reeve: 'The Romance in lofty and elevated language, describes what never happened nor is likely to happen. – The Novel gives a familiar relation of such things, as pass every day before our eyes, such as may happen to our friend, or to ourselves'.[39] The examples of prose fiction discussed in the next section demonstrate the responsiveness of late eighteenth and early nineteenth-century Irish authors to the imbrication of 'romance' and 'novel'. Presenting themselves as, at least in part, parodies of romance-reading and -writing, these works foreground their awareness of the continued debate over literary forms and their characteristics. They do so not simply to condemn romance but to comment critically upon the myriad intersections between literary forms, fact and fiction, literature and real life. In this sense, these works are concerned with the practice of reading itself as well as the place of romance, and literature more widely, in modern society.

THE WORK OF ROMANCE

At first glance, texts like *The Irish heiress*, *More ghosts!* and *The heroine* seem to participate in a longstanding anti-romance literary tradition that might be traced back to *Don Quixote* (trans. 1612) and *The mock-Clelia* (trans. 1678) through to Lennox's *The female Quixote* and Austen's *Northanger Abbey*. Yet, as has been argued recently in relation to these latter two works, *The Irish heiress*, *More ghosts!*, *The heroine* and other such titles, are much more than straightforward burlesques of existing prose fiction, whether identified as 'romance' or not. As Avril Horner and Sue Zlosnik point out, *The heroine* uses parody 'rather cleverly [to have] it both ways: it inscribes the values of the aspiring middle-class ... but simultaneously exposes the constraints they impose on the imaginative young woman'.[40] Indicatively, Cherry's ideological recuperation from addled romance reader to rational and decorous young woman ends not with her chastisement but with what she herself identifies as 'a true romance' conclusion: 'You see', she teases Stuart, 'after all your pains to prevent me from imitating romances, you have made me terminate my adventure like a true romance – in a wedding' (*The heroine*, p. 291).

As noted earlier in this chapter, *The heroine* pointedly undermines any sense of irrefragable difference between romance and novel as literary forms, proclaiming as it does so its interest in the acts of reading and writing themselves. As Jim Shanahan convincingly argues, *The heroine* does not simply 'lampoon what [Barrett] perceived to be bad writing' but instead, a whole host of writing, both respected and not; in this way, Barrett 'reinforces the idea that what he is burlesquing is not so much a discredited sub-genre as an entire space of experience'.[41] In William Hazlitt's terms, therefore, it would be a 'mistake' to interpret *The heroine*, or parody in general, as only 'degrad[ing], or imply[ing] a stigma on the subject'.[42] Underlined by the *The heroine*'s tongue-in-cheek conclusion is the indeterminacy shared by parody as a technique on the one hand, and literary classifications on the other. Barrett's text, in other words, is both a romance and not a romance; it is at once derisive of the romance as a form and, apparently contradictorily, mocking of those who would condemn the romance as different in kind and decidedly more dangerous than the novel. Tellingly, Cherry's playful chiding of her lover for simultaneously awakening her from and immersing her in romance is immediately followed by an apparently muddled didactic message. Upon being asked by Cherry 'with what moral will you now conclude the book', Stuart replies, 'I will say ... that virtue – no. That calamity – no. That fortitude and resignation – oh, no! I will say, then, that Tommy Horner was a bad boy, and would not get a plumcake; and that King Pepin was a good boy, and rode in a golden coach' (*The heroine*, p. 291). Horner and Zlosnick read this concluding sentence as an indication that 'the moral of *The heroine* should be absolutely clear to the reader, otherwise Stuart might as well be telling a pack of lies' (*The heroine*, p. 338). Barrett's suggestion, though, is not that prose fiction should contain a didactic message, but that readers should be allowed to discover any such message themselves. Through parody, therefore, *The heroine* advocates a relaxed attitude towards generic distinctions, arguing, as Stuart himself does, that any threat associated with the act of reading derives from the manner, rather than the matter, of reading.

A similar argument is put forth in Anne Fuller's *The convent; or, the history of Sophia Nelson* (1786), which focuses on the virtuous and orphaned young heroine, Sophia Nelson, as she deftly negotiates the perils of life with her ignorant and obnoxious cousins, the Woodvilles. All of Sophia's relatives present poignant comparisons either to Sophia herself or to her honourable suitor, Mortimer Stanhope. Most egregiously, Miss Cassandra Woodville is described as suffering from the effects of a misguided education in romance. With her name recalling the eponymous heroine of the chivalric romance *Cassandre* (1644–50), Cassandra is presented as an unreformed female Quixote, 'squar[ing] her conduct exactly by [the] rules' of her romances.[43] Embarrassed by Cassandra's long speeches, sighs, and belief that she will one day discover that the Woodvilles are not her family at all, the more rational Sophia laments the 'wrong education [that] has so overclouded' Cassandra's natural virtues (*The convent*, vol. 1, p. 71). Yet, *The convent* ultimately rewards Cassandra with an appropriate romance ending: the chivalric courtship of a lover and the (distant) promise of marriage. Moreover, the novel reserves its most pointed criticism for readers of history and modern novels, such as Sophia's uncle and guardian, Mr Woodville, who is shown to be seriously misled by his incomplete understanding of history and antiquarian scholarship. His home – Woodville Hall – is described by Sophia as 'in a ruinous condition', possibly, it is suggested, by Woodville's own design. Sophia aligns the 'true Gothic stile' of Woodville Hall with its owner's ridiculous pretensions to genealogical greatness; the house is throughout hung 'with portraits of grim-faced knights, and smiling damsels', considered by Woodville as 'inestimable relicks', the proof of his august lineage (*The convent*, vol. 1, p. 26). When Mortimer Stanhope first visits Woodville Hall and meets both Sophia and her guardian, he is struck by the mistaken and ludicrous understanding of the past displayed by Woodville: 'In short, he jumbled Normans, Danes, Saxons, and Britons together, till at length he arrived at the Romans, and from them he called out no less a person than Julius Caesar himself, for the head of his family' (*The convent*, vol. 1, p. 64).

No less ridiculous than Woodville is his second daughter, Eleanor. '[I]ndebted for all her knowledge to an ignorant country school mistress, and our modern novelists', Eleanor is depicted as even more seriously misguided than her sister, Cassandra (*The convent*, vol. 1, p. 16). Although tedious and irrational, Cassandra is nevertheless committed to feminine modesty and virtue. In contrast, Eleanor is not only jealous and mean-spirited, but also determined to get what she wants, even if that means engaging in unfeminine activity. In a telling incident, therefore, Eleanor writes to Stanhope to express her love for him. In so doing, Eleanor confirms her 'fallen' nature. Stanhope accordingly begs Cassandra to persuade her sister back into 'the fold of modesty and maidenly reserve' (*The convent*, vol. 1, pp. 214–15). Finding herself shunned by Stanhope, Eleanor eventually marries the 'good looking' but 'savage enough' Irishman, Heremon O'Flaherty, who ultimately turns out to be a fortune-hunter: 'Uncivilized and all bog-trotter as he is, I am convinced his rib's beauties, personal or mental never attracted him. No, no, he certainly had a hint about Nelson's will, and depending on his beau pere's villainy, wisely puts up with a partial inconvenience, in expectation of a future good' (*The convent*, vol. 2, p. 61). When this 'future good' proves illusory, O'Flaherty unceremoniously deserts his wife, unwilling to be saddled with a ridiculous woman without the benefit of a good settlement.

Why Eleanor should meet this disappointing end and Cassandra be rewarded with the kind of conclusion she has long envisioned for herself has much to do with the value given to 'modern' or 'fashionable' novels in *The convent*. As part of the 'wrong education' provided to fashionable young women, such fiction teaches ladies 'to consider nothing valuable, but as it contributes to excite admiration' (*The convent*, vol. 1, p. 261). Eleanor has received just this kind of education, as evidenced by her extreme attention to dress, often with laughable results, as when the sheep she ties to herself as ornaments of her shepherdess costume first rudely overturn her, then escape their tethers, forcing her to chase after them in a ridiculous state of dishabille. The remedy to such folly is, the narrative suggests, 'a proper, useful and refined education' (*The convent*, vol. 1, pp. 262–3). As with Lady Delacour in Edgeworth's *Belinda* (1801), therefore, Eleanor appears to function as a 'fashionable reader [who] misuses her literary knowledge ... to support a rapidly altering sequence of personas whose novelty and daring enable her to maintain her public preeminence'.[44] In contrast to Lady Delacour, however, Eleanor is both inept in her manipulation of fashionable reading and finally unreformed. Where Lady Delacour at length embraces an appropriate course of reading and, correspondingly, the proper domesticity she has hitherto eschewed, Eleanor never does.[45]

Notwithstanding Eleanor's failure to reform, *The convent* is clearly interested in the issue of appropriate fictional reading material, especially for impressionable young females. This is made clear by the extended praise accorded to Fanny Burney (1752–1840), who is described with much enthusiasm as 'a young female, who does honour to her sex and country':

> At an age when other women give themselves wholly up to dissipation, she devotes her time and her talents to the benefit of human kind. In the pleasing guise of a novellist [sic], she gives the noblest lessons of morality; and has found the art of adorning fiction with the robes of truth. In a word I sincerely wish that all my female acquaintance resembled Miss Burney. (*The convent*, vol. 1, p. 263)

In this encomium of Burney, *The convent* points to a conservative understanding of the proper role of the novel in contemporary society. Like Henry Fielding, Fuller propounds an idea of 'safe' and 'appropriate' prose fiction as that which educates its young (female) reader by way of didactic realism.

Its apparent conservatism notwithstanding, *The convent*'s treatment of its characters suggests a liberal agenda along the lines of that put forth by *The heroine* – one that implies that, perhaps more important than *what* one reads is *how* one reads.[46] The education Eleanor has received from her fashionable novels helps to win her a husband but provides no comfort when the fortune-seeking O'Flaherty absconds. Similarly, Woodville's misguided investment in history and antiquities proves the means to his end, and he dies after being attacked by robbers in Dijon, admitting on his deathbed that he had intended 'to make away with Sophia, some way or other' (*The convent*, vol. 2, p. 307). In contrast, Cassandra is rewarded, for all intents and purposes, flouting any notion of the text as wholly dismissive of chivalric romances. Moreover, Sophia herself becomes the subject of a romance plot rivalling that of Radcliffe herself: Woodville rudely rejects Stanhope and insists instead that Sophia marry her dim-witted cousin, Dick. When she refuses, he sends her to a convent in France, where she endures repeated attacks on her Protestantism, before being eventually freed by her concerned friends. Her release precipitates Woodville's death and frees her from his control. The tale then concludes with Sophia's own 'true romance' conclusion: marriage to Stanhope.

The convent thus hovers knowingly between the borders of fact and fiction, novel and romance. While it condemns certain reading practices, as exhibited by Woodville and Eleanor, and extolls what Marilyn Butler calls 'intelligent detachment', it nevertheless suggests that imaginative fiction may not be as delusive as the proponents of didactic realism insist.[47] More emphatically parodic in nature, Mrs F.C. Patrick's *More ghosts!* also straddles the line between condemnation of romance and a broader critique of indiscriminate reading. Presented by Patrick as a self-conscious burlesque of literary forms condemned by critics as misleading, including novels, chivalric romances, and 'terror fiction', *More ghosts!* begins with its putative editor noting the universally acknowledged truth that 'the best way to procure manuscripts, containing authentic histories is by a journey into the country'.[48] Correspondingly, the editor – identified in the preface as both 'an Officer's Wife' and '*An Officer's Widow*' (*More ghosts!*, vol. 1, pp. i. vi, xiii) – describes wandering into the dairy of the country farmhouse at which she has boarded while on holiday. There she espies 'a bundle of written papers' negligently stacked on a shelf for the mundane purpose of wrapping butter (*More ghosts!*, vol. 1, pp. i–ii). She rescues the manuscript from this ignominious end and discovers the story of naive young Thomas Grey, the ward of Reginald Morney, owner of Morney Abbey, a ruinous 'Gothic structure' in Yorkshire (*More ghosts!*, vol. 1, p. 16).

Much like the later, romance-misled heroes of Maturin's *The wild Irish boy* (1812) and Scott's *Waverley*, Grey allows his tendency to credit superstition and the supernatural to guide his conduct, with disastrous results. Manipulated by Betsey Bolton into believing that his kindly guardian is actually his villainous father, responsible for secretly and bigamously wedding Grey's mother and then discarding her, Grey confronts Morney and soon after finds himself sent away to university to correct the errors of his past mis-education. Revealing the true circumstances of the life and death of Grey's mother, Morney's own sister, Morney cautions Grey against his proclivity to irrational beliefs: 'credulity is your great fault; guard against that, and think of me as I shall deserve' (*More ghosts!*, vol. 2, p. 123). Returned to Morney Abbey after his education, Grey finds his superstitious nature rather confirmed than denied by the apparent supernatural appearance of his mother to various members of the household. Echoing the events that had led to his original disgrace, these visitations imply that Grey's belief in romance is less misguided than originally suggested. Even Morney himself witnesses the spectral return of his sister, come, it seems, to vindicate her son against Betsey's false accusations that Grey is the father of her illegitimate child.

As with the 'explained supernatural' of Radcliffe's fiction, the ghost of Morney Abbey is revealed to be flesh and blood. In a scene reminiscent of *The old English baron*, Morney determines to sit up all night in the haunted room in which the ghost of his sister had appeared to his daughter demanding justice for Grey. Once again the spectre appears, revealing herself to be Morney's sister, Isabella, in the flesh. It seems she had not died as Morney believed but had instead manufactured her own death in order to escape her past of bigamous marriages and rebellion against 'the tyranny of man' (*More ghosts!*, vol. 1, p. 186). Soon deserted by the lover for whom she had undergone death at least as far as her family and friends in England were concerned, Isabella is converted to Catholicism and enters a convent in Normandy, where she finds both a good abbess and personal peace.[49] This situation is later disrupted by the French Revolution, which forces Isabella and her companions to emigrate to England, where Isabella's natural maternal instincts prompt her to visit her unsuspecting family members in order to safeguard the character and matrimonial liberty of her son.

As in *The old English baron*, therefore, Isabella's apparently spectral return serves to rectify the wrongs committed against the hero, restoring him to his uncle's good graces as well as to his hitherto surrendered maternal inheritance. Grey's much hoped for end – marriage to Morney's daughter, Mary – does not follow, however. Although Morney had long intended that the marriage should take place, Mary's own education while Grey is at university convinces her that their union was founded on 'some romantic notions, which a knowledge of the world had cured her of' (*More ghosts!*, vol 3, p. 262). Mary's education serves as a poignant counterpart to that of her aunt, Isabella. Sent to London under the care of the 'female philosopher', Lady Newet, Mary is introduced to 'Voltaire, Rousseau, Hume, and Gibbon' (*More ghosts!*, vol 3, p. 40). Owing to these 'poisonous' books and to Lady Newet's resolute belief in all religion as mere superstition and witchcraft, Mary begins to become a philosopher herself (*More ghosts!*, vol 3, p. 53). She is at length convinced of her error by the combined efforts of her father and the kindly young clergyman, Seymour, who both recalls *The female Quixote*'s reforming Doctor and anticipates *Belinda*'s Dr X–. Mary's reformation from the moral philosophy she has developed under the influence of dangerous French texts is accompanied by a poignant reflection on her difference from upstanding novelistic heroines: 'This circumstance of her being, in some degree, led into error would have been omitted, but as serving to shew that the best disposed minds may sometimes suffer from the contagion of bad example, as our heroine was previously esteemed, in mental purity, hardly a whit behind Pamela, Harriet Biron, &c.' (*More ghosts!*, vol 3, p. 57).

With this reflection, the narrator confirms the novel's Richardsonian perspective on the importance of didactic realism and moral rectitude of popular reading material. Offering rational explanations for every moment of apparent supernaturalism in the text and depicting the necessary reformation of its erring female characters, *More ghosts!* strikes a powerfully conservative and reactionary note, especially with reference to the danger of ideas and sentiments associated with the French Revolution. Ultimately, it seems, like Mary's 'romantic notions', romance and its associated sentiment and sensibility must be controlled in order to ensure the present and future security of the British nation, exemplified in miniature by the domestic units established by the end of the novel – that of Mary and Seymour, on the one hand, and Grey and an unnamed 'very beautiful lady', on the other (*More ghosts!*, vol 3, p. 263). Reviewed glowingly by *The Critical Review*, *More ghosts!* was praised for its use of 'ghosts with a view of dissipating the horrors, lately excited in the tender breast of many a boarding-school miss, by the more artful and terrific dealers in the article'. With spectres more 'cunning than terrible', the novel was seen to entertain at the same time that it offered 'many just reflections on the errors of education and the irregularity of the passions'.[50] Still, like *The heroine*, *More ghosts!* ends on a strikingly ambivalent, if humorous note. Following the news of Mary's marriage to Seymour and Grey's impending nuptials, the narrator addresses the reader directly, promising three more volumes on 'the Mr. Morneys and Miss de Burgh' (*More ghosts!*, vol 3, p. 264). The implication is that the story is not yet finished, and that more romance, in the doubled sense of another publication as well as future romantic adventures, is to follow.

ROMANCE AND THE TERROR OF REAL LIFE

If *More ghosts!*, *The convent*, and *The heroine* all comment on the habit of condemning romances as immoral and destructive for impressionable readers, they also frequently position romance as a powerful tool for laying open the terrors of real life. In its description of the troubles faced by Sophia at the hands of her mercenary uncle, for instance, *The convent* foreshadows a trend located by Emma Clery in the prose fiction of the last decade of the eighteenth century: 'In the 1790s the idea seems to emerge, particularly among women authors, that romance, by its very inclusion of the marvellous or the apparently marvellous, can reveal the unpleasant truth about real life in a way impossible in the referential narratives of historians or realist novelists'.[51] Although *The convent*'s humorous take on readers such as Eleanor and Woodville may suggest the text's commitment to the tenet put forward by the narrator of *The heroine*, that 'to make the world laugh ... is the gravest occupation an author can chuse' (*The heroine*, p. 6), the novel is nevertheless very serious about the dangers faced by the average middle- and upper-class female in a patriarchal world. Writing to her friend and confidante about her uncle's insistence that she marry Dick, Sophia naively declares, 'Thank heaven it is not in his power (nor I hope will not be in his inclination) to force me into so preposterous an union' (*The convent*, vol. 1, p. 123). The fact is, as Woodville's dependant, even if made so by a false will, Sophia has very little control over what happens to her, as evidenced by her imprisonment in the convent. Even the freedom Sophia achieves by the end of the novel – release from the convent – results in a confinement of another sort – marriage. The only character to be left free of patriarchal authority by the end of the novel is actually the character who at first seems the most ridiculous – Cassandra. Released from her father's tyranny by his death and commanding a significant power over her lover, who must comply, on her desire, to 'the rules of romance' and therefore defer marriage for 'ten years at least', Cassandra finds herself in a position of liberation unequalled by any of her fellow female characters (*The convent*, vol. 2, p. 319). While *The convent* inscribes the judicious choice of reading material and the cultivation of 'intelligent detachment' as the basis of a proper education, therefore, it also celebrates romance's potential both to reveal startling truths about real life and to afford women power in a patriarchal world.[52]

Similarly, in Mrs F.C. Patrick's *The Irish heiress*, a consideration of the potential risks associated with reading is linked to the heroine's anxious negotiation of and, indeed, immersion in the horrors of revolutionary France. Like Patrick's later novel, *More ghosts!*, *The Irish heiress* repeatedly emphasises its material and marketable nature, as when the narrator refrains from giving details of the eponymous heiress's travels through England and France, promising instead a future publication: 'a sentimental journey ... entitle[d] ... "*The progress of a female heart thro' France, in the Year 1788*"' (*The Irish heiress*, vol. 2, p. 24). Moreover, just as is the case with Catherine Morland in *Northanger Abbey*, the reader is frequently urged not to view the novel's main character, Augusta, as a heroine. Accordingly, the narrator – an older version of Augusta herself – reflects on past events, saying, 'But, alas! for me, what am I writing for, and so totally unqualified for an heroine, that I have not the smallest ear for music, no taste for anything beyond St. Patrick's Day, &c. which I had imbibed an early predilection for, by hearing my nurse sing to me in childhood' (*The Irish heiress*, vol. 2, pp. 44–5). Later, learning of the elopement of her beloved, George Mostyn, with her evil sister, Sophia, upon the urging of her unnaturally distant mother, Augusta wishes she could take recourse in the alternatives available to heroines:

> I might have gone into a Convent – I might have lived a picture of mild placid woe – I might have taken a fever, and raved alternately of Mostyn and my lap dog. – Undoubtedly there are many models extant of ladies deserted, or I believe deceived rather into such a belief, for who ever deserted a heroine? But, alas! I could not copy models I had never viewed, and nature alone guided me. (*The Irish heiress*, vol. 2, pp. 117–18)

In the wake of George's desertion, Augusta decides to divert herself with 'books of a lighter nature' but is 'soon disgusted with French novels[:] they were so full of sentiments, many of them not more foolish than wicked, but so gilded over with the finery of language, that they might be often dangerous' (*The Irish heiress*, vol. 2, p. 124). She reserves particular disdain for Rousseau's *Confessions* (1787):

> I believe I ought to blush when I acknowledge that I read Rousseau's confessions, but I have some obligations to that book, since to my shame (I suppose) be it spoken, though my state of mind was not the merriest in nature, yet it gave me frequent opportunities of laughing over his most serious affairs, they appeared to my foolish imagination to be managed so ridiculously. (*The Irish heiress*, vol. 2, p. 125)

In its ridicule of Rousseau and contempt for the 'foolish' and 'wicked' sentiment of French literature, *The Irish heiress* reads as a reactionary text anxious to restrain, partially through contemptuous laughter, 'the true threat to orthodoxy': 'the moral relativism implicit in the sentimental movement'.[53]

At the same time, while laughing at Rousseau and the threatening, radicalised sensibility he had come to represent in the British consciousness during the revolutionary period, *The Irish heiress* subtly removes emphasis from reading material to actuality in describing the terrors of its heroine's life. In other words, rather than depict Rousseau's text and other such literature of sentiment and sensibility as subversive – a prominent tendency in a period in which prose fiction was increasingly feminised and radicalised – *The Irish heiress* subtly valorises romance by describing Augusta as caught up in a tale of horror all too real in the revolutionary period. Deserted by Mostyn, Augusta reluctantly follows her father's advice and marries the Irishman, Mr Connor, while in Paris, where she has been exiled by her unfeeling mother. A staunch defender of the Crown, Connor reverences 'the sacred character of [the French] king' and apparently falls in defence of the king at the Siege of Tuileries on 10 August 1792 (*The Irish heiress*, vol. 2, p. 52). With a careful specificity about dates, the third volume of *The Irish heiress* relates the bloody terrors of the French Revolution from Augusta's perspective, describing how she must tread over a multitude of dead bodies in the street with the chilling belief that she will soon be trodden upon herself. Later, having been reunited with Connor, who had not been killed after all, she witnesses him being brutally and unceremoniously beheaded after his existence is betrayed to authorities by apparent friends. Driven mad by the sight of her husband's dismembered body, Augusta wanders senselessly through Paris, her newborn child in her arms, before eventually being taken to prison, where she witnesses the people who attempt to assist her falling victim, one after another, to revolutionary zeal.

At length, she returns to Ireland, disfigured from a near-fatal bout of smallpox, only to be denied by her mother, who is anxious that Sophia retain the inheritance meant for Augusta. When she finally proves her identity and assumes her rightful inheritance, Augusta finds further obstacles presented by her Catholicism. Although she has been careful, on her father's advice, never publicly to reveal her conversion from Protestantism, Augusta finds her ownership of her ancestral estate challenged by her mother. When Augusta eventually takes possession of her familial lands she is again troubled by her Catholicism, this time because her Protestant mother-in-law applies to authorities to have Protestant guardians appointed for her grandson. By the end of the novel, it seems likely that Augusta will be separated from her child, and the tale concludes with a sense of ominous incompletion: '[Mrs Connor] still ... means to take from me that child, for whose sake I live, and for whom all my cares are engaged; she will take him from me, if I do not prevent her by some stratagem' (*The Irish heiress*, vol. 3, p. 184).

With this conclusion and its promise of future woes – and perhaps future publications – to come, *The Irish heiress* highlights the finally unresolved tension between fact and fiction, romance and novel presented in its pages. A similar ambivalence, albeit more optimistic in nature, concludes Alicia Le Fanu's *Strathallan*. Finally married to the eponymous hero after a lengthy series of heart-breaking separations occasioned by a keen sense of duty and virtue, Matilda Melbourne receives a letter from her friend, Arbella Sowerby, congratulating her on her long delayed happiness:

> When I consider the mournful and strange events, which so fast followed upon each other before your final re-union could take place, I think I see you, like Balsora and her lover, in the beautiful Eastern tale, two pure and lovely spirits, passing hand in hand, through the glooms of death, to the opening gate of Paradise. Go, happy pair, and ... may never the rude blast of misfortune disturb the Eden, of which your hearts are the centre. Go, blest Matilda, and taste, without fear, the happiness you so well deserve, with your long-lamented, your twice-restored Strathallan.[54]

The 'mournful and strange events' to which Arbella refers are not supernatural, despite the suggestion of death and resurrection attending the description of Strathallan as 'long-lamented' and 'twice-restored'. Instead, as in *The convent* and *The Irish heiress*, *Strathallan* depicts reality as inherently stranger and more dangerous than fiction, as it follows Matilda in her quest to navigate the treacherous vagaries of contemporary British society and still maintain her virtue – moral and sexual. Introduced into society by Lady Torrendale, the well-educated and rational Matilda meets a series of women prey, unlike herself, to 'literary mania'.[55] Matilda's discernment, both in terms of the literature she reads and the individuals she meets, contrasts boldly with the parodic female readers with whom she is surrounded. Lady Torrendale, for her part, is a fashionable reader, concerned only with the appearance and display of reading, and is, as Matilda admits '*all outside*' (*Strathallan*, p. 280). Though she professes to be 'dying for the Missionary [by Sydney Owenson]', her desire for the book stems from the text's popularity; while at Hookham's circulating library, Lady Torrendale melodramatically laments, 'One, two, three, four, five, – twenty on the list, I declare already for the Missionary ... how provoking to be so late!' (*Strathallan*, p. 242). Miss Mountain, in contrast, is a romance reader, who has come to expect from 'her chivalrous reading ... [a] general gallantry and deference, which, as she did not always receive, she applied herself to obtain by a variety of means, that ... gained her often the imputation of coquetry, while it was in fact only an ill understood pride' (*Strathallan*, p. 53). Miss Langrish, meanwhile, is addicted to 'modern "Horrors"', and is almost overcome by her extreme sensibility at the reading of works such as 'Lenora, Donica, the Grim White Woman, the Little Grey Man, the second book of the Last Minstrel, the Eve of St. John, the Haunted Beach ... Otranto, Udolpho, Montorio' (*Strathallan*, p. 66).[56]

The various readers included in *Strathallan* illustrate Le Fanu's desire, as outlined in the novel's preface, '[to hold] a medium both in principle and language, between that severity which forbids the existence of passion ... and that enthusiasm, which, dazzled by its wild and fitful splendors, mistakes, or wilfully [sic] confounds, in every page, its destructive fires, with the awful and lovely lights of virtue' (*Strathallan*, p. 2). In other words, Le Fanu wants not wholly to condemn romance and its associated sensibility but to promote instead readerly 'discrimination'.[57] A key example in this advocacy of detached and discriminating reading is the flighty and flirtatious Arbella Ferrars. Although intrinsically good-natured and kind of heart, Arbella too easily adopts the principles of the texts she reads, without due consideration of their merits and demerits. For this reason, she at one point espouses a philosophical abhorrence of religion derived from certain books 'in Lord Torrendale's extensive library (where poison and its antidote lay side by side)', in which she had found 'food for doubts and conjectures, which were sooner to be roused than laid asleep again' (*Strathallan*, p. 334). Matilda patiently and repeatedly counsels her friend, but it is only Mr Sowerby, the well-educated man who acts as Matilda's chief instructor, who can teach Arbella the dangers of her reading habits. Married to Sowerby by the close of the novel, Arbella seems, if not completely reformed, at least domesticated and given to the guidance of a capable and willing preceptor, much like her namesake in *The female Quixote*.

Despite this conservative sponsorship of the domestic ideology flouted by Lady Torrendale and the corresponding practice of detached or discriminating reading, *Strathallan* almost simultaneously conjures situations 'just like what one reads about' (*Northanger Abbey*, p. 114). The group assembled at the home of Lord and Lady Torrendale early in the novel, for instance, receives the news that the family's eldest son, Strathallan, has fallen in the battle of Corunna (16 January 1809). Days later, the mourners are astounded by the return of Strathallan himself. Miss Langrish hysterically declares it is Strathallan's ghost, but, it seems, the report of his death had been mistaken, and Strathallan has returned, in the flesh, to his family and home. Although it soon becomes clear that Strathallan and Matilda are kindred spirits, Lord Torrendale intends to wed Strathallan to the unfeeling and unsympathetic Miss Mountain, on account of a promise he made to his late wife, Strathallan's mother. No amount of persuasion will convince him to relinquish this promise, and Matilda, bound by her sense of duty and virtue, refuses to consider any other action than that of a paternally sanctioned marriage. Later, when Miss Mountain prematurely dies in a hunting accident, Matilda feels compelled once again to deny Strathallan, having been violently forced by her father's eccentric entailed heir, Sir Harold Mountain, to promise never to marry another man while he is alive. Later again, upon Sir Harold's death, Matilda sees her chance to marry Strathallan thwarted once more by his service in the Peninsular War (1807–14) and the associated intrigues of Lady Torrendale, who convinces Strathallan not only that Sir Harold is still alive but that he has married Matilda. Eventually, Strathallan returns to England, is informed of his error, and finally weds Matilda with the full consent and encouragement of Lord Torrendale, who repents having made his son earlier '[sacrifice] the dearest affections of his heart to my interest, peace, and honor' (*Strathallan*, p. 472).

The events described as delaying the long-awaited marriage with which *Strathallan* ends, though sometimes apparently supernatural in nature, are systematically revealed to be caused by the mundane, if no less horrific, realities of life – war and the vagaries of human passions, interests, and ambitions.[58] In this, *Strathallan* comments poignantly on the deep imbrication of romance and reality in everyday life, suggesting that the terrors experienced by its characters are all the more frightening than those proceeding from the supernatural precisely because they are real. Correspondingly, while Le Fanu, like Fuller, Patrick, and Barrett, sounds an apparently conservative call for the regulation of romance and reading in general, especially for young women, she also critiques a critical apparatus that continued to condemn romance as a dangerously misleading literary form. Not only are literary forms other than the romance proven to be deceptive when read without discrimination, but romance and reality are shown all too often to coincide with truly appalling results. Fittingly, Arbella's final letter to the new Lady Strathallan both congratulates her friend on her eventual marriage and frames her life to come as a romance, likening her to 'Balsora and her lover, in the beautiful Eastern tale, two pure and lovely spirits, passing hand in hand, through the glooms of death, to the opening gate of Paradise'. Apparently referencing 'an Oriental Tale' written by Joseph Addison (1672–1719) and published in *The Guardian* in 1713, Arbella's letter casts Matilda's marriage as a fairy tale, thus confirming the vital inherence of romance and reality presented by the novel, despite its at times cautious stance towards injudicious reading habits.[59] The clarity with which *Strathallan*, like *The convent*, *The Irish heiress*, *More ghosts!*, and *The heroine*, envisions the real terror of everyday life suggests that romance is, in fact, much closer to reality than its critics might like to believe. These works, therefore, comment critically on the essential intersection of fact and fiction. But they also suggest that to condemn romance because of its fictionality and apparent lack of didacticism is crucially to ignore the fact that, in some instances at least, reality is as horrific, if not more so, than that which one reads about.

THE NATIONAL TALE AND THE LITERARY GOTHIC

The novels discussed in earlier parts of this chapter evocatively demonstrate Siobhán Kilfeather's compelling argument that 'Irish people in the romantic period felt they were living gothic lives'.[60] Late eighteenth- and early nineteenth-century Irish authors, Kilfeather persuasively suggested, enacted in their works a general sense of socialised 'survivor guilt', producing narratives that played out the Irish people's post-1798 experience of a reality 'fractured by repeated intrusive memories of the time of danger, memories in which visual images of horror predominate'.[61] This sense of the terrific nature of reality is particularly clear in the intersection of romance and realism in texts such as *More ghosts!*, *The heroine*, and *Strathallan*. It is also one that arguably animates Irish fiction and, indeed, nonfiction more widely in the early nineteenth century.[62] Yet, Irish literary reliance on romance and related production of gothic fiction tend to go unnoticed in scholarly attention to the national tale and the historical novel, now considered the dominant literary forms of early nineteenth-century Ireland. Indeed, critical focus on the national tale's totalising narratives of allegorical union and closure has effected an erasure of continued Irish gothic literary production at the turn of the century.⁶³ As a result, the common assumption is that the gothic simply died away in the years following the Anglo-Irish Union as regional fiction, the national tale, and the historical novel took its place and attempted to effect a symbolic reconciliation of England and Ireland. This is why Charles Robert Maturin's *Melmoth the wanderer* (1820) is considered such an oddity: too late for the real vogue of gothic literature and too early for the so-called 'Irish Gothic' conventionally located at the close of the nineteenth century. But Maturin's novels 'were more or less contemporaneous' with 'the Faustian gothic of Godwin, Byron, Shelley, and Hogg', as Kilfeather pointed out.⁶⁴ Moreover, as attested to by the publication and circulating library lists for William Lane's prolific Minerva Press – discussed in greater detail in Chapter 4 – English and Irish writers alike continued to produce gothic fiction well into the nineteenth century. Maturin's *Fatal revenge* (1807) and *Melmoth the wanderer* are the obvious examples of post-Union Irish gothic literary production, but lesser-known works include *Lussington Abbey* (1804), *Villa Nova; or, the ruined castle* (1805), *The discarded son; or, haunt of the banditti* (1807), *The festival of St Jago; a Spanish romance* (1810), and *Villasantelle; or, the curious impertinent* (1817), among many others.

With titles that immediately evoke the literary gothic, thus pointedly underlining continued Irish gothic literary production of the early nineteenth century, the works just noted might seem remote from contemporary texts now commonly understood as national tales. But even these, including *Castle Rackrent* (1800), *The wild Irish girl* (1806), and *Ennui* (1809), to name but a few, reveal a significant, if now often undervalued, reliance on the literary gothic's themes, images, and tropes. Take Edgeworth's *Castle Rackrent* as an example: it purposely manipulates readerly expectations in its title, which, in conjuring the expected architectural settings of gothic literature, marketed the narrative as a similarly gothic tale.⁶⁵ Scott does this as well, particularly in the names chosen for *The black dwarf* (1816), *The monastery* (1820), and *Castle Dangerous* (1831), and while Edgeworth later constructs the gothic fiction called to mind by *Castle Rackrent*'s title as socially and personally perilous in the hands of *Ennui*'s Lord Glenthorn, her attempt to overthrow its power within the narrative, like Scott's effort to distance himself from it in his own works, proves incomplete.⁶⁶ Owenson's *The wild Irish girl*, in its turn, self-consciously differentiates itself from the gothic fiction that preceded it, proclaiming its newness in its subtitle, 'a national tale'. Nevertheless, its interest in national reconciliation and its 'Glorvina solution' are paralleled by a keen concern with competing notions of Ireland's historical and cultural evolution as well as several themes and tropes now more readily associated with gothic literature.[67] Moreover, its innovativeness is undercut by its similarities to Owenson's earlier tales, *St Clair; or, the heiress of Desmond* (1803) and *The novice of Saint Dominick* (1806).[68] Both of these novels indicatively conjure the gothic in their titles' references to the stock figures and exotic names identified by Miles as marketing cues for terror fiction.[69]

As is the case with Scott, Owenson's emphasis on originality in *The wild Irish girl* has been taken more or less at face value, and the text's similarities to contemporary gothic fiction minimised in comparison to its formulation of the 'national marriage plot' understood to form the heart of the national tale.[70] Owenson's later fictions – national tales and otherwise – have tended to lend themselves more readily to analysis as gothic hybrids. Gary Kelly, for instance, classifies *The missionary* (1811) as gothic, including it in the six-volume *Varieties of female gothic* (2002), while Jim Kelly reads *Florence MacCarthy* (1818) as 'demonstrat[ing] … [that] the Irish landscape and the visible scars of conflict provided a Gothic text in its own right'.[71] W.J. McCormack, for his part, includes excerpts of *The O'Briens and the O'Flahertys* (1827) in his influential section on 'Irish gothic and after' in *The Field Day review*, though he argues that the novel has no 'direct link to the gothic tradition'.[72] Julia M. Wright nevertheless identifies the novel's use of gothic conventions as significant, contributing as it does to a literary hyper-hybridity as well as an ambivalence towards the cultural nationalism promoted by *The wild Irish girl*.[73] Raphaël Ingelbien, moreover, links *The princess; or, the Béguine* (1835) to fin-de-siècle Irish gothic fiction in its '[turn] to continental material to write indirectly about Ireland'.[74] Owenson's increased reliance on the literary gothic as her career progressed is in keeping with her growing scepticism about the potential for political stability in Ireland. It also fits in well with conventional readings of the evolution of the national tale as a form. Both Ina Ferris and Katie Trumpener suggest that, from its inception in 1806, the national tale was influenced by but distinct from the literary gothic, preserving that difference for several years before the gothic dramatically (re)introduced itself. Ferris thus claims that Maturin's *The Milesian chief* 'pushes the travel plot of Morgan's political romance into a limit zone', and, in so doing, 'invents Irish Gothic'.[75] Trumpener, meanwhile, contends that the convergence of national tale and historical novel in the wake of Scott's *Waverley* results in the fracture of cultural wholeness and the breakdown of allegorical marriage, producing tragedy on both personal and national scales. The introduction of 'the dislocations of the historical novel' to the national tale, Trumpener writes, creates 'a new literary schizophrenia' more at home with twentieth- and twenty-first-century conceptualisations of the literary gothic than the national tale.[76]

Recent scholarship by Anne Fogarty, Bridget Matthews-Kane, Julie Donovan, and Clíona Ó Gallchoir has begun to dismantle this stadial approach to the national tale and its relationship to the literary gothic, interrogating the use of gothic topoi and the evocation of the Gothic past in *The wild Irish girl*.[77] Such assessments are key to an understanding of the inherence of gothic and national literary modes from the origins of 'the national tale' through its various evolutions and transformations in the early nineteenth century. With its supernatural figures, crumbling castles, abortive marriage ceremonies, deathbed scenes, and overriding sense of a violent past that continues to erupt in the present, *The wild Irish girl* is not so different from earlier, more obviously gothic novels such as Roche's *The children of the abbey* (1796) and Stephen Cullen's *The castle of Inchvally; a tale – alas! too true* (1796). These tales, in twinning their spectres, odious Catholic priests, ruinous castles, and sexually predatory villains with Irish settings and a clear interest in contemporary Irish affairs, strikingly anticipate later 'national' fictions such as *The wild Irish girl*. It is unsurprising, therefore, that *The children of the abbey*, though now recognised as a best-selling gothic romance of its day, has also been called 'the earliest Irish national tale'.[78] *The castle of Inchvally*, assessed upon publication as yet another popular gothic romance, has similarly been understood as 'the first Irish novel clearly aimed at [an] English readership'.[79]

Unlike later 'national' fictions such as *Castle Rackrent* and *The wild Irish girl*, though, *The children of the abbey* and *The castle of Inchvally* are generally seen to hover rather uncomfortably between gothic and national literary forms. Thus, as both Derek Hand and Claire Connolly argue, while Cullen's explanatory footnotes in *The castle of Inchvally* look forward to those in *Castle Rackrent*, they nevertheless fall short of Edgeworth's national intent and literary achievement.[80] Erratic and 'miscellaneous' in nature, Cullen's footnotes have 'the potential to open up spaces of cultural mediation', but this latent conciliatory effect is cancelled out by the novel's gothicism, expressed in 'a plot that depicts the world of contemporary Catholicism, replete with deceitful illusions and supernatural trappings, as dangerously vital'.[81] *The children of the abbey*'s gothicisim is likewise seen to war with its presciently allegorical marriage between Irish heroine, Amanda Fitzalan, and *her* Mortimer, not Horatio as in *The wild Irish girl*, but Henry. Miranda Burgess contends that *The children of the abbey*'s notable 'generic instability' functions 'as the sign of a trauma attributable to cultural and political history'.[82] Finally unable to eradicate 'the traces of political history' through a narrative of domestic settlement as later national tales were better able to do, *The children of the abbey* signals its discomfort with the national marriage plot later familiarised by Owenson by retaining a sense of gothic violence at its close. Later national tales, Burgess asserts, more successfully separate culture and political history, correspondingly moving away from the literary gothic in a more decisive manner than Roche was able to manage.[83]

Yet, *The children of the abbey* dramatically highlights the manner in which, as Burgess writes, 'allegory in the national tale is visibly decaying from the start'.[84] Indeed, the 'emotions of the most painful nature' and 'violent' tears experienced by Amanda Fitzalan upon her apparently celebratory return to Ireland in *The children of the abbey* are echoed repeatedly in later national tales.[85] They appear in the 'convulsive shriek', maniacal laughter, and feverish sobbing with which Glorvina grieves her father and, at almost the same moment, offers Horatio an equivocal consent – 'such hope as the heart of a mourning child could give to the object of her heart's first passion' – to marriage.[86] Six years later they re-emerge in Grace Nugent's angry outburst – 'My mother! – my mother! – my mother!' – at the revelations that both enable her marriage to Lord Colambre and elucidate the history of injustice committed against her and her mother.[87] And we see them again, in slightly different form, in Owenson's second self-proclaimed national tale, *O'Donnel* (1814). In marrying the Dowager Duchess of Belmont, formerly the Irish governess, Miss O'Halloran, Roderick O'Donnel, dispossessed and impoverished heir of Red Hugh O'Donnel (1572–1602), King of Tyrconnell, regains his ancestral lands and property, allowing him to forsake service in foreign militaries and once again live permanently in Ireland. Like the female national heroines that have preceded him, O'Donnel greets this revolution in his personal circumstances with mixed feelings. Although he experiences 'joyous emotions' at marrying the woman he loves, he, too, is prey to 'some feeling of melancholy' derived from his recognition that his corresponding reinstatement at Tirconnell House owes to private rather than public means:

> He was willing to owe his best felicity to the hand of love; but he would have wished to have obtained the re-possession of his rights by means more consonant to the spirit of the gentleman, the dignity of the man, and the general interests of his country.[88]

One of O'Donnel's first actions upon being restored to 'the domains of his inheritance' is tellingly to reclaim the sword of O'Donnel the Red, sold earlier in the novel to fund O'Donnel's first trip to London (*O'Donnel*, vol. 3, p. 305). Recalling the display of 'coats of arms, spears, lances and old armor' in *The children of the abbey* as well as the collection of 'national antiquities, and national curiosities' in *The wild Irish girl*, O'Donnel's proudly exhibited sword mixes the forces of cultural nationalism with a potentially disruptive memory of the past.[89] Early in the novel, O'Donnel glibly but pointedly observes to Mr Glentworth on the question of educating the Irish: 'in good policy, the first lesson you should teach the Irish, should be the art of forgetfulness' (*O'Donnel*, vol. 1, p. 217). O'Donnel himself repeatedly maintains his loyalty to British rule, refusing, for instance, to serve in any army currently fighting against England and asserting his belief that, rather than political independence, the Irish people desire sympathy and understanding from the English. Against such fidelity to the Crown, his reverence for his ancestor's sword evocatively calls into question his ability to master forgetfulness.

Highlighting the weapon's unruly symbolism, its retrieval and proud display at the close of the novel reminds readers of its first introduction, when Lady Singleton and her party take refuge in O'Donnel's cottage, not knowing to whom it belongs. There, they are regaled by O'Donnel's faithful servant, M'Rory, with stories about 'the great O'Donnel', whose apparently recent and violent feats have left bloody reminders on the sword exhibited above the mantelpiece and are recorded in a manuscript presented by M'Rory to Lady Singleton (*O'Donnel*, vol. 2, p. 4). Ferris observes that M'Rory's arguably deliberate misunderstanding of Lady Singleton's query about the recent nature of the great O'Donnel's escapades conflates past (late sixteenth century) and present (late eighteenth century). As it does so, it pointedly links long-ago violence with current Whiteboy activity, fears over which had initially driven the English tourists to O'Donnel's cabin.[90] This interpolated text, understood by the visitors as either a brief diversion or proof of the present O'Donnel's romantic nature, nevertheless 'testifies to the simultaneous circulation within the nation of unassimilable kinds of memory and desire':

In the hands of M'Rory (who literally gives the text to Lady Singleton) the fragment serves to unsettle the colonial story, while in the fugitive bands of White Boys this text of the past finds a material echo and re-enactment. The gothic swerve of interpolation thus takes on a decided political edge, foregrounding a sense of national time not only as dense and layered but as an ongoing contestation between asymmetries of remembering and forgetting.[91]

In this continued memory of the past, signalled in particular by 'the gothic technique of embedded texts', *O'Donnel*'s 'Glorvina solution' is fatally undermined by the slippery boundary between past and present.[92] It thus points to the national tale's powerlessness to effectively resolve the issue of Irish nationalism without accompanying political action. Accordingly, while Lady Llanberis commends the Duchess of Belmont for her enviably romantic domestic settlement, the novel itself ends with a desire to extrapolate private happiness into political change. Extolling his master's virtues, M'Rory declares, 'And so, ... if it was *God's will*, there is no *rayson* in life why he should'nt be a great parliament man' (*O'Donnel*, vol. 3, p. 332).

M'Rory's resort to divine power apparently de-politicises his wish for O'Donnel's enfranchisement, casting the future of Catholic Emancipation into the realm of supernatural romance rather than violent political action. Here again, however, the ostensibly harmless desire voiced by M'Rory takes on an aggressive edge when we consider the ways in which Owenson, like Maturin before her in *The Milesian chief*, establishes Ireland as the home of 'the most wild and incredible situations of romantic story'.[93] Just as Maturin set out in *The Milesian chief* to describe 'the scenes of actual life', as outrageous as they might seem, Owenson concerns herself in *O'Donnel* with 'the "flat realities of life"'; but she reminds her readers throughout, that, in Ireland, '*le vrai n'est pas toujours le vraisemblable*' (*O'Donnel*, vol. 1, p. ix; vol. 3, p. 317).[94] Accordingly, while her English tourists conceive of O'Donnel as the fitting inhabitant for the 'fantastically beautiful' natural landscape they encounter on the coast of Antrim, Owenson repeatedly calls attention to their dangerously misleading dismissal of Ireland and its inhabitants as mere objects of romance (*O'Donnel*, vol. 1, p. 130). Presented as of gigantic proportion, capable of heroic feats, impervious to fear, and inclined to the use of hidden passages and revolving portraits that seem borrowed directly from Radcliffe, O'Donnel is, to his English visitors, an exotic object of curiosity derived directly from myth or folklore. Having read the manuscript of '*O'Donnel The Red, or The Chiefs of Tirconnel. A Fragment*', Lady Florence tellingly reports that afterwards 'she had dreamed of Irish chiefs and heroes the whole night', thus transforming O'Donnel's family history into a kind of myth or fairy tale (*O'Donnel*, vol. 2, pp. 7, 70). Later, upon arriving in London, O'Donnel finds himself recommended to the Countess of Llanberis as the subject of 'a tale of wonder' that prompts her to refer to him as 'our hero' and invite him to her home as a personage likely both to amuse her and to catch the attention of fashionable society (*O'Donnel*, vol. 2, pp. 154, 153).

O'Donnel is immediately wary of the 'exaggerated descriptions' that could have led to the Countess's invitation to him as a 'hero', feeling the term fundamentally at odds with the reality of his situation: poverty, exile, and political disenfranchisement (*O'Donnel*, vol. 2, p. 153). He nevertheless accepts her hospitality and soon finds his mistrust well placed. Insulted by Lord Charles Savill, Lady Llanberis's accepted lover, O'Donnel challenges him to a duel in which Lord Charles is injured. Outraged, Lady Llanberis turns on Lady Singleton and accuses her of imposing upon her hospitality a man whose sordid reality failed to live up to the romance: 'the man was no more the thing you described, as least that *I* expected. He was, I think, pretty much like other persons, but not the very least amusing' (*O'Donnel*, vol. 3, p. 221). The cause of her current troubles, Lady Llanberis suggests, was believing Lady Singleton's 'tales of wonder about kidnapped chiefs, and the Castle of Dublin, and his fighting a whole German legion, and all that nonsense', when all along she should have listened to Lord Charles's insistence that O'Donnel was nothing more than an Irish adventurer (*O'Donnel*, vol. 3, p. 220). When Lord Charles proves likely to recover from his injury and O'Donnel is married to the Duchess of Belmont in a union that re-possesses him of much of his lost ancestral inheritance, however, O'Donnel returns once again to the realm of romance, at least in the minds of his English acquaintances. Lady Llanberis thus congratulates the Duchess on her fiction-worthy life: 'I have no idea of any thing finer than being the wife of a chief ... your following him to Ireland – the Duke of Belmont having left you the property that once had been his – in short, it is all a romance, and I wish Mrs. St. Leger would take it up' (*O'Donnel*, vol. 3, p. 324).

Dismissing O'Donnel's marriage and the private rectification of past public wrongs it represents as mere romance, Lady Llanberis naively overlooks the fact that, when it comes to Ireland, romance can do little to contain 'the Gothic horror of history'.[95] Having once changed her hero from Red Hugh O'Donnel himself to his 'more polished descendant in a more refined age', Owenson recorded her recognition that to write of the former was to 'raise a veil which ought never to be drawn, and renew the memory of events, which the interests of humanity require to be for ever buried in oblivion' (*O'Donnel*, vol. 1, pp. xii, xi). In the resulting narrative, Owenson attempts to reduce the past to a harmless fairy tale with little bearing on the present. Yet, as is clear in the continued surfacing of a violent memory of the past at odds with O'Donnel's otherwise rational acceptance of British rule and private, rather than public, enfranchisement, Owenson's Ireland remains troubled by the persistent convergence of past and present forms of violence.

CONCLUSION

Published in the same year as *Waverley*, Owenson's *O'Donnel* simultaneously looks backward to the more pessimistically ambiguous conclusion of Maturin's *The Milesian chief* and anticipates the similarly equivocal ending of Scott's *The bride of Lammermoor*. As such, following arguments presented by Trumpener and Ferris and discussed in this chapter, the novel might be taken as evidence of the re-introduction of the gothic to the national tale as it developed in the 1810s. However, closer examination of the text alongside earlier examples of gothic-national fiction proves that it is, in fact, revelatory of a much longer established generic fluidity and interdependence that prevents any easy distinction between gothic novel and national tale from the last decade of the eighteenth century into the first two decades of the nineteenth. In its pointed use and interrogation of romance as a tool for describing an often fantastic and horrific reality, moreover, *O'Donnel* links itself to contemporary tales such as *The convent*, *The heroine*, *The Irish heiress*, and *Strathallan*. As it does so, it underscores the enduring production of the literary gothic by late eighteenth- and early nineteenth-century Irish writers.

That all of the texts discussed in this chapter share a concern with local settings, Irish and British, is of note. Not only do these novels dismantle conventional scholarly conceptions of genre and form in this period, but, as Chapter 3 discusses, they also speak to the inaccuracy of current emphasis on the Catholic Continent as the primary setting for gothic fiction of the late eighteenth and early nineteenth centuries. The focus on domestic settings in much Irish gothic fiction of this period signals the wider attention to local rather than foreign geographies in British gothic as a whole, while the particular use of Irish locales in the works of Elizabeth Griffith (1727–93) helped to combat and reconfigure prevailing English perceptions of Ireland itself as a peculiarly strange and estranging landscape.

NOTES

1. James Kelly, 'Gothic and the Celtic Fringe, 1750–1850', in Glennis Byron and Dale Townshend (eds), *The gothic world* (London: Routledge, 2013), p. 38.
2. John Banim, *Revelations of the dead-alive* (London: W. Simpkin & R. Marshall, 1824), p. 96.
3. *The Critical Review*, 67 (May 1789), 330, 331.
4. *Ibid.*, 331, 332–3.
5. *Gentleman's Magazine*, 60 (June 1790), 550.
6. *Ibid.*
7. James White, *The adventures of John of Gaunt, Duke of Lancaster*, 3 vols (London, 1790), vol 3, p. 243. Further references are to this edition and are given in parentheses in the text.
8. *The Critical Review*, 69 (June 1790), 713.
9. *Ibid.*, 714.
10. Henry Fielding, *The history of the adventures of Joseph Andrews and of his friend Mr Abraham Adams*, ed. Douglas Brooks-Davies, introd. Thomas Keymer (1742; Oxford: Oxford University Press, 2008), pp. 3, 15.
11. James Beattie, *Dissertations moral and critical* (London, 1783), pp. 573–4.
12. Clery, 'The genesis of "Gothic" fiction', p. 32.
13. *Ibid.*, p. 25.
14. Punter, *The literature of terror*, vol. 1, p. 47.
15. *Ibid.*, vol. 1, p. 44.
16. Brean Hammond and Shaun Regan, *Making the novel: fiction and society in Britain, 1660–1789* (Basingstoke and New York: Palgrave Macmillan, 2006), p. 7. Clery similarly notes that 'the novel *needed* romance as the measure of its own achievements; there was a dialectical relation between the two, an interdependency'; she further adds, 'in spite of the rhetoric[,] the dividing line between novel and romance was not absolutely clear-cut'; Clery, 'The genesis of "Gothic" fiction', p. 23.
17. The full titles of these works are as follows: *The castles of Athlin and Dunbayne; a highland story* (1790); *A Sicilian romance* (1790); *The romance of the forest, interspersed with some pieces of poetry* (1791); *The mysteries of Udolpho, a romance, interspersed with some pieces of poetry* (1794), and *The Italian, or the confessional of the Black Penitents; a romance* (1797).
18. *The Critical Review*, 13 (March 1762), 252. Added emphasis.
19. Williams, *Art of darkness*, pp. 2–3.
20. For the suggestion that Mrs F.C. Patrick may not be the author of *The Irish heiress*, see Ian Campbell Ross, Review of *A guide to Irish fiction*, *Eighteenth-century Ireland*, 22 (2007), 225.
21. Anna M. Fitzer, 'Introduction', in Alicia Le Fanu, *Strathallan* (London: Pickering & Chatto, 2008), p. ix.

22 Rolf and Magda Loeber point out that only six Irish novels published from 1806 to 1846 used the term 'national' in their titles, and three of these works were by Owenson herself; *A guide to Irish fiction*, p. lxii.
23 Eaton Stannard Barrett, *The heroine, or, adventures of a fair romance reader*, ed. Avril Horner and Sue Zlosnik (1813; Kansas City, MO: Valancourt Books, 2011), pp. 286–7. Further references are to this edition and are given in parentheses in the text.
24 Jane Austen, *Northanger Abbey*, ed. James Kinsley and John Davie, introd. Claudia L. Johnson (1818; Oxford: Oxford University Press, 2003), p. 25. Further references are to this edition and are given in parentheses in the text.
25 Mrs F.C. Patrick, *The Irish heiress, a novel, in three volumes* (London, 1797), vol. 1, p. 51. Further references are to this edition and are given in parentheses in the text.
26 *The Critical Review*, 2nd ser., 25 (January 1799), 119.
27 *Ibid.*
28 *Ibid.*
29 *Monthly Review*, n.s., 2 (August 1790), 414–15.
30 See, for instance, *Edinburgh Review*, 22 (October 1813), 245; *Edinburgh Review*, 22 (January 1814), 490; and *Edinburgh Review*, 27 (1816), 537.
31 Amanda Gilroy and Wil Verhoeven, 'The Romantic-era novel: a special issue', *Novel: a forum on fiction*, 34.2 (2001), 150.
32 Edward Mangin, *An essay on light reading, as it may be supposed to influence moral conduct on literary taste* (London, 1808), p. 5; quoted in Gilroy and Verhoeven, 'The Romantic-era novel', p. 150.
33 Gilroy and Verhoeven, 'The Romantic-era novel', p. 150.
34 See the Appendix for a full list of the texts considered here alongside their generic identifiers.
35 Miles, 'The 1790s: the effulgence of gothic', p. 41.
36 *Ibid.*, pp. 41–2.
37 See Pearson, 'Masculinizing the novel'.
38 See Mikhail Bakhtin, *The dialogic imagination: four essays*, ed. Michael Holquist, trans. Caryl Emerson and Michael Holquist (Austin, TX: University of Texas Press, 1981).
39 Reeve, *The progress of romance*, 211.
40 Avril Horner and Sue Zlosnik, 'Introduction', in Eaton Stannard Barrett, *The heroine, or adventures of a fair romance reader* (Kansas City, MO: Valancourt Books, 2011), p. xix.
41 Jim Shanahan, 'Escaping from Barrett's moon: recreating the Irish literary landscape in the Romantic period', in Kelly (ed.), *Ireland and Romanticism*, p. 195.
42 William Hazlitt, *Lectures on the English comic writers*, in P.P. Howe (ed.), *The complete works of William Hazlitt*, 21 vols (London: Dent, 1930–34), vol. 6,

p. 24; quoted in Graeme Stones (ed.), *Parodies of the Romantic age. Volume 1: the Anti-Jacobin* (London: Pickering & Chatto, 1999), p. xiv.
43 Anne Fuller, *The convent: or, the history of Sophia Nelson*, 2 vols (London [1786]), vol. 1, p. 15. Further references are to this edition and are given in parentheses in the text. Cassandra's resemblance to Arabella appears to have been deliberate and was commented upon in contemporary reviews: 'Cassandra Woodville is the Female Quixote'; *The Critical Review*, 62 (December 1786), 469.
44 Heather MacFadyen, 'Lady Delacour's library: Maria Edgeworth's *Belinda* and fashionable reading', *Nineteenth-century literature*, 48.4 (1994), 426.
45 *Ibid.*, 436.
46 This is an argument voiced by Marilyn Butler in relation to *Northanger Abbey*, a novel frequently understood as a simple burlesque of the 'horrid' fiction Catherine Morland loves. Contesting this simplistic view, Butler persuasively contends that Austen employs parody in much the same way as Barrett in *The heroine*, asking readers 'not ... to criticize certain novels, nor the habit of novel-reading, but rather to consider the habits of mind which the different speakers reveal'; Marilyn Butler, *Jane Austen and the war of ideas* (1975; Oxford: Clarendon Press, 2002), pp. 173, 175.
47 Butler, *Jane Austen and the war of ideas*, p. 175.
48 Mrs F.C. Patrick, *More ghosts! In three volumes* (London, 1798), vol. 1, p. i. Further references are to this edition and are given in parentheses in the text.
49 In its sympathetic portrayal of Catholicism, *More ghosts!* confirms the arguments presented by Maria Purves when she counters the critical belief that gothic fiction is generally anti-Catholic in nature. Purves contends instead that novels such as *More ghosts!* 'complicate the orthodox critical reading of Gothic as a vehicle for anti-Catholic, anticlerical sentiment. They make Catholic monastic characters heroic and use them to define and demonstrate the value and superiority of Christian piety in a world of unruly emotion and unchecked sensibility'; Maria Purves, *The gothic and Catholicism: religion, cultural exchange and the popular novel, 1785–1829* (Cardiff: University of Wales Press, 2009), p. 1.
50 *The Critical Review*, 2nd ser., 24 (October 1798), 236.
51 Clery, *The rise of supernatural fiction*, p. 129.
52 For a similar argument about the final valorisation of romance in Lennox's *The female Quixote*, see Margaret Anne Doody, 'Introduction', in Charlotte Lennox, *The female Quixote* (Oxford: Oxford University Press, 2008), pp. xxi, xxxii. See also Scott Paul Gordon, 'The space of romance in Lennox's *Female Quixote*', *Studies in English literature, 1500–1900*, 38.3 (1998), 499–516.
53 Butler, *Jane Austen and the war of ideas*, p. 33.

54 Alicia Le Fanu, *Strathallan*, ed. Anna M. Fitzer (1816; London: Pickering & Chatto, 2008), p. 492. Further references are to this edition and are given in parentheses in the text.
55 Fitzer, 'Introduction', p. xvi.
56 In her editorial notes to the 2008 Pickering & Chatto edition of *Strathallan*, Anna M. Fitzer names the works referenced here as Gottfried August Bürger's 'Leonora' (1774), Robert Southey's 'Donica' (1797), Matthew Lewis's 'The grim white woman' (1800), Walter Scott's 'The eve of St John' (1800) and 'The lay of the last minstrel' (1805), Mary Robinson's 'The haunted beach' (1806), Walpole's *The castle of Otranto*, Radcliffe's *The mysteries of Udolpho*, and Charles Robert Maturin's *The fatal revenge; or, the family of Montorio* (1807) (*Strathallan*, p. 498, n. 61).
57 Fitzer, 'Introduction', p. xiii.
58 The suggestion of supernatural agency is made most clearly in the vocabulary used to describe Strathallan's supposed death and subsequent 'resurrection' as well as in the figure of Sir Harold Mountain, who appears to harbour a spectre in the ruined part of his home. Ultimately, this ghost is revealed to be his own mother, Lady Julia Melbourne. Long believed to be dead, Lady Julia had actually been forcibly confined by her jealous husband, possibly, it is suggested, on false information provided by Lady Torrendale, and had been driven mad by her unjust imprisonment, despite her son's careful, if secret, attention. Her death shortly after her apparent resurrection precipitates that of Sir Harold.
59 *The Guardian*, 167 (22 September 1713). The untitled tale tells of Helim, physician to the tyrannical King of Persia, Alnareschin, who, having already executed 35 previous wives, demands Helim's beautiful daughter, Balsora, as his next. Aware that Balsora is in love with the King's son, Abdallah, Helim gives the lovers a sleeping potion that allows them to feign death. They then escape to a secluded mountain retreat, disguised as spirits from the after world. There, they live out the remainder of their lives, even after Alnareschin has died. Le Fanu may have been familiar with the tale in its original form, as *The Guardian* and collections of the works of Addison and Richard Steele (bap.1672–d.1729) were published throughout the eighteenth century. She may also have encountered it in one of its permutations as a moralistic children's tale popular into the late eighteenth and early nineteenth centuries. For instance, 'The story of Abdallah and Balsora' appeared in several collections of didactic tales for children in the latter half of the eighteenth century, including *The new polite instructor; or universal moralist* (London, 1771) and *The moral miscellany; or, a collection of select pieces, in prose and verse, for the instruction and entertainment of youth* (Dublin, 1774).
60 Siobhán Kilfeather, 'Terrific register: the gothicization of atrocity in Irish Romantic writing', *boundary 2*, 31.1 (2004), 60.

61 *Ibid.*
62 Jim Kelly observes that '[r]egisters, themes and images that we associate with Gothic fiction were so prevalent in Irish printed and oral culture [in the nineteenth century] that modern observers might conclude that there were aspects of the Gothic in everything'; Kelly, 'Gothic and the Celtic Fringe', p. 39.
63 See Morin, '"Gothic" and "national"?'
64 Kilfeather, 'Terrific register', 56, 55.
65 For compelling explorations of the architecture of *Castle Rackrent* and the novel's gothicism, see Killeen, 'Building bridges: Maria Edgeworth's *Castle Rackrent* and the gothic mansion', *Gothic Ireland*, pp. 191–222 and William McCormack, '*Castle Rackrent*', Ascendancy and tradition in Anglo-Irish literary history from 1789 to 1939 (Oxford: Oxford University Press, 1985), pp. 97–122. See also Kellie A. Donovan, 'Imprisonment in *Castle Rackrent*: Maria Edgeworth's use of gothic conventions', in Patricia A. Lynch, Joachim Fischer, and Brian Coates (eds), *Back to the present, forward to the past: Irish writing and history since 1798: volume 1* (Amsterdam: Rodopi, 2006), pp. 145–56.
66 Robertson, *Legitimate histories*, p. 4. On the use of gothic fiction in *The absentee* as an emblem of Lord Glenthorn's susceptibility to romantic enthrallment, the narrative's attempt to present Glenthorn's recovery from his reading-induced sensibility, and the conclusion's uncertainty about Glenthorn's security against future ontological and literary seduction, see Sharon Murphy, *Maria Edgeworth and romance* (Dublin: Four Courts Press, 2004), pp. 155–66.
67 For the identification of the 'Glorvina solution', see Robert Tracy, 'Maria Edgeworth and Lady Morgan: legality versus legitimacy', *Nineteenth-century fiction*, 40.1 (1985), 1–22.
68 On the similarities and differences between *The wild Irish girl* and *St Clair*, in particular, see Claire Connolly, 'The national tale', in Peter Garside and Karen O'Brien (eds), *The Oxford history of the novel in English; volume 2: English and British fiction, 1750–1820* (Oxford: Oxford University Press, 2015), pp. 225–6.
69 Miles, 'The 1790s: the effulgence of gothic', pp. 41–2. The clear influence of Goethe's *The sorrows of young Werther* (trans. 1779) on *St Clair* also links Owenson's novel to German literature and, what was inextricably bound with it in the contemporary British consciousness, gothic romance.
70 Trumpener, *Bardic nationalism*, p. 137.
71 Gary Kelly (ed.), *Varieties of female gothic*, 6 vols (London: Pickering & Chatto, 2002); Kelly, 'Gothic and the Celtic Fringe, 1750–1850', p. 41.
72 McCormack, 'Irish gothic and after', pp. 867–73.
73 Julia M. Wright, '"The nation begins to form": competing nationalisms in Morgan's *The O'Briens and the O'Flahertys*', *ELH*, 66 (1999), 339–65. Wright further develops the connection between the literary gothic and the national tale in more recent work, arguing that, from its inception, the national tale's 'Glorvina solution' 'is specifically a solution to a gothic problem – namely, the

need to authorize what remains marked as the illicit seizure of property ... and to assuage the gothic anxieties that such instabilities produce'; Wright, *Representing the national landscape*, p. 190.
74 Raphaël Ingelbien, 'Paradoxes of national liberation: Lady Morgan, O'Connellism, and the Belgian Revolution', *Éire-Ireland*, 42:3&4 (2007), 124.
75 Ferris, *The Romantic national tale*, p. 16.
76 Trumpener, *Bardic nationalism*, p. 142. Although Trumpener is careful to emphasise the generic 'interdependen[ce]' of the national tale and historical novel, she is less concerned with the interplay of these works and the gothic novels that preceded, co-existed with, and vitally informed them. She traces the similarities between Radcliffe's *The castles of Athlin and Dunbayne* (1789) and works by Charlotte Smith and Maria Edgeworth but does not enter into a discussion of the important influence of the literary gothic on early national tales and historical novels; *Bardic nationalism*, pp. 131, 138–9.
77 See Anne Fogarty, 'Imperfect concord: spectres of history in the Irish novels of Maria Edgeworth and Lady Morgan', in Kelleher and Murphy (eds), *Gender perspectives in nineteenth-century Ireland*, pp. 116–26; Bridget Matthews-Kane, 'Gothic excess and political anxiety: Lady Morgan's *The wild Irish girl*', *Gothic studies*, 5.2 (2003), 7–19; Julie Donovan, 'Text and textile in *The wild Irish girl*', *Sydney Owenson, Lady Morgan and the politics of style* (Palo Alto, CA: Academica Press, 2009), pp. 19–51; and Clíona Ó Gallchoir, 'Celtic Ireland and Celtic Scotland: Ossianism and *The wild Irish girl*', in David Duff and Catherine Jones (ed.), *Scotland, Ireland, and the Romantic aesthetic* (Lewisburg, PA: Bucknell University Press, 2007), pp. 114–30.
78 Miranda Burgess, 'Violent translations: allegory, gender, and cultural nationalism in Ireland, 1796–1806', *Modern language quarterly*, 59.1 (1998), 40.
79 Loeber and Loeber, *A guide to Irish fiction*, p. lxiii. For contemporary assessments of *The castle of Inchvally*, see *The Monthly Mirror*, 2 (December 1796), 479; *The Critical Review*, n.s., 20 (May 1797), 118; and *The British Critic and Quarterly Theological Review*, 11 (June 1798), 680.
80 Hand, *A history of the Irish novel*, p. 62. Connolly, 'The national tale', p. 221.
81 Connolly, 'The national tale', p. 221.
82 Burgess, 'Violent translations', p. 39.
83 *Ibid.*, p. 55.
84 *Ibid.*, p. 63.
85 Regina Maria Roche, *The children of the abbey* (1796; New York: Thomas Y. Crowell & Co., no date), pp. 582–3.
86 Sydney Owenson, Lady Morgan, *The wild Irish girl: a national tale*, ed. Kathryn Kirkpatrick (1806; Oxford: Oxford University Press, 1999), pp. 239, 245.
87 Maria Edgeworth, *The absentee*, ed. W.J. McCormack and Kim Walker (1812; Oxford: Oxford University Press, 2001), p. 256. For more detailed discussions of the violence at the heart of the apparently conciliatory marriages in *The*

wild Irish girl and *The absentee*, see, for instance, Julia Anne Miller, 'Acts of union: family violence and national courtship in Maria Edgeworth's *The absentee* and Sydney Owenson's *The wild Irish girl*', in Kathryn Kirkpatrick (ed.), *Border crossings: Irish women writers and national identities* (Tuscaloosa, AL and London: The University of Alabama Press, 2000), pp. 13–37; Morin, *Charles Robert Maturin*, pp. 9–10, 46–7, 65–8; and Morin, ' "Gothic" and "national"?'

88 Sydney Owenson, *O'Donnel: a national tale*, 3 vols (London: Colburn, 1814), vol. 3, pp. 306–7. Further references are to this edition and are given in parentheses in the text.
89 Roche, *The children of the abbey*, p. 138; Owenson, *The wild Irish girl*, p. 102. See Burgess, 'Violent translations', pp. 60–2.
90 Ferris, *The Romantic national tale*, p. 88.
91 *Ibid.*, pp. 88–9.
92 *Ibid.*, p. 88.
93 Charles Robert Maturin, *The Milesian chief; a romance*, 4 vols (London: Henry Colburn, 1812), 1:v.
94 *Ibid.*
95 Kelly, 'Gothic and the Celtic Fringe', p. 48.

3
Gothic geographies: the cartographic consciousness of Irish gothic fiction

~

Theodore Melville's *The White Knight, or the monastery of Morne* (1802) provides both a useful instance of the convergence of regional, national, and gothic literary forms considered in Chapter 2 and a helpful starting point with which to discuss the geographic settings of Romantic-era Irish gothic literature. Published just two years after *Castle Rackrent* (1800), *The White Knight* presents itself as a quasi-historical account of Irish antiquity and is set entirely in Ireland, with the main activity of the tale occurring in fifteenth-century Munster and Ulster. Melville's preface explains that its subject matter – the White Knight himself – was a real person: '*There were formerly three branches of the family of Fitzgerald, distinguished in Ireland by the titles of the* White Knight, *the* Knight of Kerry, *and the* Knight of Glynn. *The first, which I have chosen as the subject of the following pages, is now extinct*'.[1] The narrative that follows clearly aligns itself with a Radcliffean tradition of gothic romance in its prominent use of the 'explained supernatural' and its tale of abduction, imprisonment, and thwarted love centred in the secret, subterranean passageways of Glanville Castle, the Castle of Dromore, and the nearby Monastery of Morne. At the same time, it bears a significant resemblance to the regional and national fictions of Edgeworth and Owenson. Its conclusion, envisioning the amicable end to the violent clan warfare at the heart of its narrative, maps the political onto the private in the symbolic marriages of once feuding families, thus evoking the nationally significant unions associated with the national tale. Similarly, its attempts to inform its (English) readers about Ireland and its people through lengthy descriptions of Irish landscape as well as explanatory details about Irish language and folklore, recall *Castle Rackrent*'s glossary and foreshadow Owenson's dense use of topographical and antiquarian material to establish Ireland's cultural significance in *The wild Irish girl* (1806).

As in the cases of Roche's *The children of the abbey* (1796) and Cullen's *The castle of Inchvally* (1796), *The White Knight* has arguably been neglected because of its association with popular gothic romance.[2] The novel is therefore seen not to seriously engage in the kind of cultural nationalist work associated with Edgeworth, Owenson, and even Melville's later novel, *The Irish chieftain, and his family* (1809).[3] The flaws in such arguments are discussed in Chapter 2. Melville's Irish setting reinforces the claims made in Chapter 2 about the formal fluidity of national, regional, and gothic forms; the novel's publication so soon after *Castle Rackrent's* draws attention to contemporary and earlier instances of Irish writing about Ireland – many of them gothic – that situate Edgeworth's text as part of a long-standing tradition of Irish engagement with specifically Irish material.[4]

If *The White Knight's* resolute attention to Irish geography encourages us to see a longer, larger trend in Irish literary representations of Ireland, it also highlights some of the problematic issues associated with Romantic-era depictions of the country, especially those composed with an English audience in mind. In particular, Melville's portrayal of Ireland as a peculiarly gothic landscape appears to confirm the stereotypically English view of Ireland as 'a spatial and temporal anomaly'.[5] Attention to Irish writers' acceptance of a colonial 'version of Ireland as a Gothic madhouse' has tended to dominate discussion of Irish gothic literature, particularly in psychoanalytically driven criticism of texts by Anglo-Irish authors.[6] Such awareness is not without merit in the case of works by Roche, Maturin, and Owenson, who, in Kilfeather's terms, 'establish[ed] Ireland as a primary gothic setting', in keeping with the understanding that Irish reality brooked no comparison to the wildest romance.[7] As Maturin memorably put it, Ireland is 'the only country on earth, where, from the strange existing opposition of religion, politics, and manners, the extremes of refinement and barbarism are united, and the most wild and incredible situations of romantic story are hourly passing before modern eyes' (*The Milesian chief*, vol. 1, p. 54). Significant as these writers have become in the historiography of Irish gothic literature, though, it is worth reflecting on deviations from the norm they are seen to constitute – one based, as many of the accepted traits of Irish and British gothic literature of this period are, on relatively few titles, which are themselves, often too simplistically understood. The variety of (non)interactions with Ireland offered by a wider selection of late eighteenth- and early nineteenth-century texts underlines a much richer, more complex approach to gothic geography than is commonly attributed to Irish writers.

Focus on the diversity of settings in Romantic-era Irish literary gothic also emphasises the falsity of our assumption that contemporary English gothic literature almost universally deploys Catholic Continental locales. Far from anomalous in the British gothic output of his day, Melville's evocative depictions of local geography represent an established pattern that has been all too often dismissed. As Kilfeather has noted, 'critical attention to the eighteenth-century female gothic novel has been so dominated by readings of Ann Radcliffe that Radcliffe's Italian and French settings have been defined as almost essential to the genre'.[8] Yet, closer examination of Radcliffe's *oeuvre* reveals that even *she* was not as attached to Catholic Continental settings as we now tend to think. In fact, Radcliffe's earliest novel *The castles of Athlin and Dunbayne* (1789) shuns a medieval Catholic European setting in favour of the sublime scenery of contemporary Scotland. If this gestures towards the equation of the so-called 'Celtic Fringe' with a barbarity equally terrifying, if not more so, than that of the Catholic Continent, it also refers back to the local, English settings of earlier texts such as Leland's *Longsword* (1762), Reeve's *The old English baron* (1777), Sophia Lee's *The recess* (1783–5), and Fuller's *Alan Fitz-Osborne* (1787). Moreover, it anticipates the native Irish and British landscapes of later gothic texts, including, as we have seen, White's *The adventures of John of Gaunt* (1790), Maturin's *The Milesian chief* (1812), and Le Fanu's *Strathallan* (1816). This is not to deny the importance of distant and distancing geography in the literary gothic but instead to argue for a reconsideration of the local in our understanding of gothic literature of the late eighteenth and early nineteenth centuries. What is needed, this chapter suggests, is an expansion of Clery's observation: 'Radcliffe may have favoured southern Europe, [but] her followers generally set their novels in Britain.'[9]

Clery's supposition is that, from the 1790s, the literary gothic experienced a steady movement from the geographical otherness of exotic locations to the uncanny familiarity of 'home', just as it gradually transitioned from distant temporal periods to more recent, even contemporary, times. Although persuasive in their insistence on the renegotiation of both temporal and geographical gothic landscapes, Clery's arguments fail to account for the decisively British settings of texts such as *The castles of Athlin and Dunbayne* and *The old English baron*. This latter text, it is worth remembering, was one of the few novels actually to call itself 'Gothic', a term it applied specifically to the 'times and manners' of fifteenth-century Yorkshire.[10] The interest in indigenous scenery, not to mention characters and events, evidenced in these and a multitude of other works in this period forcefully indicates that landscape in the literary gothic is not simply a question of displacement. Rather, much as with the names and titles authors gave to their works, the setting of a given piece of fiction can represent a very particular choice, one with both narratological and ideological import. To ignore the significance of this preference, this chapter contends, is fundamentally to misconstrue the literary gothic.

Here, as in the assessment of titles and nomenclature, quantitative analysis offers a particularly instructive vantage point, allowing us strikingly to visualise the geographical settings of the literary gothic. Figure 3 demonstrates that the vast majority of the works considered in this study locate their narratives primarily in the British Isles, which, for the terms of this discussion, means mainland England, as well as Wales, Ireland, and Scotland. A much smaller percentage of works feature the Catholic Continental settings – France, Italy, Spain, and Portugal – that we have come to expect from eighteenth- and nineteenth-century gothic works. Two reject both Britain and Europe for the more exotic locations of the Holy Land and Scandinavia.[11]

Secondary, tertiary, and quaternary geographical settings show a general authorial awareness of and interest in more distant locations, but often

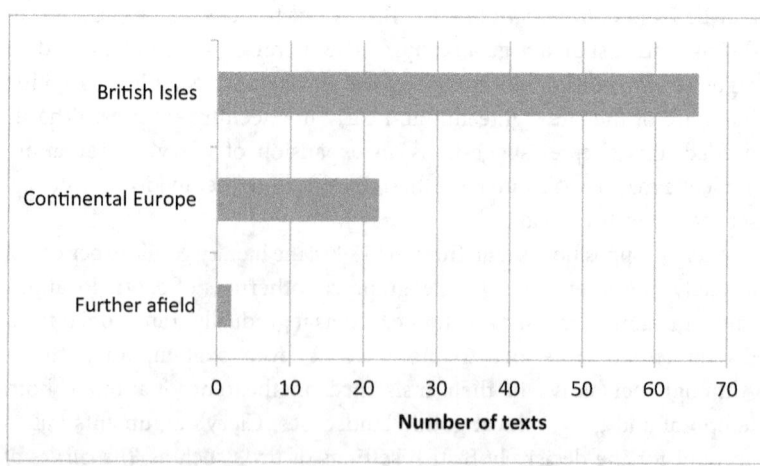

Figure 3 Irish gothic novels and their primary geographic settings

via narrative subplots that serve as temporary diversions from the main story line and, as such, never completely draw attention away from the local. Indeed, in many of the works assessed here, foreign locations are frequently framed as the place from which characters continuously strive to return home. As such, they are sites of exile, hardship, enslavement, and imprisonment, but very often only momentarily, as in the case of *Longsword, The convent,* or *Alan Fitz-Osborne*. At the same time, the distant geographies in these texts frequently help highlight the terrible disruption, violence, and distress to be discovered at the long-desired home. In other works, as discussed in the final section of this chapter, the characters' experiences abroad, although often presented as digressions from a more central concern with Ireland, are positively construed as the key to the restoration of rights at home and the construction of new national identities in the wake of the 1798 Rebellion and the Anglo-Irish Union.

These figures strikingly evidence a decided interest in 'home' settings in Romantic-era Irish gothic literary production. Certainly, a number of texts adopt the Catholic Continental settings traditionally associated with contemporary gothic: Stephen Cullen's *The haunted priory; or, the fortunes of the house of Rayo* (1794), the Reverend Luke Aylmer Conolly's *The friar's tale; or, memoirs of the chevalier Orsino* (1805), Marianne Kenley's *The cottage of the Appenines, or, the Castle of Novina* (1806), and Charles Maturin's *The fatal revenge; or, the family of Montorio* (1807). But a significant portion of Irish gothic fiction in this period turns its attention to native – specifically English – settings. The thirteenth-century English landscape of Leland's *Longsword* is only one instance of such topography found in a number of politically engaged gothic romances. These include, as we have seen, Fuller's *Alan Fitz-Osborne* and the works of James White, but also, for instance, Fuller's *The son of Ethelwolf* (1789) and Anna Milliken's *Corfe Castle* (1793). All of these novels speak to the trend in late eighteenth-century British gothic literature '[to] accentuate the "native" associations of the Gothic and of romance, [while] reasserting the dignity of ancestors in the name of a belligerent patriotism'.[12] In doing so, they exemplify both the overlap of gothic and historical modes discussed in Chapter 1 and the now overlooked tendency in both English and Irish gothic fictions of this period to reject Catholic Continental settings and thus bring terror imaginatively closer to home.

Drawing attention to the local geography of Irish gothic fiction, the first part of this chapter traces the use of Irish topography in the *oeuvre* of Elizabeth Griffith (1727–93), considering her works as indicative of the literary gothic's nuanced engagement with Ireland in the Romantic period. As already noted in the Introduction, Griffith's fiction has been situated at the start of gothic literary production in Ireland, particularly in its representation of the country as part of the sublime geographical fringes of the British nation.[13] In their emphasis on Ireland as a strange and estranging terrain, works such as *The history of Lady Barton* (1771), *The story of Lady Juliana Harley* (1776), and 'Conjugal fidelity' (1780) might be considered to embrace rather than reject prevailing English understandings of Ireland as a marginal zone of incomprehensible strangeness. Correspondingly, they lend apparent credence to more recent critical assessments of Irish gothic literature's obsessive interest in Ireland's dangerously enchanting geography. Examined collectively, though, Griffith's works reveal rich and varied constructions of Ireland. In both *The history of Lady Barton* and *The story of Lady Juliana Harley*, for example, the colonial cause of Ireland's unfamiliar and forbidding reputation is repeatedly emphasised, drawing attention away from Irish topography to a lengthy history of violent invasion and dispossession. Indeed, in much of her fiction, Griffith carefully reverses accusations of Irish savagery by investigating the import of terror into Ireland, frequently depicting English villains victimising a blameless, innately noble Irish people. Elsewhere, Griffith employs local and exotic scenery that contributes to a subtle but no less scathing commentary on the state of English modernity.

The second part of the chapter continues the discussion of the first, concentrating on the use of English settings in a selection of generally overlooked Irish gothic fictions. Julia M. Wright has recently claimed that part of what makes Irish gothic literary production distinctive from English gothic is 'its use of English settings'; 'to locate gothic narratives in England', Wright argues, 'is unusual in English gothic fiction before the sensation fiction of the 1860s'.[14] While Wright fails adequately to consider the resolutely local settings of earlier English examples of gothic, basing her conclusion on a handful of 'leading examples of the gothic novel', her argument is compelling in its emphasis on the ideological importance of local settings in Romantic-era Irish gothic fiction.[15] The works assessed here, including Fuller's *The convent* (1786) and *The son of Ethelwolf*, Milliken's *Corfe Castle*, and Catharine Selden's *The English nun* (1797), evidence Irish writers' frequent rejection of the Catholic Continental settings traditionally associated with gothic fiction in order to focus on English locales described as equally dangerous as foreign climes, if not more so. They thus invite their readers to view England as characterised by an unsettling violence and irrationality normally linked to the Continent and its superstitious, pre-modern, radicalised cultures.

The final section of the chapter charts Irish literary gothic's participation in the new 'cartographic consciousness' that emerges in early nineteenth-century Irish fiction as writers explore 'the different ways in which place can be inscribed in literature'.[16] Connolly argues that the imagined cultural encounters between England and Ireland in the national tale help forge a 'new relationship to place' in the nineteenth-century Irish novel,[17] as writers deploy Irish and English settings to '[map] developmental stages topographically, as adjacent worlds in which characters move and then choose between'.[18] The scenes of Anglo-Irish encounter familiar from *The wild Irish girl*, *The absentee*, *The wild Irish boy*, and *The Milesian chief* have been well documented: through his transformative movement from England to Ireland, and his subsequently enlightening experience of the Irish landscape and its people, the national tale's hero overturns his prejudices about the country and cements his newfound appreciation of its culture by marriage to its allegorical female representative. Less well recognised are the symbolic cultural interactions between Ireland and countries other than England in contemporary Irish fiction.[19] The final section of this chapter accordingly explores the more far-reaching cultural exchanges of several nationally minded gothic romances. These works – Henrietta Rouvière Mosse's *The old Irish baronet; or, manners of my country* (1808) and Roche's *The tradition of the castle; or, scenes in the Emerald Isle* (1824) – adapt the ideas of cultural encounter and national vindication manifest in the national tale, earlier gothic romances, and contemporary travelogues in order to construct various forms of travel as the key to a post-Union Irish national identity that is primarily transnational in nature.

(UN)GOTHICISING IRELAND: A CASE STUDY OF ELIZABETH GRIFFITH (1727–93)

A prolific writer of drama, fiction, and literary criticism, Elizabeth Griffith is best known today for her career as a playwright and comedies such as *The platonic wife* (1765), *The double mistake* (1766), *The school for rakes* (1769), and *A wife in the right* (1772). While her fiction has been 'appreciated' by scholars,[20] it is telling that only one of her three novels has appeared in a modern edition, whereas her plays have all recently been anthologised.[21] Kilfeather's pioneering work on Irish gothic literature, particularly that by women writers, gestured to the significance of a wider recognition of

Griffith's fictional achievements. Arguing that '[a] history of Irish gothic fiction might begin with adultery in the works of Frances Sheridan and Elizabeth Griffith', Kilfeather not only expanded the usual chronology of the 'Irish Gothic' but also positioned Griffith's novels and short stories as important, early instances of the Irish literary gothic.[22] Her focus on Griffith's use of Irish topography and depiction of symbolic journeys to Ireland amounted to a call for more detailed analysis of late eighteenth-century Irish gothic literature's engagement with native geography at the same time that it invited further consideration of the connections to be made between Griffith's gothic fictions and later forms such as the national tale.[23] This section addresses the as-yet-unmet demand for further examination of Griffith's fiction, concentrating on her short stories and novels as interrogating and deconstructing contemporary depictions of Ireland as 'an exotic tourist resort' at best and a hellish zone of perversity and savagery at worst.[24]

Griffith's earliest novel, *The delicate distress* (1769), offers what might be considered a displaced reflection on English disdain for Ireland. Published as one of two fictions in *Two novels in letters. By the authors of* Henry and Frances. *In four volumes*, the work was situated as a companion piece to another publication, *A series of genuine letters between Henry and Frances* (1757–70).[25] The first two-volume installment of *that* text, published in 1757, presented Griffith's correspondence with her husband Richard Griffith (d. 1788) before their clandestine marriage on 12 May 1751. As Elizabeth Eger notes, the Griffiths' epistolary collection 'caused an immediate literary sensation', and they went on to publish several more volumes of *Genuine letters*, which was also reprinted a number of times before the end of the century.[26]

Shaun Regan has compellingly traced the 'significant, if at times uncertain, role' Ireland plays in the *Genuine letters*, noting the manner in which the letters of the first edition are addressed largely from England, not Ireland, where much of the original correspondence took place.[27] *Genuine letters* thus appears to renounce Ireland, a repudiation that reflects the complex '[a]cts of positioning, literary and geographical' that mark eighteenth-century Irish fiction and its primarily Protestant authors' attempts to negotiate their relationship to both Ireland and England.[28] It also indicates the Griffiths' wariness, in the midst of 'financial desperation', to introduce any controversial or unpopular sentiments into a work whose financial success they sorely required.[29] The necessity for such caution was borne out by the Griffths' experience of re-introducing Irish geographical reference points in subsequent instalments and editions of the *Genuine letters*. This act of relocation proved unpopular with readers and elicited mocking responses from reviewers.[30]

The knowledge gleaned from publishing *Genuine letters* may have advocated caution to Griffith in her engagement with Ireland in her subsequent fiction. Certainly, *The delicate distress* omits all but the occasional reference to Ireland: in volume 1, a minor character is said to 'liv[e] in Ireland, where her husband had a very large fortune' – a fact that keeps her from her friends for extended periods.[31] Volume 2 contains a lengthier nod to Ireland with its inclusion of a brief poem titled 'Verses written at the fountain at Mallow, in the county of Cork, in Ireland' (*Delicate distress* vol. 2, p. 84). The lines are sent by the novel's heroine, Lady Woodville, from her home in York, to her sister elsewhere in England, with the explanation that they were 'written upon a particular occasion, at a water-drinking place in Ireland, called Mallow, some years ago' (*Delicate distress*, vol. 2, p. 83). Lady Woodville identifies the poem's 'unfortunate subject' as 'a much admired character in that place … dignified by the title of Sappho' (*Delicate distress*, vol. 2, p. 83). Although no reference is given, the poem had earlier appeared in *The memoirs of Mrs Laetitia Pilkington* (1748): 'Mr. Worsdale to Mrs Pilkintgon'.[32] Its association with the infamous Pilkington allows Griffith thematically to emphasise the idea of female moral frailty driving the narrative proper, recalling for readers the accusations of adultery and sexual impropriety levelled at Pilkington by her husband from 1737.[33]

Neither allusion to Ireland in *The delicate distress* draws particular attention to the country, which instead becomes conspicuous by its very absence, especially in light of the pronounced negative treatment England receives. Set in an English countryside made treacherous by the ravages of smallpox, the machinations of a lustful marchioness who directs her 'ensnaring wiles' at the overly sensible and recently married Lord Woodville, and the unjust edicts and actions of a number of tyrannical fathers inclined to imprison their daughters in Continental convents, *The delicate distress* charts an explicitly English geography of terror (*Delicate distress*, vol. 1, p. 25). The novel's periodic episodes in France and Italy serve not so much to highlight England's comparative enlightenment as simply to accentuate the borderlessness between iniquities committed abroad and those enacted at home. The narrative's particular focus on England and English locations thus helps to bear out this study's contention that local settings are much more prevalent in early gothic fiction than is generally believed. It also subtly suggests Griffith's desire to exonerate Ireland from contemporary accusations of savagery linked to the 'Celtic Fringe' or 'Celtic periphery'. Ireland's notable exclusion from its pages, in other words, assumes a real significance, underlining what Kilfeather calls '[e]arly Irish gothic fiction[']s] ... surprising reluctance to permit local [Irish] horrors'.[34]

A similar displaced engagement with Ireland is evident in Griffith's unproduced dramatic poem, *Amana* (1764), published just five years before *The delicate distress*. Clearly indicating the multi-generic nature of eighteenth-century Irish gothic literature, *Amana* ostensibly concerns itself with a vindication of British modernity by way of comparison with an archaic past represented by 'Gothic' Egypt.[35] Its exotic, oriental setting calls upon contemporary understanding of the Gothic past and prompts a reading of the text alongside Leland's *Longsword* and Reeve's *The old English baron* as a dramatic version of Watt's 'Loyalist Gothic romance'.[36] The work's praise of Britain as the home of 'native liberty' and the propagator of political freedom around the world functions as a rhetoric of patriotism used to validate British intervention in international conflict and to reassure readers of British greatness during a time of continued concern over France following the Seven Years' War and increasing conflict with the colonies in America (*Amana*, p. 53).[37]

In this context, Ireland seems to act simply as a part of the 'thrice happy kingdoms' Griffith proclaims to be the seat of 'peculiar blessings of liberty' (*Amana*, p. iv). Yet, Griffith's dedication of her play suggests a deep-seated concern with exclusively Irish, not British, national valorisation. Recommending *Amana* to the attention of Elizabeth Percy, the Countess of Northumberland, whose husband acted as Lord Lieutenant of Ireland from 1763 to 1765, Griffith reminds Percy of her family lineage, extolling 'the names of *Percy* and *Seymour*' as virtually synonymous with 'Liberty' and 'Glory' (*Amana*, [p. v]). She moreover praises Percy herself for her 'humanity, benevolence and affability', calling the latter 'the characteristic of true nobility, in opposition to that haughtiness which is frequently observable in those who have sprung from obscurity' (*Amana*, [p. v]). Apparently laudatory, Griffith's comments are nevertheless barbed, ridiculing a woman whose love of lavish entertainment was both well known and much criticised. Horace Walpole – no stranger himself to excess – called her 'junketaceous' and considered her 'aristocratic but vulgar'.[38] Percy's husband catered to her desire for opulence while in Ireland but struggled in his position there, especially with Edmond Pery (1719–1806) and his group of parliamentary patriots demanding constitutional concessions such as an Irish Habeas Corpus Act, reform of the pensions list, and a dramatic overhaul of the treasury system applied to Ireland.[39] Exasperated, Northumberland appealed to Westminster to be allowed to punish Pery and other troublemakers but was counselled to conciliate them instead. Soon after, but not soon enough for Northumberland, one suspects, he left the post of Lord Lieutenant of Ireland to take up that of vice-admiral of all America.

Griffith's dedication to the Countess of Northumberland, read in the light of the latter's brief but tempestuous stay in Ireland, undermines the piece's concern with British liberty and suggests instead a veiled commentary on the current state of the Irish nation. In particular, it implicates the Countess of Northumberland, whose attention to political matters was well noted, in the success or failure of the liberation, however limited, of Ireland represented by Pery's demands. Calling on Percy to do justice to her noble forebears who, as Griffith writes, took '[l]iberty [as] their crest', Griffith invites England itself to do justice to its own 'Gothick Constitution' by rethinking its relationship to Ireland (*Amana*, [p. v]).[40]

The indirect but no less significant deliberations on Ireland, England, and Anglo-Irish relations via non-Irish settings in *Amana* and *The delicate distress* anticipate the more obvious and extended treatments of Irish geography in *The history of Lady Barton* (1771) and *The story of Lady Juliana Harley* (1776). In both of these novels, Ireland is presented as, alongside Scotland and Wales, an intriguingly liminal area of the British nation that could function, at one and the same time, as retreat or refuge and uncanny, near otherworldly space. Evidently influenced both by Burke and contemporary travel writing, while also foreshadowing the scenes of geographical and cultural encounter made familiar in the national tale and historical novel, *The history of Lady Barton* opens with its heroine's descriptions of wild Celtic scenery. Having just been married to the Anglo-Irish Lord Barton, Lady Louisa Barton recounts her adventures travelling from her family seat in England to her husband's home in Ireland. Upon reaching Holyhead, Louisa writes of her unfamiliar surroundings in explicitly Burkean terms:

> The wildness, or even horror, of this place, for we have had a perpetual storm, is so strongly contrasted with the mild scenes of Cleveland Hall, or indeed any other part of England that I have seen, that one would scarce think it possible for a few days journey to transport us into such extremes, of the sublime and beautiful –.[41]

Describing the Welsh landscape as an 'enchanted ground' (*The history of Lady Barton*, vol. 1, p. 7), Louisa establishes an immediate social and geographic distinction between England and Wales.[42] Days later, Louisa couches the description of her first encounter with Ireland in similar terms of mystical strangeness. After the ship from Holyhead nearly sinks, Louisa and her party find themselves 'upon what may almost be called a desert island ... uninhabited by every thing but a few goats, and some fishermen, who are almost as wild as they' (*The history of Lady Barton*, vol. 1, pp. 14–15). Louisa's husband promptly ventures out 'to *reconnoitre la carte païs, de la terre inconnuë, ou nous etions*' (*The history of Lady Barton*, vol. 1, p. 15).[43] As Kilfeather persuasively contended, the use of the French language to speak of this strange new world poignantly highlights Ireland's foreign nature, one later reiterated in Louisa's account of the Irish people she meets:[44] The old Irish families stile themselves Milesians, from Milesius, a Spaniard, who brought over a colony of his countrymen to people the island. – But I should think, from their manners, as I hinted at before, that they were originally derived rather from the French (*The history of Lady Barton*, vol. 1, p. 54).

For Kilfeather, the implications of this passage are clear: on the one hand, it constructs Ireland and its people as intrinsically foreign, more akin to the Catholic Continent than to England. On the other, by underlining the Irish people's claim to a Milesian identity, it points to the contested nature of the country's history. Although the Irish families to whom Louisa refers deploy the term 'Milesian' as a mark of pride in their lineage, the reminder of their august heritage is also a reminder that, as Kilfeather put it, 'England is only the latest in a series of colonial powers to invade Ireland, and that the country has no native identity'.[45]

The notion of colonial invasion is supported in the text by the character of Colonel Walter, an early version of the absentee landlord, who has decided to travel to Ireland 'to take possession of his estate, and a seat in parliament for a borough he never saw' (*The history of Lady Barton*, vol. 1, p. 10). On this information, Louisa pointedly comments, 'I am no politician, or I should animadvert a little upon this subject' (*The history of Lady Barton*, vol. 1, p. 10). While she refuses openly to admit her disapproval of Colonel Walter, her experiences in Ireland overwhelmingly prove the danger he represents. In fact, it is largely through Colonel Walter's machinations that Louisa's once charming husband becomes a tyrannical and jealous brute, viewing Louisa with intense suspicion and fundamentally contributing to her eventual death from grief and (largely imagined) guilt. *The history of*

GOTHIC GEOGRAPHIES

Lady Barton thus forcefully suggests that, while Ireland may be a strange and enchanting world, villainy is not native to its soil.

The story of Lady Juliana Harley describes a similar passage from the mundane reality of life in London and Bath to the sublime environs of Wales and Ireland. If, in *The history of Lady Barton*, travel to the geographical margins of the nation is a bewildering and terrifying experience, in *The story of Lady Juliana Harley* it is a much more bland, albeit bemusing, affair. Undertaking his journey in order to forget his love for the eponymous heroine, a young widow around whom some mystery ever hangs, Charles Evelyn tells his correspondent, 'We arrived at Holyhead – But I shall not attempt to describe the delightfully romantic wildness of the country through which we passed to it – From thence we embarked for Dublin; and without storm, tempest, or any other sinister accident, arrived there in about eight hours.'[46] Charles and his companions decide 'to make a tour of this country and visit some of the natural beauties it contains' (*Juliana Harley*, vol. 2, p. 9). Enraptured by Killarney Lake, Charles summarises it as 'past description', adding that '[t]he beautiful and sublime are here mingled in the superlative degree; the great Creator's works, unspoiled by art, rush on the mind, and fill it with delight and awe' (*Juliana Harley* vol. 2, pp. 34, 35). But Charles's romantic views of Ireland take a more disturbing tone when he journeys to Roscommon, an area surrounded by land 'less cultivated than any part of Ireland than I have yet seen' and almost entirely devoid of human society except that promised by 'a few miserable huts, made up of mud and straw, which appear to be scarcely inhabitable' (*Juliana Harley*, vol. 2, p. 38). Romance and reality collide even more spectacularly in Roscommon town, where Charles discovers the windowless home of the Prince of Coolavin, whose 'ancestors were lords of this wide domain' and whose 'proud spirit cannot bear to look upon those lands, which he considers as by right his own, though Cromwell tore the inheritance from his family, and reduced his patrimony to the scanty pittance of two hundred pounds a year' (*Juliana Harley*, vol. 2, p. 39). Unlike the proud but sympathetic Prince of Inismore in Owenson's *The wild Irish girl*, the Prince of Coolavin is offensive in his arrogance, presiding over his household from 'an oak great chair' with an iron hand, refusing to allow his wife to eat with him because she does not derive from royal blood, and maintaining always at the side of his throne, in testament to the respect owed to him, 'an immense large coffin' adorned with his ancestral heraldry and flanked by 'hundreds of wooden cups' to be filled with whiskey for those who attend his funeral (*Juliana Harley*, vol. 2, p. 42).

~ 125

While this 'old savage', as Charles calls him, stands as evidence of a misguided attachment to past glories, he is more absurd than threatening (*Juliana Harley*, vol. 2, p. 43). Taken together, the Irish episodes of *The story of Lady Juliana Harley* seem calculated to support, if not a positive image of Ireland itself, a least an impression of mainstream English society as infinitely more threatening. Ireland may be a 'land of genealogers' obsessed with powerless royal lineages and historic wrongs, but the vestiges of a glorious past never threaten to rise against the present, as they do in a text such as Roche's *The children of the abbey* (*Juliana Harley*, vol. 2, p. 32).[47] Instead, in *The story of Lady Juliana Harley*, violence and atrocity reside elsewhere, specifically in England, where Juliana repeatedly finds herself a victim to the demands of patriarchal society. Eventually taking refuge in a Continental convent, Juliana discovers peace and the 'earthly happiness' available to her only in 'seclusion' from England and its 'world of woe' (*Juliana Harley*, vol. 2, pp. 133, 134). And, while 'the absent forms of those from whom she is banished haunt her retirement', Juliana prefers the 'visions' and 'spectres' of her 'solitary cell' to her English home, even after her brother – the latest male family member attempting to exert a villainous control over her – repents and begs her to return (*Juliana Harley*, vol. 2, p. 65). The novel accordingly ends with the news that Juliana has taken her vows and become Sister Mary Magdalen, finding the support and affection refused to her by suspicious family members and treacherous friends at home, in the 'sensible' and 'good' society of her fellow nuns (*Juliana Harley*, vol. 2, p. 134).

With this conclusion, *The story of Lady Juliana Harley* reverses the vilification of the Continent usually associated with 'the Gothic novel', locating atrocity instead in a domestic, English setting. At the same time, it counters English stereotypes of Ireland's gothic terrain. Although its treatment of Irish geography and culture is more tangential and apparently flippant than that of *The history of Lady Barton*, it nevertheless constructs a striking contrast between Ireland and England that upsets conventional ideas about the 'Celtic Fringe' and its relationship to the cosmopolitan centre. Here, despite its sublime landscape, Ireland is an unthreatening realm of hospitality and harmless nostalgia for the past, while England is haunted by the cruelties enacted upon a young heroine who has the misfortune to fall afoul of patriarchal authority.

Griffith's later fiction continues the attention to English treachery evident in *The story of Lady Juliana Harley* and *The history of Lady Barton*. Two of the stories included in *Novellettes, selected for the use of young ladies and gentlemen* (1780) are particularly worth noting in this regard. As discussed in the Introduction, 'Conjugal fidelity' appears to confirm stereotypes of gothic Ireland in its focus on a seventeenth-century Irish terrain overwhelmed by 'storms' – natural and otherwise – and its detailing of the terrors of the 1641 Rebellion ('Conjugal fidelity', p. 186). It nonetheless complicates narratives of Protestant victimhood, in part by suggesting that political and religious strife arrived in Kilkenny with Pansfield's sixteenth-century English ancestors. As in *The history of Lady Barton*, however, the Elizabethan conquest of Ireland is only one instance in a long history of successive acts of colonisation. Tellingly, Elvina Butler's identity as 'a near relation to the Ormond family' links her to an illustrious Old English family whose claim to their extensive estates in Munster and Leinster dated back to the twelfth-century Norman invasion, thus emphasising repeated foreign incursions into Ireland over the centuries ('Conjugal fidelity', p. 182). Moreover, while Elvina herself is a Catholic and apparently sympathises with the confederates' cause, her name conjures James Butler, 1st Duke of Ormond (1610–88), who, against his family's wishes, was raised a Protestant and took an active role in royalist resistance to the 1641 Rebellion.[48] As it does so, it emphasises the continued presence and power of alien forces in Ireland.

In contrast to 'Conjugal fidelity', 'Story of Lady Fanny Beaumont and Lord Layton' omits Ireland altogether to concentrate on an unambiguously English setting. The relationship between its eponymous characters, the married couple Lady Beaumont and Lord Layton, anticipates the violence of male oppression so common to later British gothic fiction. Like Shakespeare's Romeo and Juliet, Lady Beaumont and Lord Layton are star-crossed lovers belonging to rival families. When they fall in love, they elope to Scotland and find themselves 'curse[d]' by their parents.[49] Horrified by the effects of her filial disobedience, the scrupulous Lady Beaumont soon learns to regret her clandestine marriage for other reasons as well when Lord Layton proves a fickle lover. Four years after their marriage and two after the birth of their daughter, Lord Layton conceives an all-consuming passion for a young Frenchwoman named Louisa. Desperate to be rid of his wife so that he can persuade Louisa to accept his advances, Lord Layton banishes his wife to a 'dismal Castle' in Westmoreland, '[un]inhabited by any of his family for above a century' ('Story of Lady Fanny Beaumont and Lord Layton', p. 198). In a twisted perversion of the ruse by which Romeo and Juliet intend to be united, Lord Layton convinces his wife to consent to a plan by which she will first feign sickness and death, then allow herself to be taken from the castle in a hearse, only then to conceal herself on the Continent for the rest of her life. Unable fully to commit herself to Lord Layton's designs, Lady Beaumont decides, like Elvina in 'Conjugal fidelity', to take matters into her own hands, fatally stabbing herself with a rusty dagger that she discovers in the castle. As in *Romeo and Juliet*, however, there is a moment of dreadful realisation that death was not necessary: the noises Lady Beaumont had taken for the beginning of Lord Layton's plot are actually her young daughter, come to find her after Lord Layton had been mortally wounded in a duel with Lady Beaumont's brother, thus freeing her from both literal and figurative confinement.

At the conclusion of her tale, Griffith provides the following moral: 'From this sad Story let the young and thoughtless learn, that the smallest deviation from the paths of virtue is liable to plunge the soul and body into the extremes of vice and misery; for none can say to themselves, "Thus far, and no farther will I go"' ('Story of Lady Fanny Beaumont and Lord Layton', p. 202). The tale's straightforward warning against excessive sensibility looks forward to similar cautions that appear in later gothic fictions such as *The mysteries of Udolpho* and *The Italian*, but there is an intriguing twist here. Not only is it a man, rather than a woman, who is seen to be the principal victim of unbridled emotion, it is a well-respected English peer. In this, Lord Layton prefigures the English villains of William Godwin's fiction, at the same time that he evinces Griffith's interest in linking England, not Ireland, to gothic atrocity in the form of dangerous sensibility as well as patriarchal violence and oppression. 'Story of Lady Fanny Beaumont and Lord Layton' thus constructs an explicitly English topography of terror, symbolically re-locating barbarism and savagery from Ireland and the Continent to England.

MAPPING THE ENGLISH LANDSCAPES OF ROMANTIC IRISH GOTHIC FICTION

The many, varied (non)representations of Ireland evident in Griffith's *oeuvre* underline the often subtle, often complex nature of eighteenth-century Irish literature's engagement with questions of identity, origins, and national affiliation.[50] Exploring and charting Irish terrain, but also conspicuously ignoring it at times, Griffith's works reveal early Irish gothic's nuanced considerations of Ireland's placement in the period's '"map" of Gothicity'.[51] As they do so, they embody the overlooked trend in late eighteenth-century Irish and British gothic literary production to focus on local, autochthonous

– rather than foreign, Continental – settings. Griffith's frequent depiction of England as a peculiarly gothic landscape is particularly worth noting in this regard. Whereas Ireland and the 'Celtic Fringe' might reasonably be associated with the Catholic Continent and considered exotic and bizarre in this period, mainland England was supposed to be different: enlightened, rational, civilised. Hence, the conventional argument goes, English gothic literature deployed European settings as a method of tacitly confirming English modernity. Yet, many Romantic gothic texts anxiously interrogate English political and cultural progress by way of native settings that allow for meaningful explorations of the Gothic past and its relationship to present-day England. This is evident in the historic English settings of works such as *The old English baron*, *The recess*, and Richard Warner's *Netley Abbey; a gothic story* (1795).[52] Similarly, as we have already seen in Chapter 1, many Irish authors, including Thomas Leland, Anne Fuller, and James White, adopt medieval English settings in their gothic fictions as a method of debating eighteenth-century society's advancement – or lack thereof – from the past.

Examination of the native geography of several further examples of historical gothic fiction demonstrates the central – if varied – role English settings played in the development of Irish and English gothic literature. Fuller's *The son of Ethelwolf* (1789) considers the reign of Alfred the Great (r. 848/9–99), who is described as valiantly resisting the incursions of the 'licentious [Danish] invaders who disturb his throne, and deluge his country with blood!'[53] His eventual triumph over the Danes is lauded as a pivotal moment in English history: restored to the throne, Alfred is said 'to dispense the blessings of peace and security to his people', through the exercise of 'his military abilities' and 'his just and vigorous laws' (*Son of Ethelwolf*, p. 277). Under his leadership, '[c]ommerce, till then unknown or neglected, poured the products of far distant realms into his dominions, and learning, cherished by his fostering care, broke the fetters with which superstitious ignorance had bound her' (*Son of Ethelwolf*, p. 277). Fuller's valorisation of Alfred – 'the paradigmatic hero of reformist patriotism in the eighteenth century, an iconically "English" figure widely credited with the institution of a bicameral national Parliament, as well as trial by jury' – aligns her novel with contemporary English works such as Joseph Cottle's *Alfred, an epic poem* (1800) and Henry Pye's *Alfred; an epic poem* (1801).[54] As it does so, it suggests her interest – shared with a number of Irish as well as English writers – in the 'construction of a living – and sometimes explicitly Gothic – past with an exemplary meaning for the present.'[55]

If Fuller's *The son of Ethelwolf* participates in the broadly apologist vein of the Loyalist gothic romance identified by Watt, Mrs F.C. Patrick's later text, *The Jesuit; or, the history of Anthony Babington, Esq.* (1799), deploys its historic English setting to a much more critical end.[56] Set during the religious warfare of the reign of Elizabeth I (1558–1603), *The Jesuit* catalogues the series of events by which its eponymous protagonist becomes embroiled in, and condemned for, treasonous plotting against the queen. Although he has been committed from his youth by his zealously Catholic father to such activity, Babington finds himself appalled by the sectarian horrors he witnesses and is convinced of 'the consequences of rebellion and disturbance'.[57] Nevertheless, Catholicism repeatedly overcomes Babington's better nature and the 'glimmerings of a Protestant conscience' that momentarily cause him to hesitate in his loyalty to his father's religion.[58] While, as Connolly argues, the novel's 'iconography of anti-Catholicism' implicates it in a prevailing tendency of late eighteenth-century English gothic fiction, it also refuses solely to displace the violence and upheaval of sectarian discord to the Continent.[59] Babington's recognition of the desirability of 'a well-regulated settled government' is prompted by the assassination of the Duke de Guise in France, but his experience of his homeland is of a nation similarly riven by bloody religious disputes (*The Jesuit*, vol. 3, p. 20). After all, it is in England, as Babington admits in his prison-cell confession, that 'the artifices to which, throughout my whole life, I have been the victim' were conceived and deployed; it is in England, Babington writes, that he first embarked on the series of events that transformed him into little more than 'a monster' (*The Jesuit*, vol. 3, p. 336); and it is England, the novel suggests, that continues to evidence the markers of an atavistic, Gothic savagery supposedly left behind in the ensuing centuries of progress and enlightenment.

The Jesuit's questioning of English modernity by way of its setting assumes a particularly poignant significance in Patrick's overt linking of it to recent rebellious activity in Ireland. Presenting the novel as a redacted manuscript containing Babington's eyewitness testimony, Patrick encourages her readers to use it 'to penetrate into the *real* motives of revolutions' (*The Jesuit*, vol. 1, p. x).[60] Coming so soon after the 1798 Rebellion, Patrick's advice strikingly conflates past and present at the same time that it suggests the ways in which English settings could be used by Irish gothicists to explore issues of Anglo-Irish relations, often in defence of Irish patriotism. Meanwhile, despite its Loyalist perspective, Fuller's *The son of Ethelwolf* might be read as commenting negatively on the English presence in Ireland, reflecting a revolutionary zeal no doubt connected to the fall of the Bastille and the start of the French Revolution in the year of the novel's publication. Indicatively, Loeber and Loeber present the novel as 'an allegory of contemporary conditions in Ireland';[61] Kilfeather, meanwhile, argued that it prompts comparisons with eighteenth-century Ireland in its representation of the Danes 'as colonial destroyers' pitted against a noble but usurped king described as 'a patriot sovereign'.[62]

Similar arguments might be advanced about Milliken's *Corfe Castle* (1793), which, much like Leland's *Longsword* and Fuller's *Alan Fitz-Osborne*, explores the disastrous effects of a 'weak minded' king – Ethelred the Unready (r. 978–1013, 1014–16) – too easily swayed by the influence of villainous confidants at a time when strong leadership is most needed: the Danish invasions of England in the early eleventh century.[63] With the bloodthirsty Danish warrior Swain having temporarily vanquished Ethelred from his throne, the people lament their powerless and imperiled position:

> Those were the days of England's mourning! when an usurper sat upon her throne! when her Nobles were slaughtered, and their treasures sent into a foreign land! when her matrons toiled to deck the spoilers out in gorgeous weeds! when her trembling Virgins were torn from the arms of their widowed mothers, to gratify the brutal passions of those, who had murdered their sires! when the temples dedicated to the worship of their God! were turned into scenes of the most savage riot! – when avarice and oppression laid her cities waste, and all were subject to a tyrant[']s will! – those were days of mourning! – those were days of horror! (*Corfe Castle*, vol. 1, pp. 266-7)

The language of usurpation, tyranny, rapine, and pillage anticipates the graphic descriptions of government force in what Niall Gillespie has identified as Irish Jacobin gothic, a form that became increasingly popular after 1795 and the violent disarmament of the then illegal United Irishmen Society.[64] The novel's consideration of the reign of Ethelred the Unready moreover conjures the related historical crises in Ireland, namely Brian Boru's death at the Battle of Clontarf (1014) and the succession crisis that followed. With Brian Boru often quasi-mythologised as the victorious liberator of Ireland from the bloodthirsty Vikings, the narrative's implied connection to ongoing unrest in contemporary Ireland assumes an even keener edge.[65]

Ultimately, Milliken's novel sounds a conservative note. With the accession to the English throne of Swain's son, Canute, order is restored under a ruler who, though foreign, is presented as merciful, just, and capable. Unlike either the Anglo-Saxon Ethelred or his own father, Swain is said to look to 'his people's happiness', seeking to ensure it 'by the institution of wholesome laws, and the impartial administration of justice' (*Corfe Castle*, vol. 2, p. 283). His marriage to Emma, Ethelred's widow, ensures political continuity, not least because Emma accepts Canute only on condition 'that his children by her should inherit the crown of England in preference to any others he might hereafter have, and in case of a failure of issue by this marriage, that the sons of Ethelred or [Ethelred's son] Edmond should be restored to their right' (*Corfe Castle* vol. 2, p. 304).

Canute's ability to bring peace to the land and broker a lasting union between Anglo-Saxon and Danish peoples, partially through his own marriage, speaks presciently to Irish politics in the run-up to the 1798 Rebellion and ensuing Anglo-Irish Union while it anticipates the allegorical marriages of the later national tale. Caution is needed, of course, in the interpretation as allegorical of texts such as *Corfe Castle* and *The son of Ethelwolf*, as Jarlath Killeen reminds us.[66] These works are not textbook examples of literary allegory; nevertheless, contemporary Ireland frequently becomes symbolically spread through their narratives by way of romance's tendency '[to provoke] alternative meanings'.[67] Although neither text is directly about Ireland, they both contain paratextual reminders of their authors' home country that frame their interpretations of English history. Milliken, for instance, dedicates her novel to the Irish MP Henry Boyle, 3rd Earl of Shannon (1771–1842) and numbers among her patrons, as does Fuller, several prominent Irish peers, as indicated in the subscription lists included in both of their novels. Milliken's decision to publish her novel with Cork-based James Haly, moreover, suggests her targeting of a specifically Irish readership.[68] Fuller's *The son of Ethelwolf*, too, though initially published in London, was immediately reprinted in Dublin, revealing both its general popularity and its perceived appeal to an Irish audience.[69]

The material history of these novels, like their paratextual reminders of Ireland, does not, in itself, make them allegorical, but an awareness of it can – and often does – inflect our reading of their versions of English history. While, therefore, these texts are not unique in their use of England's past, drawing attention instead to the widespread focus on local historical settings in contemporary Irish and English gothic literature, they point to the potential added interest Irish writers had in exploring the annals of British history. At the same time, these texts are not simply evidence of 'the Irish gothic's much-discussed concern with the colonial problem'; rather they underline eighteenth- and early nineteenth-century Irish literature's frequent 'engage[ment] with the gothic to critique English structures on broader terms'.[70] As is the case with texts such as *Longsword* and *The castle of Otranto*, *The son of Ethelwolf* and *Corfe Castle* adopt a historical perspective that works effectively to collapse the distance between past and present, thus expressing doubts about eighteenth-century England's enlightened modernity. In these novels, 'the myth of English modernity' is alternately confirmed and eroded as Fuller and Milliken revisit and rewrite moments of transition from pre-modernity to modernity.[71]

Where *Corfe Castle* and *The son of Ethelwolf* use the past in order to displace, at least temporally, any negative understandings of England's Gothic identity, other Irish gothic texts offer much more urgent, present-day constructions of the English landscape. By refusing any kind of imaginative displacement, they force their readers to consider the sheer proximity – geographically and temporally – of gothic atrocity. In these works, England is never a place of security, nor does it allow readers to indulge in a mental buttressing of rational, Protestant English-ness. Instead, contemporary England itself becomes the seat of horrifying misery, iniquity, and religious prejudice, placing in question the reader's understood equation of the English nation with modernity and the Catholic Continent with backward barbarism. As an example, Fuller's *The convent* (1786) repeatedly affirms the danger represented to the English home by recurrent memories of a violent and unsettling past. Initially, the novel appears to engage in a vindication of England by way of a denigration of the Catholic Continent, adding potency to its depiction of Sophia battling an army of French nuns and priests by its clearly contemporary setting.[72] Sophia's assertions of her national loyalties – 'I have friends ... who will not tamely see me injured – detain me therefore at your peril! I am a British subject, and you have no right to control me' (*The convent*, vol. 2, pp. 184–5) – reflect concerns over increasing revolutionary unrest in France and the potential threat it posed to English national security. They also appear to voice the defences of English national identity and character now understood to underwrite 'the Gothic novel' as it develops at the close of the eighteenth century. As such, *The convent* might be read as confirming traditional critical views of the use of Continental settings in 'the Gothic novel' as intended to allow its 'middle-class Protestant readership ... to thrill to the scenes of political and religious persecution safe in the knowledge that they themselves had awoken from such historical nightmares'.[73]

Yet, the terrors faced by Sophia in France are a secondary narrative focus. Indeed, Sophia's convent immurement occupies a relatively brief interlude and is relayed to readers in the curiously indirect manner of letters exchanged by Sophia's friends and family members. Sophia herself remains largely silent, and the details of her experiences in France are primarily secondhand. A partial consequence of the novel's epistolary format, this oblique treatment of the titular convent serves not so much to underscore French treachery as to draw attention to the more obvious and pronounced villainy of Sophia's own family in England, her guardian Mr Woodville in particular. Sophia may be subject to zealous Catholic evangelism in France, but, the novel forcefully indicates, the real danger to both her life and her liberty resides at home with her scheming uncle. Only with his death can Sophia achieve true freedom from fear; even then Sophia is reminded of the power Woodville wields as well as the reasons behind her exile to France. Confessing, on his deathbed, that he had intended 'to make away with Sophia some way or other', Woodville confirms the threateningly violent terrain of Sophia's own home in England (*The convent*, vol. 2, p. 307).

In a similar manner, Selden's *The English nun* (1797) places a marked emphasis on England as a disturbing landscape haunted continuously by patriarchal violence and its long-lasting effects. Relating the sufferings of Louisa Percy, the daughter of the Catholic Scottish Peer, the Earl of Montrose, the novel tells of her abrupt removal from the English convent in Portugal in which she is educated to England upon the deaths of her three elder brothers. It is her father's intention 'literally to be disposed of [her]' through marriage, but he disapproves of her chosen lover, Lord Edward Lumley, the third son of the Duke of Beaufort.[74] As it happens, Edward's father also objects to Louisa, who is presented to him as a 'Caledonian belle' and a 'pretty papist beggar' (*The English nun*, pp. 11, 78). With both fathers insisting that their children have nothing to do with each other, Louisa and Edward resign themselves to separation, and Edward soon after travels to Switzerland, intending to remain there for several years. While he is gone, Louisa's parents die, leaving her a penniless orphan, and she returns to the English convent in Portugal with the purpose of immediately taking the veil.

Louisa's journey to Portugal is pregnant with her devastation over leaving her native land, an exit that becomes chillingly linked to her own impending change in cultural and social status. Embarking on the ship that will take her to Portugal for what she assumes will be the rest of her life, Louisa is struck with 'the painful idea of abandoning her native land' (*The English nun*, p. 114). Upon arriving in Portugal, Louisa sends a miniature portrait of herself to Edward's sympathetic mother, the Duchess of Beaufort, begging her to look upon it occasionally and 'remember that such a being as myself once existed' (*The English nun*, p. 121). Banishment from her home country, Louisa's words suggest, coincides with the existential death of Louisa Percy and her replacement by Sister Louisa. For the rest of the narrative, this imagery of Louisa as somehow other-worldly will persist, as when, for instance, she once again sees Edward upon an unexpected return to England to claim the property left to her by a distant relation. Arguing against Edward's frantic insistence that, with the Duke of Beaufort now dead, they can obtain an absolution of Louisa's vows and marry, Louisa conjures him, 'Consider me as your sister; fancy that I am the one you most loved, risen from the grave, and then I shall glory in your affection' (*The English nun*, p. 186). Styling herself as Edward's long-dead twin sister, Frances, risen again, Louisa affirms her supernatural existence, one that fits her only for future, rather than present, happiness with Edward. Accordingly, once her business in England is completed, Louisa returns to Portugal and is soon after made abbess of the English convent in Lisbon. Edward, in his turn, enlists in the Russian army to fight against the Turks and is killed in battle. Days after hearing this news, Louisa herself succumbs not so much to grief but to a belief that now, finally, she and Edward might be together: 'It is now no violation of the tenderest friendship to wish to die. Lumley no longer lives, to have his sad existence embittered by my death. He expects me in a better world, and I hasten to rejoin him' (*The English nun*, p. 211).

While it is exile from their native land that is associated with the death of Louisa and Edward's wishes for a future together, England is repeatedly presented as a barren landscape hostile to its sons and daughters. Contemplating a return to England after having lived in Portugal for seven years, Louisa says that to do so would not make her content but would instead revive the bitter memories of her youth: 'wherever I lay me, my bed will be strewed with thorns; for where is the oblivious cup that will annihilate memory?' (*The English nun*, p. 126). Although Edward accuses Louisa of having 'a memory so little retentive', the problem is that she, like Edward himself, can only wish for 'some charm to banish recollection' (*The English nun*, p. 135). For him, England can never be his home again, because 'the contrast that it every moment presents, between the present time and the past, is too wounding to feelings irrascible [sic] by nature, and rendered more so by affliction' (*The English nun*, p. 135). Even with the concluding deaths of Edward and Louisa, England retains its strangely disconsolate character. Upon his brother's death, the profligate William

Harcourt Lumley suddenly reforms, cares for his grieving mother, assumes his position as the new Duke of Beaufort, and marries the sister of Louisa's last remaining relative, the Earl of Montrose. Louisa's former admirer, the Marquis of Halifax, marries the sister of Lady Emmeline, a young woman of whom Louisa had become fond during her education at the English convent in Portugal. Together, these families 'lived in the most perfect union' and 'would have been perfectly happy', were it not for occasional reminders of the escapades of remaining unruly relatives (*The English nun*, p. 214). Referring to a past that continues to disrupt a settled and contented present, these traces of discontent find their contrast in the continued memory of Louisa and Edward:

> They were all too sensible of the happy release from sorrow that death had afforded to their beloved friends, to mourn for them without measure, or without end; but they never forgot them: and Emmeline and Julie often held up as an example to their daughters the virtues of the *English nun*. (*The English nun*, p. 215)

These constant reminders of Louisa and Edward, however positively construed, nevertheless refer the reader back to Edward's earlier descriptions of England as a peculiarly haunted mental, if not geographical, landscape. Moreover, when combined with the disruptive potential of Edward's jealous sister, Cecilia, who had purposely assisted her father in thwarting the love between Edward and Louisa because of her own disappointment in not securing the Marquis of Halifax for herself, this gentle and commemorative memory of the now happy couple threatens to transform, suddenly and violently, into a dangerous force of ongoing destruction and misery.

Asserting the veracity of her account of an English landscape so inhospitable as to be dismissed for a Portuguese convent, Selden refers her reader to the 'the well known circumstances mentioned by Mr. Barretti [sic], in the First Volume of his Travels through Spain and Portugal' (*The English nun*, [p. ii]). Evidently referencing Joseph Baretti's *Journey from England to Genoa* (1770), Selden appears to call upon traditional, anti-Catholic depictions of the Continent in a bid to triumph English modernity. Baretti's travelogue, as Nathalie C. Hester notes, depicts Portugal 'on the far-flung margins of Europe', both geographically and culturally, using this portrayal as a method of aligning Italy with England and thereby 'confirm[ing] Italy's enduring centrality to western civilization'.[75] In its pointedly negative stereotyping of Portugal, Baretti's account sits comfortably alongside contemporary English texts such as Richard Twiss's *Travels through Portugal and Spain* (1775), William Dalrymple's *Travels through Spain and Portugal, in 1774* (1777) and Alexander Jardine's *Letters from Barbary, France, Spain, Portugal* (1788), which emphasise the country's barbarism, primarily through its continued attachment to Catholicism.[76] Whereas Baretti, Twiss, Dalrymple, and Jardine focus on Portuguese depravity in order to contrast the country with more enlightened English and, in Baretti's case, Italian societies, Selden offers a much more sympathetic account of Portugal that reverses these dichotomies. By doing so, Selden upsets the comparative framework of eighteenth-century British travelogues – one also traditionally linked to gothic literature in this period – and locates, both imaginatively and geographically, the bewildering violence enacted against her heroine at home rather than abroad.[77]

That Selden, like Fuller before her, chooses a deliberately contemporary time period makes her depictions of a gothic English landscape even more unsettling, as it insists on both the temporal and geographical proximity of barbarism.[78] In these works, the map of gothic atrocity is re-centred from the Catholic Continent (and the 'Celtic Fringe') to mainland England. Like contemporary and near-contemporary works interested in particular periods of English history, therefore, *The convent* and *The English nun* urge a reconsideration of current literary criticism's view of the traditional settings of Romantic gothic literature, pointing to a pronounced late eighteenth-century concern with England's precarious state of modernity.

IRISH GOTHIC FICTION AND THE CULTURAL NATIONALISM OF INTERNATIONAL TRAVEL

In their multi-faceted and varied interactions with Ireland and England, the works discussed in this chapter evidence the decidedly autochthonous focus of late eighteenth-century Irish gothic literature. By the first two decades of the nineteenth century, such local and regional settings would become a hallmark of the national tale and its defence of the Irish people by way of an extensive exploration of customs, culture, and geography. Traditionally understood, the national tale revolves around an imaginative juxtaposition of Ireland and England, allowing readers to learn, alongside the usually uninformed and prejudiced hero, of the beauties of the Irish countryside, the innate nobility of its people, and the august nature of its culture. The English or Anglo-Irish hero's experience of the foreign landscape and people of Ireland convinces him of its worth and helps to reconcile England to political union. For this reason, Ina Ferris has spoken cogently of the national tale as instituting a 'dynamic notion of culture as encounter, often of an abrasive kind'.[79] But the symbolic, often fraught meetings of the national tale do not always occur between England and Ireland, as conventional readings of the form would suggest. *The fair Hibernian* (1789), for instance, may be classified as an early example of the national tale and focuses, as Ian Campbell Ross notes, on 'a clash of cultures – though not, interestingly, the more familiar Irish-English one but rather Irish-French relations'.[80] Owenson's *The missionary* (1811), subtitled 'an Indian tale', but frequently read as a displaced consideration of Irish national politics, envisions a fatal meeting of Eastern and Western cultures in its concentration on seventeenth-century India.[81] Similarly, Owenson's *The novice of Saint Dominick* (1805) operates as what Wright identifies as an 'outsider national tale', or '[a] national [tale] about nations of which the author is not a member'.[82] Its consideration of fourteenth-century France and its interfaith marriage of Catholic heroine and Huguenot hero point to the complex ways in which Irish authors looked beyond Anglo-Irish encounters in their works to negotiate and define modern nationhood in the early nineteenth century.

Underlining the varied nature of the national tale and the cultural encounters it envisions, Miranda Burgess claims that it is predominantly 'dialogical' in nature, 'reproducing diverse accents, vocabularies and sometimes languages as it attempts to provide an overview of a national community – a national community that is continually in contact with representatives from other nations'.[83] Burgess's emphasis on the international aspect of the national tale harmonises well with recent analyses of Irish fiction presented by Wright and Connolly, amongst others. For her part, Wright argues that nineteenth-century Irish nationalist writing 'often explicitly draws on larger geographical networks that establish wide-ranging international comparisons'.[84] Connolly, meanwhile, contends that much nineteenth-century Irish fiction displays 'a transnational dimension' devolving from the Irish novel's location at the 'intersection of [the] dynamics of proximity and distance' inherent to the realities of the contemporary print industry: with native publishing annihilated in the wake of Union, the migration of Irish authors to London intensified just as the numbers of Irish novels specifically concerned with Ireland or the Irish people markedly increased.[85]

Chapter 4 considers in more detail the transnational element of gothic fiction produced by Irish émigré authors publishing with the Minerva Press, a notorious London-based producer of popular hack fiction, gothic romances in particular. The discussion here, though, focuses on two rarely read Irish gothic narratives that translate the national tale's ideas of cultural encounter into explorations of the role of travel in the assertion of a new Irish national identity following the 1798 Rebellion and Anglo-Irish Union. These novels, Henrietta Rouvière Mosse's *The old Irish baronet; or, manners of my country* (1808) and Roche's *The tradition of the castle; or, scenes in the Emerald Isle* (1824), exemplify the overlap of gothic and national forms in the late eighteenth and early nineteenth centuries, twinning an interest in the legacy of the past and a related examination of romance with extensive explorations of Irish national identity. Significantly, they do so through heroes and heroines who are not purposefully grounded in Ireland, like Glorvina O'Melville is, but are instead inveterate travellers and exiled wanderers, functioning as exemplars of both the disastrous effects of rebellion and dispossession as well as the potential advantages of the consequent Irish exposure to international communities and participation in global events. Although written from varying perspectives and at differing historical junctures, these novels attest to the significance of travel in the renegotiation of Irish national identity in the first three decades following the 1798 Rebellion and the Anglo-Irish Union.

Published just two years after *The wild Irish girl*, Mosse's *The old Irish baronet* appears, at first glance, to be an opportunistic imitation of Owenson's model.[86] It tells the tale of the apparently orphaned and inconspicuous tutor Ferdinand Sylvester as he discovers his true parentage, is reinstated as the heir apparent to the Duncarty family estate in Co. Kildare, and validates his newfound identity by way of the national tale's characteristic 'Glorvina solution'. The marriage between Sylvester (really Mr Netterville, future Lord Duncarty of Princely Hall) and Ellen O'Callaghan, daughter of the man who had assumed ownership of the Duncarty estates in the absence of its rightful owner, signifies a union of legal and inherited rights, much as do the nuptials in *The wild Irish girl* and *The absentee*. There is a difference here, however. Although Netterville has spent much of his youth and early adulthood outside of Ireland and, in this sense, assumes the role of 'stranger' inhabited by Horatio Mortimer and, later, Lord Colambre, as suggested by the temporary, albeit involuntary, suspension of his identity,[87] he nevertheless represents, like Glorvina and Grace Nugent, the dispossession and political allegiances of Gaelic Ireland.[88] This is apparent in the associations conjured by his various names. 'Ferdinand Sylvester' recalls the eighteenth-century antiquarian, Sylvester O'Halloran (1728–1807), while 'Netterville' raises the spectre of the recusant John

Netterville, 2nd Viscount Netterville of Dowth (d. 1659), and his father, both of whom were implicated in the 1641 Rebellion and consequently lost both title and estates.[89]

Mosse's novel thus envisions a triumphant return of native Irishness in both Netterville's physical relocation to Ireland and his reinstatement as heir apparent to the Duncarty estate. His marriage to Ellen O'Callaghan, although outwardly suggestive of a cross-cultural, Anglo-Irish accord, further reinforces the novel's interest in Catholic re-possession, recalling as her name does Cornelius O'Callaghan, 1st Baron Lismore (1741–97), the eighteenth-century descendant of one of the few native families gifted with an Irish peerage.[90] Rather than unsettle the country, Netterville's relocation to Ireland and marriage to Ellen is applauded as 'a happy pledge' of future 'bounty'.[91] More than that, it implicitly helps to put an end to the superstitious beliefs of credulous servants who understand that Netterville's father was 'carried off for a sartinty by the good people' (*The old Irish baronet*, vol. 1, p. 16). Allowing for the reinterment of his grandparents, whose bones periodically and inexplicably unearth themselves in the ruined chapel graveyard of Princely Hall, Netterville's return concludes – even as it also confirms – the local belief that their bodies 'never will rest in peace till the lawful heirs of those deceased persons are discovered' (*The old Irish baronet*, vol. 1, p. 15).

Gifted with this inheritance, Netterville does not, like Mortimer or Colambre, require an education in Irish customs, society, or culture, despite his long absence from his homeland. While Mortimer and Colambre must travel through Ireland and come to an appreciation of its true nature and worth in order to assume their positions of privilege, Netterville is instead empowered to re-inhabit his ancestral home in Ireland as he travels through Britain, Europe, and, figuratively at least, North America as well. Accompanying Sir Thomas O'Callaghan on a European tour after the peer has been deprived of his seat in parliament by Union, Netterville discovers the treachery enacted against his grandparents in the abduction of their only son by the duplicitous Fr Jeronome, former confessor to Netterville's Spanish great-grandfather, who had disapproved of his daughter's marriage. This revelation restores Netterville to his rightful identity and position, paving the way for his eventual return to Ireland in his capacity as gentleman and landowner. But travel plays a more significant role in the novel than simply the setting for the disclosures by which Netterville becomes himself, as it were. Indeed, travel is portrayed as the key to the 'amelioration' of governance at home (*The old Irish baronet*, vol. 1, p. 198). It is travel, the narrative maintains, that allows for domestic reform, not simply through a comparison of modern Britain with more Gothic geographical zones on the Continent, but through a recognition of current deficiencies in present-day British institutions. Specifically countering the geographical and ideological dichotomy associated with English gothic fiction of this period, *The old Irish baronet* suggests that travel broadens the mind and prompts a consideration of potential areas of improvement in systems at home. It cautions its readers, moreover, against the assumption that nineteenth-century Britain had reached the pinnacle of enlightenment: '[t]he elements that compose the present edifice of British freedom, are excellent. ... But let us not evoke the bugbear of antiquity to oppose their practical amelioration' (*The old Irish baronet*, vol. 1, pp. 197–8). Britain, Mosse's tale contends, is not that far removed – temporally or geographically – from the barbarity it detected in foreign cultures:

> The present degree of perfection to which the structure of public weal has attained, is the result of successive improvements, and the farther we trace back our steps (and reform has no other meaning), the nearer we come to those times when barbarism and servitude went hand in hand. (*The old Irish baronet*, vol. 1, pp. 197–8)

Recalling the native geography of atrocity found in *The convent*, *The son of Ethelwolf*, *Corfe Castle*, *The English nun*, and the works of Elizabeth Griffith, *The old Irish baronet* turns attention to the potentially atavistic elements of the British nation, suggesting that these Gothic remainders lie primarily in Anglo-Irish relations. Ned Newburgh, the '*fashionable*' gentleman and profligate absentee set to inherit from O'Callaghan before the discovery of Netterville's true identity is particularly noteworthy in this regard (*The old Irish baronet*, vol. 1, p. 139).[92] Apparently as modern as they come, Newburgh nevertheless represents irresponsibly outdated attitudes and behaviours. His plan to deforest Princely Hall in order to pay his many creditors while continuing to live in London epitomises negligent English and Anglo-Irish stewardship of Ireland, emphasising the culpability of those Sir Thomas calls 'noble aliens' in the rebellious feelings of the Irish peasantry and the devastation of the Irish economy (*The old Irish baronet*, vol. 1, p. 180). Netterville's return and the promise of a Catholic restoration envisions a new future for Ireland enabled by travel, which, the novel suggests, provides for the 'successive improvements' lauded as the key to the present-day 'perfection' of the British state. The importance of mobility is further reinforced by Netterville's transnational

Irish identity, bequeathed to him by his Canadian Quaker mother and Spanish Catholic grandmother. He thus gestures towards an 'amelioration' of Ireland and, concomitantly, Britain dependent not just on the restoration of Gaelic Catholic rights but also on a transcontinental and transatlantic perspective underwritten by various forms of travel, including tourism, but also exile and trade.[93]

Roche's *The tradition of the castle* even more forcefully delineates the importance of travel in its many guises to the future of the nation. Like *The old Irish baronet*, it appears, at first glance, to offer a conventional national tale narrative and conclusion revolving around the return of the Anglo-Irish hero, Donaghue O'Brien – a direct descendant of Brian Boru himself – to Ireland to take up residence there and correct the misdeeds of his father, who had not only moved to London with the establishment of Anglo-Irish Union but had also voted that Union into place. A heavily intertextual novel, *The tradition of the castle* most immediately recalls Edgeworth's *The absentee* as it sketches the O'Brien family's relocation to London, against the wishes of Donaghue's mother, and their subsequent experiences of 'severe mortification' upon realising that 'the rank and fortune that in [their] own country were thought so much of, [were] here, comparatively, little regarded'.[94] Like Lady Clonbrony before him, O'Brien senior attempts to dissuade his son from returning to Ireland by describing it in the most disadvantageous terms as

> a place from which every person of respectability had fled since the union, leaving it in possession of a set of beings, who, neither the one thing nor the other, still disgusted by their imprudent assumption of consequence; while the land was rude and uncultivated, the tenantry lawless, and the common people, in short, no better than a set of wild savages, ready to start into rebellion on the slightest imaginary provocation. (*The tradition of the castle*, vol. 1, p. 48)

Such representations of Ireland find further purchase in Donaghue's mind by the arguments of his would-be lover, Lady Jane Doyle, who resembles *The absentee*'s Lady Dashfort in her prejudicial views of Ireland as a 'sweet land of blunders' peopled by 'wild savages' (*The tradition of the castle*, vol. 1, pp. 50, 51). Unlike Colambre, Donaghue is much swayed by these narrow-minded perceptions of Ireland, finding 'much to censure, but nothing to admire' upon his first arrival (*The tradition of the castle*, vol. 1, p. 57). So intolerant of the country has he become, that Donaghue refuses to socialise with any but a few select acquaintances from London forced for financial reasons to 'rusticat[e] amidst the barbarous wilds of Ireland' (*The tradition of the castle*, vol. 1, p. 69). In the process, he offends both his mother and the woman she intends for his bride, Eveleen Erin. He soon after leaves for London, thoroughly unreformed.

While in London, Donaghue's life takes a strange and unexpected turn. There, he discovers that his father has become an inveterate gambler in his absence, partially in an attempt to recoup the extensive financial ruin he has hidden from his family. When confronted, O'Brien becomes violent, stabbing Donaghue in the chest before drowning himself in the Thames. Donaghue's mother later dies, and Donaghue, now deprived of his rightful inheritance due to his father's debts, accepts a commission in the British army and departs for the Continent, where he undergoes the kind of alienating experience traditionally associated with the depiction of Catholic European countries in 'the Gothic novel'. Travelling to Spain after serving in the British army at Waterloo, for instance, Donaghue is taken prisoner by the Inquisition and, in a scene reminiscent of Maturin's *Melmoth the wanderer*, is forced to escape via underground passages led by a suspicious figure acting as an agent of the Inquisition.[95] Repeatedly linked to the Goths and an associated, pejoratively construed Gothic civilisation, the Spanish people are represented as credulous in the extreme, blindly committed to Roman Catholicism, and trapped in a deeply unenlightened way of life. Return to England, in this context, is presented as a welcome homecoming. In England, Donaghue's travelling companion, Rosebud, asserts, 'we neither fear racks on one side, or stilettos on the other'; here, 'the accusation of man against man is bold and open as his own nature'. It is in short, a 'region of liberty' characterised by 'virtuous and generous sentiments' and enjoying 'a peculiar Providence' that 'watch[es] over and bless[es] the land that has been instrumental to restoring man to his natural charter' (*The tradition of the castle*, vol. 2, p. 56).

If *The tradition of the castle*'s depictions of Spain appear to conform to conventional understandings of the geography of contemporary gothic literature, the descriptions of Ireland upon Donaghue's later return there also recall the estranging encounters with the 'Celtic periphery' familiar from *The history of Lady Barton*, *The wild Irish girl*, and *The children of the abbey*. Journeying home after his experiences abroad, Donaghue is filled with 'painful feelings' and describes his ancestral home as 'cold', 'dreary', and 'desolate' (*The tradition of the castle*, vol. 2, pp. 160, 161). Such emotions are directly related to the death of his mother, whose absence affects Donaghue acutely:

> [I am now] returned to my home. But what a home! without a being to sympathize in my feelings – what a contrast to that of past times, when I had the first, the most exalted of women, the tenderest of mothers, to recover me, sooth any care that might have obtruded by her mild counsel, or check any impatience. (*Tradition of the castle*, vol. 2, p. 170)

More broadly, the negative contrast of past and present renders the country as a whole a miserable landscape of devastation and ruin, haunted by the memory of former greatness. Contemplating the scenery as he approaches Dublin harbour, Donaghue picks out the spot at which his ancestor was said to have fallen and reflects on the decline of the country since Brian Boru was alive:

> [N]o wonder he conquered [at Clontarf], for neither the physical strength, nor the spirit of Irishmen, in those days, was impaired or crushed. A chief was then a father to his followers, nor fled to another land, forgetful of their claim on his kindness, and took care not to squander what he wrung from their toil, or acquired through their valour. – 'But now!' Donaghue sighed at the melancholy contrast. (*Tradition of the castle*, vol. 2, p. 63)

Here, Donaghue's re-encounter with his homeland conflates personal and political loss, suggesting that the cause of Ireland's current degradation is the profligate absenteeism represented by Donaghue's own father. The Spanish people may misguidedly persist in antiquated manners and customs bequeathed by former generations, the narrative suggests, but Ireland too easily squanders its noble heritage. As a result, Irish and Spanish geographies become equally gothicised, if for different reasons.

The solution to alienating domestic and public environments, the novel proposes, is a rejection of the absentee landlordism that had first caused problems for Donaghue and Ireland alike. In this, Roche offers a conventional national tale conclusion, contending that 'many of the evils now complained of [in Ireland] would be avoided' if Irish men and would women would make '*the land of their forefathers ... their permanent residence*' (*The tradition of the castle*, vol. 3, p. 222).[96] As in *The old Irish baronet*, however, this denouement is enabled not by the tours around Ireland familiar from *The wild Irish girl* and *The absentee*, but by Donaghue's experiences abroad. It transpires, in fact, that Donaghue's persecutor in Spain is none other than the son of the greedy agent who had manufactured O'Brien's pro-Union vote, encouraged his extensive debts, and entailed the O'Brien estates to himself.[97] Donaghue's encounters with don Callan/O'Callaghan in Spain enable a decisive meeting in Ireland by which Donaghue is re-possessed of his ancestral estates. More than that, Donaghue's travels are attendant upon his entry into the British military, a step he is all but forced to take by his father's actions. Effectively exiled from Ireland, as suggested by the novel's epigraph, excerpted from the famous ballad, 'The exile of Erin' (1801),[98] Donaghue becomes involved in key moments of British and Continental history, fighting at the Battle of Waterloo, for example, and escaping from the Inquisition just days before its abolition by Spanish authorities. In this, he exemplifies the tendency, located by Wright in a number of Irish Romantic texts, to 'suggest … that the abjection of Irish men through exile ironically allows the demonstration of their merits'.[99] Donaghue's travels thus function as 'a kind of colonial Grand Tour' by which he can counter 'colonial disempowerment' through '[the demonstration] of individual merit in a larger international arena'.[100]

As with Netterville's return to Ireland in *The old Irish baronet*, Donaghue's reinstatement as rightful owner of his ancestral home and estates reads as a wilful act of Catholic enfranchisement. Descended from Brian Boru on his father's side and, on his mother's from both 'O'Donaghue, lord, by descent, of the lakes, but known in after times as king' and 'Cormac M'Culinan, at once archbishop and king of Cashell' as well as author of 'The Psalter of Cashell', Donaghue represents a long history of colonial violence, dispossession, and Gaelic resistance (*The tradition of the castle*, vol. 1, pp. 35, 36).[101] His return to Ireland after an absence depicted as imposed upon him insists that the solution to Ireland's ills lay not just in the overthrow of absenteeism but in the restoration of Catholic rights.[102] In both novels, indeed, the atavistic elements of Irish society are insistently coded as Anglo-Irish rather than Catholic, with the 'return' of the latter – both physically and imaginatively – portrayed as the key to modern Irish nationhood. As is the nature of returns, though, these movements are only made possible by absence, however forcefully inflicted. Against the irresponsible and destructive absenteeism of O'Brien and Ned Newburgh, the travels and military escapades of Donaghue and Netterville instil in them the necessary perspective, insight, and qualities with which to assume their rightful positions at home.

CONCLUSION

Written by émigrée authors who were themselves all but forced out of Ireland for personal and professional reasons, *The old Irish baronet* and

The tradition of the castle imagine remigration to Ireland at the same time that they invest travel and exile themselves with the potential to recover Irish cultural and economic, if not political, power. In these novels, Irish experiences of other cultures and communities become precisely that which enables the righting of historic wrongs at home, consequently brightening Ireland's future prospects. These works thus adapt the scenes of cultural encounter made familiar by the contemporary national tale and gothic fiction alike in order to enlarge the geography underpinning Irish national identity. As they do so, they underline the exceptionally expansive map of topographical settings drawn by late eighteenth- and early nineteenth-century gothic literary production. Far from simply confining themselves to the Catholic Continental and 'Celtic Fringe' zones commonly linked to gothic fiction of this period, the works assessed in this chapter evidence the widely varied use of local and exotic geography in Romantic-era gothic. More than that, as Chapter 4 contends, they reflect the increasing mobility of Irish authors themselves as well as the expanding material circulation of Irish gothic literature in the Romantic literary marketplace.

NOTES

1 Theodore Melville, *The White Knight, or the monastery of Morne. A romance*, 3 vols (London: Crosby & Letterman, 1802), vol. 1, [p. iii]. Further references are to this edition and are given in parentheses in the text. Original italics.
2 Anthony Mandal notes the manner in which publication with Crosby would have branded *The White Knight* as a particular kind of fiction – a 'run-of-the mill' gothic/sentimental romance unworthy of serious scholarly attention; *Jane Austen and the popular novel: the determined author* (Basingstoke and New York: Palgrave Macmillan, 2007), p. 67.
3 Tellingly, *The White Knight* is excluded from the list of Ireland-related fiction included in Jacqueline Belanger, 'Some preliminary remarks on the production and reception of fiction relating to Ireland, 1800–1829', *Cardiff Corvey: reading the Romantic text*, 4.2 (2000), 1–31, www.cf.ac.uk/encap/corvey/articles/cc04_n02.html, accessed 15 June 2017. Nothing has been written of it in recent accounts of the Irish novel, including edited collections and monographs such as Jacqueline Belanger (ed.), *The Irish novel in the nineteenth century: facts and fictions* (Dublin: Four Courts Press, 2005); Connolly, *A cultural history of the Irish novel*; Foster, *The Cambridge companion to the Irish novel*; and Hand, *A history of the Irish novel*. And, while it appears in the Loebers' *A guide to Irish fiction*, the narrative synopsis attached to it seems partly based on another

novel altogether; see *A guide to Irish fiction*, p. 896. For the recognition of *The Irish chieftain* as fully engaged in cultural nationalist attempts to prove and vindicate Ireland's cultural worth, see Trumpener, *Bardic nationalism*, p. 45.

4 For a problematisation of the conventional positioning of *Castle Rackrent* as 'the first Irish novel' and an enumeration of some of the earlier instances of Irish fiction interested in Ireland and Irish characters, see Ian Campbell Ross, 'Fiction to 1800', in Seamus Deane (ed.), *The Field Day anthology of Irish writing*, vol. 1 (Derry: Field Day Publications, 1991), p. 682; Aileen Douglas, 'The novel before 1800', in Foster (ed.), *The Cambridge companion to the Irish novel*, pp. 22–38; and the essays collected in Aileen Douglas, Moyra Haslett, and Ian Campbell Ross (eds), *Irish fiction, 1660–1830*, special issue of *Irish university review*, 41.1 (2011).
5 Killeen, *The emergence of Irish gothic fiction*, p. 9.
6 Ibid., p. 10.
7 Siobhán Marie Kilfeather, ' "Strangers at home": political fictions by women in eighteenth-century Ireland', Ph.D. dissertation (Princeton University, 1989), p. 277. Kilfeather referred specifically to Owenson and Roche in her commentary, but Maturin equally contributed to the literary emphasis on Ireland as, in his own words, a land of 'dark, desolate and stormy grandeur' (*The Milesian chief*, vol. 1, p. 54).
8 Kilfeather, 'Origins of the Irish female gothic', 36.
9 Clery, *The rise of supernatural fiction*, p. 129.
10 Reeve, *The old English baron*, p. 2.
11 This graph is based on a sampling of 90 texts drawn from the 114 titles catalogued in the Appendix, which indicates both the works included in this sampling and their geographical settings.
12 Watt, *Contesting the gothic*, pp. 43–4.
13 See Kilfeather, 'Origins of the Irish female gothic', 37–8, and Kilfeather, 'The gothic novel', pp. 80–1.
14 Wright, *Representing the national landscape*, p. 131.
15 Ibid.
16 Connolly, *A cultural history of the Irish novel*, p. 48.
17 Ibid.
18 Trumpener, *Bardic nationalism*, p. 141.
19 On the overlooked 'international focus' of the national tale, see Karen Steele, 'Irish incognitos: transnational mobility in the national tales of Maria Edgeworth and Sydney Owenson', *Éire-Ireland*, 50.3/4 (2015), 94–112.
20 Siobhán Kilfeather, 'The profession of letters, 1700–1810', in Angela Bourke, Siobhán Kilfeather, Maria Luddy, Margaret Mac Curtain, Gerardine Meaney, Máirín Ní Dhonnchadha, Mary O'Dowd, and Clair Wills (eds), *The Field Day anthology of Irish writing: volume 5* (Cork: Cork University Press, 2002), p. 832.

21 See Elizabeth Griffith, *The delicate distress*, eds Cynthia Booth Ricciardi and Susan Staves (Lexington, KY: The University Press of Kentucky, 1997); Betty Rizzo (ed.), *Eighteenth-century women playwrights. Volume 4: Elizabeth Griffith* (London: Pickering & Chatto, 2001); and Melinda C. Finberg (ed.), *Eighteenth-century women dramatists* (Oxford: Oxford University Press, 2001). For the argument that Griffith herself saw drama as her primary literary calling, see Elizabeth Eger, 'Griffith, Elizabeth (1727–1793)', *Oxford dictionary of national biography* (Oxford, 2004; online edn, 2009), www.oxforddnb.com, accessed 15 June 2017.

22 Kilfeather, 'Origins of the Irish female gothic', 38.

23 *Ibid.*, 38–41.

24 Killeen, *The emergence of Irish gothic fiction*, pp. 7, 6.

25 The other novel to appear alongside *The delicate distress* was Richard Griffith's *The Gordian knot*.

26 Eger, 'Griffith, Elizabeth'.

27 Shaun Regan, 'Locating Richard Griffith: genre, nation, canon', *Irish university review*, 41.1 (2011), 901.

28 Douglas, 'The novel before 1800', p. 22.

29 Eger, 'Griffith, Elizabeth'.

30 Kilfeather, 'The profession of letters, 1700–1810', p. 796. For a particularly sardonic review, see the *Monthly Review*, 26 (1767), 154–5.

31 [Elizabeth Griffith], *The delicate distress, a novel: in letters*, 2 vols (1769; Dublin, 1787), vol. 1, p. 63. Further references are to this edition and are given in parentheses in the text.

32 Griffith, *The delicate distress*, eds Ricciardi and Staves, p. 261.

33 *Ibid.*, pp. 261–2.

34 Kilfeather, 'Origins of the Irish female gothic', 42.

35 'A Lady' [Elizabeth Griffith], *Amana; a dramatic poem* (London, 1764), p. 35. Further references are to this edition and are given in parentheses in the text. The castle of the despotic Egyptian ruler – the villain of the piece – is specifically described in the stage directions as '*A Gothic building, representing the palace of Sakara*' (*Amana*, p. 35). Original emphasis.

36 Watt, *Contesting the gothic*, p. 49.

37 In the course of the play, Britain's 'protector' – presumably George III – is lauded as one 'Who not in Britain's cause alone sustains / The toils of council, and of hostile plains: / The world's great champion, born for all mankind, / In whom the oppressed a certain refuge find: / Whose sword, but like the lancet, wounds to heal, / Where moral lenitives can naught avail; / Whose olive bearing laurel peace restores, / And calms the discord of contending powers' (*Amana*, p. 54).

38 John Cannon, 'Percy [formerly Smithson], Hugh', *Oxford dictionary of national biography* (Oxford, 2004; online edn, 2008), www.oxforddnb.com, accessed

2 July 2013; Harriet Blodgett, 'Percy, Elizabeth', *Oxford dictionary of national biography* (Oxford, 2004; online edn, 2008), www.oxforddnd.com, accessed 2 July 2013.

39 See Patrick M. Geoghegan, 'Pery, Edmond Sexten 1st Viscount Pery', *Dictionary of Irish biography*, eds James McGuire and James Quinn (Cambridge: Cambridge University Press, 2009), http://dib.cambridge.org, accessed 26 May 2015.

40 For a more detailed consideration of *Amana* as well as the manner in which it highlights the multi-generic nature of gothic literary production in eighteenth-century Ireland, Britain, and Europe, see Morin, 'Theorizing "gothic" in eighteenth-century Ireland'. It is tempting to read Griffith's dedication of *The delicate distress* to John Russell, 4th Duke of Bedford (1710–71), who acted as Lord Lieutenant of Ireland from 1756 to 1760, in a similar manner. In that case, however, the brief words of gratitude Griffith includes seem to owe to Bedford's granting of a post to Richard Griffith in 1760 or thereabouts, though few details of the transaction survive. See Sidney Lee, 'Griffith, Richard (*d*. 1788)', rev. Ian Campbell Ross, *Oxford dictionary of national biography* (Oxford, 2004; online edn, 2008), www.oxforddnb.com, accessed 15 August 2013.

41 Elizabeth Griffith, *The history of Lady Barton, a novel, in letters*, 3 vols (London, 1771), vol. 1, p. 7. Further references are to this edition and are given in parentheses in the text.

42 Kilfeather, 'Origins of the Irish female gothic', 39. On eighteenth-century conceptualisations of Wales as, like Ireland, a liminal and uncanny space that lent itself very well to the gothic literary mode, see Elizabeth Edwards, 'Iniquity, terror and survival: Welsh gothic, 1789–1804', *Journal for eighteenth-century studies*, 35.1 (2012), 119–33.

43 Original italics.

44 Kilfeather, 'Origins of the Irish female gothic', 40.

45 *Ibid*.

46 Elizabeth Griffith, *The story of Lady Juliana Harley, a novel. In letters*, 2 vols (Dublin, 1776), vol. 2, p. 7. Further references are to this edition and are given in parentheses in the text.

47 Burgess, 'Violent translations', 62.

48 See Michael Perceval-Maxwell, 'Butler, James', *Dictionary of Irish biography*, eds James McGuire and James Quinn (Cambridge: Cambridge University Press, 2009), http://dib.cambridge.org, accessed 21 June 2017.

49 Elizabeth Griffith, 'Story of Lady Fanny Beaumont and Lord Layton', in Griffith and Goldsmith (eds), *Novellettes*, pp. 192–202. Further references are to this edition and are given in parentheses in the text.

50 See Douglas, 'The novel before 1800'.

51 Robert Mighall, *A geography of Victorian gothic fiction: mapping history's nightmares* (Oxford: Oxford University Press, 1999), p. xvii.

52 Like Reeve's *The old English baron*, *Netley Abbey* is one of the few novels of the period purposely to refer to itself as gothic.
53 Anne Fuller, *The son of Ethelwolf; an historical tale* (Dublin [1789]), p. 4. Further references are to this edition and are given in parentheses in the text.
54 Watt, *Contesting the gothic*, pp. 51–2, 52–3.
55 *Ibid.*, p. 58.
56 See *Ibid.*, Chapter 2, 'The Loyalist gothic romance', pp. 42–69.
57 Mrs F.C. Patrick, *The Jesuit; or, the history of Anthony Babington, Esq., an historical novel*, 3 vols (Bath, 1799), vol. 3, p. 20. Further references are to this edition and are given in parentheses in the text.
58 Connolly, *A cultural history of the Irish novel*, p. 132.
59 *Ibid.*
60 Original emphasis.
61 Loeber and Loeber, *A guide to Irish fiction*, p. 478.
62 Kilfeather, 'The profession of letters, 1700–1810', p. 812.
63 Anna Milliken, *Corfe Castle; or, historic tracts. A novel, in two volumes* (Cork: James Haly, 1793), vol. 1, p. 61. Further references are to this edition and are given in parentheses in the text.
64 Gillespie, 'Irish Jacobin gothic', pp. 58–73.
65 Seán Duffy, *Brian Boru and the Battle of Clontarf* (2013; Dublin: Gill & Macmillan, 2014), p. 239.
66 See Killeen, 'Breaking stories: religion, identity, and the emergence of narrative instability in post-revolutionary Ireland', *The emergence of Irish gothic fiction*, pp. 79–105.
67 *Ibid.*, p. 88. The notion of 'symbolic spread' is Northrop Frye's; see Frye, *The secular scripture*, p. 59
68 Connolly, *A cultural history of the Irish novel*, p. 6.
69 Loeber and Loeber, *A guide to Irish fiction*, p. 478. As Mary Pollard notes, eighteenth-century Irish publishers as a rule 'chose the most readable and popular material from London publications' to reprint; *Dublin's trade in books, 1550–1800* (Oxford: Clarendon Press, 1989), p. v.
70 Wright, *Representing the national landscape*, p. 132.
71 *Ibid.*, p. 133.
72 There is little indication of the time period in Fuller's novel. The letters exchanged between the characters remain undated, and, while there are many plot similarities to Radcliffe's later, more temporally and geographically distanced novels, the letters' pointed interest in female modesty and the containment of excessive sensibility, as discussed briefly in Chapter 2, creates an immediacy that places the novel directly within contemporary debates about fiction and its revolutionary potential. It is thus fundamentally linked to a late eighteenth-century English cultural and geographic landscape. On these debates and the epistolary form, see, for instance, Linda S. Kauffman,

Discourses of desire: gender, genre, and epistolary fictions (Ithaca, NY: Cornell University Press, 1986); Ruth Perry, *Women, letters, and the novel* (New York: AMS Press, 1980); and Watson, *Revolution and the form of the British novel*.
73 Baldick and Mighall, 'Gothic criticism', p. 219.
74 Catharine Selden, *The English nun; a novel* (London, 1797), p. 8. Further references are to this edition and are given in parentheses in the text.
75 Nathalie C. Hester, 'Geographies of belonging: Italian travel writing and Italian identity in the age of early European tourism', *Annali d'Italianistica*, 21 (2003), 298, 294.
76 On enduring eighteenth-century British dread of the Portuguese Inquisition and the accompanying understanding of Lisbon 'as a city of violent death', characterised in British accounts of the period by frequent reference to underground Inquisition torture chambers and nuns immured behind convent walls, see Richard Hamblyn, 'Notes from underground: Lisbon after the earthquake', *Romanticism*, 14.2 (2008), 113–16.
77 On the 'binary, symmetrical oppositions between the familiar and the foreign' in eighteenth-century British travel writing, see Chloe Chard, *Pleasure and guilt on the Grand Tour: travel writing and imaginative geography, 1600–1830* (Manchester: Manchester University Press, 1999), p. 40. See also the discussion of the similarities between eighteenth-century English travel writing and gothic fiction in Mighall, *A geography of Victorian gothic fiction*, pp. 16–26.
78 The date of the events in *The English nun* can be pinpointed by the passing reference made upon Sister Louisa's return to England to the beginning of the Swedish Revolution on 19 August 1772. The concluding events of the novel, including Edward's death fighting in the ongoing Russo-Turkish wars (1768–74) and Louisa's own subsequent death, occur within months of this date. Earlier events in the novel may be dated to approximately seven years previously, for Louisa is said to pass seven years in the convent before returning to England to claim her inheritance.
79 Ferris, *The Romantic national tale*, p. 9.
80 Ian Campbell Ross, 'Irish fiction before the Union', in Belanger (ed.), *The Irish novel in the nineteenth century*, p. 40.
81 Wright reads *The missionary*'s Indian setting as 'a contrivance for addressing colonialism and the attendant issue of religious intolerance while apparently dislocating them from Owenson's main sphere of interest, nineteenth-century Ireland, by nominally rooting them in seventeenth-century Portugal and India'; Julia M. Wright, 'Introduction', in Sydney Owenson, *The missionary: an Indian tale*, ed. Julia M. Wright (Ontario: Broadview Press, 2002), p. 19.
82 Wright, *Representing the national landscape*, pp. 173–4.
83 Miranda Burgess, 'The national tale and allied genres, 1770s–1840s', in Foster (ed.), *The Cambridge companion to the Irish novel*, p. 40.
84 Wright, *Representing the national landscape*, p. xiii.

85 Connolly, *A cultural history of the Irish novel*, p. 6; Loeber and Loeber, *Guide to Irish fiction*, p. lxii.
86 Claire Connolly includes *The old Irish baronet* in her list of novels 'that prove the instant marketability of *The Wild Irish Girl* formula'; 'Irish Romanticism, 1800–1829', in Kelleher and O'Leary (eds), *The Cambridge history of Irish literature*, p. 415.
87 Ferris, *The Romantic national tale*, p. 57.
88 Pittock, *Scottish and Irish Romanticism*, pp. 178–9.
89 Pádraig Lenihan, 'Netterville, John, second Viscount Netterville of Dowth (d. 1659)', *Oxford dictionary of national biography* (Oxford, 2004; online edn, 2008), www.oxforddnb.com, accessed 8 September 2016.
90 B.H. Soulsby, 'O'Callaghan, Sir Robert William (1777–1840)', rev. James Falkner, *Oxford dictionary of national biography* (Oxford, 2004; online edn, 2008), www.oxforddnb.com, accessed 8 September 2016.
91 Henrietta Rouvière Mosse, *The old Irish baronet; or, manners of my country. A novel*, 3 vols (London: Lane, Newman & Co., 1808), vol. 3, pp. 251, 252. Further references are to this edition and are given in parentheses in the text.
92 Original emphasis.
93 Netterville's own father, for instance, is effectively banished from Ireland after being abducted from his parents and sent to live in secret seclusion in England. The next chapter will return to the issue of the print trade and the manner in which the dissemination of Irish gothic fiction became central to contemporary discourses of both nationalism and transnationalism in Ireland and elsewhere.
94 Regina Maria Roche, *The tradition of the castle; or, scenes in the Emerald Isle*, 4 vols (London: A.K. Newman & Co.,1824), vol. 1, p. 42. Further references are to this edition and are given in parentheses in the text.
95 Further suggesting Roche's debt to Maturin, a minor character in the novel bears the name of don Alonzo de Guzman, recalling two separate characters from *Melmoth* – Alonzo di Monçada and the wealthy merchant known simply as Guzman. Later, a character named Brennan conjures the Brennan of Maturin's *The Milesian chief* and is implicated in a similar tale of long-cherished rebellion and star-crossed love that forms the 'tradition of the castle' linked to Donaghue's Irish home, Altoir-na-Grenie.
96 Original italics.
97 Here again, Roche's intertextuality appears evident, with the deceptions practised on O'Brien echoing those of the hapless Sir Condy in Edgeworth's *Castle Rackrent*. I am grateful to Ian Campbell Ross for highlighting these similarities to me.
98 A poem lamenting the exile enforced upon individuals involved in the 1798 Rebellion, 'The exile of Erin' is popularly attributed to Thomas Campbell but may have been written by George Nugent Reynolds. See Wright, *Representing*

the national landscape, p. 277 note 2 and Frank Molloy, 'Thomas Campbell's "Exile of Erin": English poem, Irish reactions', in Lynch, Fischer, and Coates (eds), *Back to the present*, pp. 43–53.
99 Wright, *Representing the national landscape*, p. xiii.
100 *Ibid.*, p. xiv.
101 This genealogy links Donaghue's mother to the historical O'Donoghue family of Co. Kerry, which, as Seán Ó Tuama observes, made a name for itself at the start of the eighteenth century as 'resistance leaders' opposed to 'the new Williamite colonists but also to … old Anglo-Irish colonists'. Quasi-fictional O'Donoghues would later feature prominently in Charles Lever's novel, *The O'Donoghue: a tale of Ireland fifty years ago* (1845), functioning, in Jim Shanahan's terms, as tools with which 'to reject [the] thesis of compromise, process and progress' of Scott's historical novel. For Roche, though, the O'Donoghue pedigree establishes Grace O'Donoghue's native aristocratic origins, thus asserting her worthiness to marry O'Brien and underlining the novel's keen attention to Catholic rights. The reference to Cormac, king of Cashel (846–908), reinforces Donaghue's august Gaelic matrilineage. See Seán Ó Tuama, *Repossessions: selected essays on the Irish literary heritage* (Cork: Cork University Press, 1995), p. 104; Jim Shanahan, 'Charles Lever, Walter Scott, and the Irish national tale', in Paddy Lyons, Willy Maley, and John Miller (eds), *Romantic Ireland: from Tone to Gonne; fresh perspectives on nineteenth-century Ireland* (Newcastle upon Tyne: Cambridge Scholars Publishing, 2013), p. 301; Aidan Breen, 'Cormac', *Dictionary of Irish* biography, eds James McGuire and James Quinn (Cambridge: Cambridge University Press, 2009), http://dib.cambridge.org, accessed 14 September 2016.
102 Roche's own religious affiliations and sympathies are a matter of some debate, with several scholars actively identifying Roche as Catholic and others detecting a strong pro-Catholic perspective in her works. See, for example, Purves, *The gothic and Catholicism*, p. 122 and Killeen, *Gothic Ireland*, pp. 182–90. Diane Long Hoeveler contested such views, querying attempts to read a Catholic agenda in *The children of the abbey* and, indeed, in female gothic as a whole; 'Regina Maria Roche's *The children of the abbey*: contesting the Catholic presence in female gothic fiction', *Tulsa studies in women's literature*, 31.1/2 (2012), 137–58.

4
Gothic materialities: Regina Maria Roche, the Minerva Press, and the bibliographic spread of Irish gothic fiction

∽

Evocative of the nationally transformative potential of travel sketched in *The old Irish baronet* (1808) and *The tradition of the castle* (1824), Regina Maria Roche's *The castle chapel* (1825) establishes the global journey of one of its two protagonists as the key to restored and refreshed identities at home. Compelled by his dependent status to conciliate the favour of a rich uncle by travelling first to India and then throughout Europe, William Delamere returns to Ireland considerably wealthier, materially and experientially, than when he left. There, literally and metaphorically enriched by his travels, he marries his childhood sweetheart, Grace O'Neil, restoring her family to the status and prosperity denied to them by a lengthy history of violent dispossession and metatextually reworking a similar union in Edgeworth's *Ennui* (1809). In *that* novel, Lord Glenthorn's marriage to Cecilia Delamere and assumption of his wife's name is a symbolic act of rebirth that both reinvests him with an aristocratic identity and signals, in Clíona Ó Gallchoir's terms, 'the collapse of the patrilineal system', as suggested by the translation of 'de-la-mère' as 'of-the-mother'.[1] *The castle chapel*, by contrast, places emphasis on another possible translation of Delamere – 'de-la-mer' or 'of-the-sea' – in order to suggest the centrality of mobility to Ireland's future. Against Glenthorn's alternately purposeless and boredom-driven travel throughout Europe and Ireland, *The castle chapel* imagines instead the personally and publicly restorative power of travel when combined with an 'inquisitive mind' and 'ardent imagination'.[2] In this, the novel resonates with *The old Irish baronet* and *The tradition of the castle*, portraying Delamere and his various movements as the key to a new transnationally inflected Irishness.[3]

Roche's novel further reflects on the usefulness of travel in the negotiation of nineteenth-century Irish identities through its exploration of the literary endeavours of its second protagonist, Eugene O'Neil. Presenting himself to a Dublin publisher in the hope of becoming a 'successful competitor with "the Great Unknown"', O'Neil finds he must follow his dreams elsewhere, thanks to the devastation of the Irish print industry in the wake of Anglo-Irish Union and the consequent application of English copyright law to Ireland (*The castle chapel*, vol. 1, p. 121). '[I]t's not by an Irish press you must hope to be introduced to the world', O'Neil is told, before being given a letter of introduction to Mr C– in London and all but escorted to the Dublin port (*The castle chapel*, vol. 1, p. 252). Once arrived in London, O'Neil meets with a series of disappointments that convince him of the 'gross' and 'immoral' tendency of popular literary tastes, demanding, as he sees it, nothing short of authorial 'prostitution' (*The castle chapel*, vol. 1, p. 258). O'Neil eventually abandons his literary aspirations, not least because they prove the tool by which his secret enemy, Mr Mordaunt, manages to have him imprisoned for treason and subsequently incarcerated in a private asylum for the insane.[4] While O'Neil's literary career, like his travels themselves, ultimately proves disastrous for him, it serves several important purposes. First, it highlights the wholesale migration of Irish print culture in this period. Second, it emphasises the precariousness of London literary life for Irish émigré authors like Roche herself. Third, it points to the acute awareness Roche shared with many of her contemporaries of her participation in what Karen O'Brien calls 'a borderless and mobile European and transatlantic culture of fiction' that enabled and encouraged cultural transfer and an ongoing reconfiguration of Irishness during the Romantic period.[5]

Offering compelling parallels with Roche and her experiences as an émigré author in London, O'Neil ably represents the increasing numbers of Irish writers seeking professional advancement outside of Ireland at the start of the nineteenth century. Responding to Anglo-Irish Union, the subsequent application of English copyright law to Ireland, and a long-standing perception that a successful literary career was only truly possible abroad, many Irish authors felt compelled, like O'Neil, to pursue their literary ambitions elsewhere. His experience of creative 'prostitution' further speaks to the difficulties Roche and countless contemporaries – Irish and otherwise – underwent in attempting to secure financial stability and popular acclaim in the cut-throat world of the London literary market. O'Neil's career finally proves abortive and his absence from Ireland a fatal impediment to his symbolic marriage to Rose Cormack – Mordaunt's unacknowledged daughter and thus the 'descendant of him to whose treachery [the O'Neil family] imputed the loss of the rich possessions of their famed and royal ancestor [O'Neil, the high king of Ulster]' (*The castle chapel*, vol 1, p. 175). It nevertheless implicitly speaks to the evolving material and bibliographic contexts in which novels such as *The castle chapel* were published. As Andrew Piper cogently observes, writers in the Romantic period became increasingly aware of their texts as they related to 'a bibliographic elsewhere'.[6] As a consequence, the question of narratological settings considered in Chapter 3 became twinned with a new attention to bibliographic and material placement, including the geographic location of a text's publication, its physical and/or figurative position amongst contiguous or related texts, and its relation to books that preceded and followed it. This in turn fed into a developing consciousness of literary globality, as Piper contends: 'romantic concerns with problems of bibliographic placement were simultaneously connected to those of geographic placement … Reading romantic books means reading a growing attention to the international circulation of trends and texts'.[7]

With all fifteen of her novels originally printed or republished by the notorious Minerva Press established in 1790 by William Lane and headed, from Lane's death in 1814, by A.K. Newman,[8] Roche was arguably at the forefront of the Romantic period's increasing expansion of literary production and dissemination.[9] Thanks, at least in part, to Lane's pioneering development of the circulating library system and his savvy establishment of trade partnerships, Roche saw her novels frequently reprinted and translated on a global scale. Yet, while she published to spectacular international acclaim, her works were routinely subject to critical censure linked to concerns over the growth of the literary marketplace, its perceived pandering to a growing middle-class readership, its disconcerting dominance by female readers and writers, and its effect on both the worth and accessibility of literature. The principal publisher of popular novels in Romantic-era Britain,[10] Lane was understood by critics to drive the period's troubling 'bibliographic surplus' and the associated '"quantitative" rather than qualitative rise' of the novel.[11] 'Minerva' thus became a contemptuous buzzword for the kind of cheap, imitative fictions – gothic romances in particular – that, in the minds of critics, threatened to reduce authorship to mere hack-work.[12]

As one of Lane's bestselling female authors, Roche often suffered from the blanket condemnation of Minerva Press publications as cultural trash.

GOTHIC MATERIALITIES

Fellow Minerva authors, including the Irish writers Captain Thomas Ashe (1770–1835), Eaton Stannard Barrett (1786–1820), Nugent Bell (*fl.* 1817), Alice Margaret Ennis (*fl.* 1817), Alicia Le Fanu (1791–1844?), Mrs Sarah Green (*fl.* 1790–1825), Theodore Melville (*fl.* 1802), Henrietta Rouvière Mosse (d. 1835), Anna Milliken (*fl.* 1793), Mrs F.C. Patrick (*fl.* 1797), Mrs Frances Peck (*fl.* 1808), and Catharine Selden (*fl.* 1797), many of them also emigrants to London, similarly found their works pithily dismissed by reference to their choice of publisher. Even in reviews where the Minerva Press was not specifically mentioned, Lane's publications tended to be condemned as typical circulating library fodder, evidence of the current degraded state of literary production.[13] Such assessments ignored, as Deborah Anne McLeod notes, the real diversity of Minerva press publications and authors, as well as the quality of much of the literature Lane produced.[14] They have also ensured that twentieth- and twenty-first-century scholarship remains unnecessarily disparaging of or, what is perhaps worse, largely unfamiliar with a great deal of literature that, in its appeal to and widespread dissemination amongst the reading public, bears distinct cultural significance.[15]

This chapter focuses particular attention on Roche's now all too frequently overlooked novels, which, as McLeod suggests of Minerva Press publications more widely, '*should* be of interest if only because they were often the most widely read and enjoyed literature of the period'.[16] Certainly, Roche's gothic romances provide a kind of litmus test as to the prevailing literary tastes of the average circulating library reader in the late eighteenth and early nineteenth centuries, not just in Britain, but throughout Europe, North and South America, and the British colonies. More than that, they offer a perceptive account of the cartographic consciousness of nineteenth-century Irish authors and the extensive, if now underestimated, bibliographic spread and influence of Irish gothic fiction in this period. Distinctly aware of themselves as fictive, as Aileen Douglas has persuasively written, Roche's novels reflect an author heavily invested in manipulating both the conventions of genre and readerly expectations.[17] They also underline Roche's keen awareness and knowing narratological replication of her fiction's place in local and global literary arenas. Producing bookish characters that trace the trade routes by which her novels were consumed by a worldwide readership, Roche's novels comment shrewdly on the central position occupied by Irish gothic fiction in the transnational expansion of the Romantic-era book trade. Understood today as above all else secondary, much like Irish gothic literary production in this period more generally,

Roche's fictions amply repay further study. In particular, they highlight the extent to which her contemporary fame and insightful engagement with expanding bibliographic networks situated Irish gothic fiction at the centre of a newly understood transcontinental and transatlantic gothic literary production – an enduring cultural activity that spanned international borders and concomitantly contributed to, just as it was shaped by, transnational and cross-cultural exchange.

The first part of this chapter accordingly offers a brief contextual consideration of Roche's career in London as well as the contemporary critical reception of her works. Despite rivalling in popularity Ann Radcliffe (1764–1823) and Isabella Kelly (c.1759–1857) from the publication of *The children of the abbey* (1796) and *Clermont* (1798), Roche remained plagued with financial insecurity, as documented by her correspondence with the Royal Literary Fund. That she continued exclusively to publish with a publisher known '[to pay] his authors notoriously little' until her death in 1845 indicates that Lane's appeal comprised something other than financial security.[18] Just what he offered, this chapter argues, was remarkably expansive material dissemination via his burgeoning transnational network of printers, circulating libraries, and booksellers. The attraction of this network becomes clear from the careers of American novelist Charles Brockden Brown (1771–1810) and British-American novelist and playwright Susannah Rowson (1762–1824), both of whom very consciously used publication by the Minerva Press to further their own transatlantic careers.[19]

With little personal correspondence or other archival material available to us today, Roche's reasons for publishing with Minerva remain opaque. Yet, as the second section of this chapter demonstrates, her novels enjoyed the kind of extensive, long-lasting popularity and circulation now associated with canonical writers such as Austen and Scott. Moreover, they frequently reveal a critical awareness of their participation in a new international book trade. Indeed, like the works discussed in Chapter 3, Roche's novels defy conventional assumptions about gothic geography, rejecting Catholic Continental settings in favour of a constantly shifting global network mirroring contemporary trade routes. Many of these texts, in fact, narratologically replicate their material dissemination as well as the related movement of Irish peoples and print instrumental to the re-negotiation of Ireland's position in a post-Union Atlantic economy. As they do so, the final section of this chapter contends, they gesture towards the role played by these fictions in both refining an Irish cultural nationalism

ROCHE, THE MINERVA PRESS, AND THE MIGRATION OF IRISH LITERARY PRODUCTION

Born in Waterford and raised in Dublin, Roche (née Dalton) moved to London shortly after her marriage to Ambrose Roche in 1792. Having already published two novels, *The vicar of Lansdowne, or, country quarters* (1789) and *The maid of the hamlet* (1793), with two different London publishers, Roche began what appeared to be an auspicious publishing relationship with the Minerva Press in 1796. That year, *The children of the abbey* was published to spectacular acclaim. *Clermont* followed soon after, solidifying Roche's status as one of the foremost novelists of the 1790s. She wrote a further eleven novels for Minerva, which also re-issued *The vicar of Lansdowne* and *The maid of the hamlet*, but suffered enduring financial difficulties until her death in 1845. Indicatively, she published her fourteenth novel, *Contrast* (1828), by subscription and successfully appealed to the Royal Literary Fund for financial assistance on no less than three occasions between 1827 and 1831.[20] She sent her fifteenth and final novel, *The nun's picture* (1836), to Lane's successor, A.K. Newman, for publication from Ireland, whence she had returned in 1831, and later died, alone, poverty-stricken, and all but forgotten, in her hometown of Waterford.

Roche's financial troubles owed much to her husband's ill health and a prolonged chancery suit related to the unscrupulous activities of an Irish lawyer to whom the Roches had entrusted their Irish affairs.[21] They also reflect the instabilities of the literary scene in England, underlining the realities of hard work and deprivation faced by any number of aspiring authors, Irish and otherwise, who attempted to harness the potential of a newly industrialised print trade centred in London. If, in her 'Address' in *The vicar of Lansdowne*, Roche could be accused of a '*saucy humility*' revelatory of an author who 'does not deem too humbly of her own abilities', her later novels, written while living in England, reveal the failure of that initial optimistic confidence to translate into financial security within the London book market.[22] In her preface to *Contrast*, therefore, Roche pleads for the indulgence of readers and critics alike, declaring that 'at no period of her life did she take up the pen under difficulties and afflictions so overwhelming'.[23] Her correspondence with the Royal Literary Fund charts a harrowing course of destitution and need despite her 'celebrity as an Author', which, as her solicitors noted in 1827, 'has been long since acknowledged'.[24]

Roche's experiences of extreme financial hardship despite prolific and acclaimed publication parallel those of more well-known Irish émigré authors such as John Banim (1798–1842), and Gerald Griffin (1803–40), while also underscoring the devastation of the Irish print industry following the Act of Union. By this point, Irish writers had long been sending their works to England for publication, complaining of the Irish publishing industry's reliance on reprinting works produced elsewhere, and taking advantage of the monetary inducement provided by the Copyright Act of 1709.[25] Several prominent Irish authors of the latter half of the eighteenth century, including Oliver Goldsmith (1728–74), Edmund Burke (1730–97), and Richard Brinsley Sheridan (1751–1816), followed their manuscripts abroad, choosing to make their careers in England, rather than in Ireland. So, too, did a number of lesser-known writers, such as Elizabeth Griffith (1727–93), Hugh Kelly (1739–77), Arthur Murphy (1727–1805), and John O'Keeffe (1747–1833). These authors' decision to publish and live outside of Ireland in the late 1700s indicates that, even before the Act of Union, imaginative and physical migration was perceived as a near necessity for an Irish author's professional success.[26] The application of English copyright law to Ireland in the wake of Union, however, added new urgency and anxiety to the migration of Irish print culture. With the reprint trade now made illegal, the Irish publishing industry became critically depressed, and Irish writers were all but compelled to seek publishing opportunities elsewhere.

In the years immediately following Union, as Claire Connolly notes, only a handful of novels – *False appearances* (anon; 1803), Owenson's *St Clair; or, the heiress of Desmond* (1803), and Sarah Isdell's *The vale of Louisiana; an American tale* (1805) – were published in Dublin.[27] The majority of Irish fiction produced in the first three decades of the nineteenth century, including all but one of the fifteen novels collectively produced by Charles Maturin and Sydney Owenson, was published elsewhere, either in London or Edinburgh. Maria Edgeworth routinely published her fiction with London publisher Joseph Johnson, while Griffin and the Banim brothers made use of a number of metropolitan publishing houses, including those of Henry Colburn and Saunders & Otley, to produce their fiction in the late 1820s and early 1830s. Alongside the countless, often nameless, Irish writers publishing with popular presses such as Minerva, these authors attest to the migration of literary production so ably remarked upon in Roche's *The castle chapel*.

Unsurprisingly, as in *The castle chapel*, many of Roche's novels comment self-consciously on this relocation of literary culture as well as the frequently heartbreaking realities of competing in a swiftly developing marketplace. For O'Neil, failure to succeed within that 'great mart of literature, and world in itself, London' impels his return home, where, after further encounters with Mordaunt, he appears ready to assume his rightful position in Ireland through marriage, much as in the national tale popularised by Owenson and Edgeworth (*The castle chapel*, vol. 1, p. 258). As noted at the start of this chapter, though, O'Neil's projected union with Rose Cormack never comes to pass. Suffering from scruples over their pre-marital intimacy and the subsequent birth and death of their child, Rose feels 'unworthy of associating with those she loved' and resolves to retire to solitude, after having signed over her fortune and estates to the O'Neil family (*The castle chapel*, vol. 3, p. 24). But she dies before she can do so, thrown into a fatal emotional turmoil after O'Neil visits her in her Welsh refuge without her consent. He thereafter travels to the Continent and joins 'the patriot cause of Greece', vowing 'never to know a home again' following Rose's rejection (*The castle chapel*, vol. 3, pp. 283, 248).[28]

Drawing to a close '[t]wo years … [after] the melancholy event that forced Eugene from his native country' (*The castle chapel*, vol. 3, p. 283), *The castle chapel* envisions its hero as an unfortunate exile, thus referring the reader back to the epigraph provided in the novel's first chapter:

> With awe-struck thought and pitying tears,
> I view that noble, stately dome,
> Where *Ulster's* kings of other years,
> Fam'd heroes! had their royal home:
> Alas! how chang'd the times to come!
> Their royal name low in the dust –
> Their hapless race wild, wand'ring roam –
> Though rigid law cries out – 'twas just! (*The castle chapel*, vol. 1, p. 1)

An adaptation of Robert Burns's 'Address to Edinburgh' (1786), Roche's epigraph emphasises the history and consequences of dispossession suffered by the O'Neil family. As recounted in Roche's novel, the O'Neils twice found themselves on the losing side of colonial warfare and, as a result, were both stripped of their titles and estates and 'banished' from 'their goodly lands' to 'waste, sterile spots, on the sides of bleak and rugged mountains' (*The castle chapel*, vol. 1, p. 6).[29] They thus become the now humbled 'heroes' of Ulster doomed to 'wand'ring roam' eulogised in Roche's version of Burns's poem. The 'pitying tears' of Roche's narrator suggest a mournful regret for the perceived iniquities of the past as well as the dispersal and exile of 'Ulster's kings', despite the justifiable dictates of 'rigid law'. In the context of O'Neil's experiences, though, they also reflect on the hardships of emigration – a reality with which Roche was all too familiar.

If O'Neil's tempestuous career in London suggests an author embittered by personal suffering and a literary market that failed generously to reward its suppliers, it should be remembered that Roche was not unique in either her prolific publication or her failure to make an adequate living by her pen. Far from an indication of the quality of her writing, this inability to prosper by way of her literary production reflects the reality of authorship in this period.[30] As O'Brien observes, 'it was not until after 1820 that novelists themselves were able to make an independent living out of publishing their work'.[31] Whether Roche would have succeeded in supporting herself by publishing with a different, more highly regarded publisher is a moot point. William Lane's stated willingness to pay just £5 for manuscripts had certainly earned him a reputation as a particularly acquisitive publisher, who compensated his authors poorly but personally profited enormously from the sale of their texts.[32] Existing records of Lane's transactions are few, but Dorothy Blakey draws evidence from various contemporary sources to conclude that the average Lane paid for one novel in the final decade of the eighteenth century was £30.[33] Compared to the £25 average estimated from the copyright contracts of the publishing house of George Robinson, this figure indicates that Lane was not particularly parsimonious in paying his authors.[34] The sums Lane paid to authors seem to have risen in the early nineteenth century, as both the Minerva Press and the novel became more firmly established.[35] Nevertheless, it remains clear that not all of Lane's authors benefited from the same 'liberal encouragement' that was lauded by one Minerva author, Mrs Smith, in the preface to *The Caledonian bandit* (1811).[36] Moreover, even when Lane paid generously for copy, openly offering up to 100 guineas (or just over £100) for manuscripts, his authors must have frequently fallen prey to the financial insecurity attendant upon what William St Clair aptly terms the 'lumpy and unpredictable' nature of an income derived largely from copyright contracts, post-dated bills, and money advances.[37]

Roche's correspondence with the Royal Literary Fund – our chief source of information about her life – does not record the payments she received from Lane for her novels. In one of her later letters to the committee, she refers to the success of *The children of the abbey*, remarking that it 'was beyond my hopes' and noting, 'I have reason to be truly grateful to the Public'.[38] Roche refrains from commenting upon her publisher's munificence – or lack thereof – but her repeated requests to the Fund for assistance between 1827 and 1831 suggest that, by this point in her life, whatever payments he made proved insufficient for her needs. Indicatively, Roche's first correspondence with the Fund in 1827 coincided with her husband's second declaration of bankruptcy, itself precipitated by the refusal in 1826 by Irish politician Richard Martin (1754–1834) to pay the Roches £500 of rent he owed them as well as a devastatingly expensive and long-lasting chancery suit undertaken by the Roches in 1820. While Roche continued to publish steadily during these hardships, producing five novels between 1820 and 1828,[39] any money she received for them simply was not adequate to meet the debts the Roches had incurred, as detailed minutely in her letters to the Fund. Ambrose Roche's ill health from 1825, followed by his death in 1829, undoubtedly contributed to Roche's money concerns, placing more pressure on her writing as the couple's primary source of income.

What this evidence suggests is that Lane was certainly no more, but also no less, generous in his compensation of Roche. Like many of her contemporaries, Irish and otherwise, Roche clearly wrote out of financial need but, also like them, failed to make a living from her literary endeavours.[40] Roche's faithfulness to Lane, therefore, needs to be weighed in terms of the period's norms for authorship, which very rarely proved lucrative for the writers themselves. But it also needs to be assessed in terms of the less tangible forms of remuneration afforded by publication with Lane. After all, it was publication with the Minerva Press that arguably ensured Roche's accessibility to an increasingly populous readership across Britain, Europe, North America, and further afield. As Natalie Schroeder remarks, Roche's 'readers were legion' and continued to be so throughout the nineteenth century.[41] So notable was the circulation and appeal of Roche's novels that, as the *New England Weekly Review* observed in 1828, they could be found 'in the hands of every novel reader in Europe and America'.[42] The global impact of Roche's novels relied principally on Lane's transcontinental and transatlantic connections.

A key figure in the growth of a transnational literary marketplace, Lane vitally enabled the spread of the circulating library network in England while also feeding printing presses across Europe and the United States. Having founded his own popular circulating library in Leadenhall Street in or around 1784, Lane devoted himself to the spread of the library network across England, helping to establish circulating libraries 'in the chief towns of public resort', supporting enterprises of all sizes, and successfully 'induc[ing] many a petty shopkeeper to add even so small a collection as a hundred volumes to his shelves'.[43] Blakey declares Lane's promotion of a nationwide network of libraries 'the most significant of the various enterprises undertaken by the Leadenhall Street house'.[44] His success in this endeavour – one he named '*not more the Business than the Pride of my Life*' – had much to do with the advertisements he placed, like that in *The correspondents* in 1784.[45] There, he called on '*any Person, either in Town or Country, desirous of commencing a* Circulating Library' to take advantage of the '*several* Thousand *Volumes, in* History, Voyages, Novels, Plays, &c.' he kept '*always ready bound*'. More than that, Lane asserted, he was '*happy in instructing them in the Manner of keeping a Reading Library*'.[46]

Lane continued this marketing throughout the 1780s and 1790s in various forums, publishing in 1795 a two-part pamphlet including *An address to the public, on circulating libraries*, in which he notes the increasing number of circulating libraries in '*every part of this Kingdom*'.[47] He '*offer[s] those who wish to open Public Libraries, all the Information a long Experience, and a devoted Attachment to my Profession can afford them*' and, as in his 1784 advertisement, assures potential library owners that he has '*many Thousand [v]olumes, of every Description, in Literature*' ready for '*immediate Circulation*'.[48] He further asserts the continuing availability of such volumes, observing that '*Works of Merit are constantly printing, under my own Inspection, at the Minerva Press*'.[49] Moreover, indicating the manner in which 'book-borrowing and book-purchasing channels would frequently merge in the Romantic period',[50] Lane concludes his pamphlet with the information that Minerva Press publications '[m]ay be had the Day of Publication, from our numerous Correspondents, not only in this Metropolis, but also in every City or Town in this Kingdom'.[51]

The extent of Lane's circulating library network meant that publishing with the Minerva Press *should* have secured a market advantage for writers such as Roche. Certainly, Roche's novels appear repeatedly in the catalogues of circulating libraries across England, Scotland, and Ireland, and, while circulating library presence cannot accurately quantify actual readership of a given text, it does underline reading trends and point to market demand, as Franz Potter contends: 'in an industry driven by consumer interest, it is likely that titles which were included in library catalogues reflect to an extent consumer interest in the marketplace.'[52] Of course, compared to the circulating library presence of contemporaries such as Edgeworth, Owenson, and even Maturin, Roche's may seem unremarkable. According to figures derived from the *British Fiction, 1800–1829* database, the average number of circulating libraries to advertise Roche's ten novels in the period 1800–29 is nine. That for Edgeworth is 20; Owenson, 15; and Maturin, 12.[53] Superficially, these numbers seem to support the idea of canonicity. Those authors apparently more widely read in their own day also happen to fall into our prevailing idea of the canon of early nineteenth-century Irish literature. Yet, it is worth remembering here that neither Owenson nor Maturin has long enjoyed canonical status in twentieth- and twenty-first-century scholarship. Despite his contemporary popularity, Maturin has only very recently been recovered to view as an integral contributor to the development of Irish Romantic literature.[54] In the preface to his fourth novel, *Women; or, pour et contre* (1818), Maturin himself bitterly complained of his neglect: 'None of my former prose works have been popular. The strongest proof of which is, none of them arrived at a second edition.'[55] He indicated that the reason for this lack of notice was his early novels' association with 'circulating libraries', and, while he gained considerable notoriety with the publication of *Melmoth the wanderer*, critics continued to dismiss Maturin as an eccentric, imitative writer of little consequence.[56] Such condemnations have been repeated with regularity until very recently, defying the considerable reprint and translation history Maturin's novels enjoyed, while also ignoring the substantial impact Maturin had on contemporary authors and those that followed him.[57] Similarly, Owenson's controversial and flamboyant style ruled her out of much serious scholarly attention until feminist criticism in the second half of the twentieth century revived interest in her *oeuvre*.[58] Roche, too, clearly fell prey to the prevailing critical view of Minerva Press productions as debased, derivative, and unworthy of serious scholarly attention.

Despite critical condemnation, Roche found considerable favour amongst readers. Analysis of the market evidence indicates that the gratitude to the public Roche expressed in her correspondence with the Royal Literary Fund was not ill-placed.[59] In addition to maintaining a respectable circulating library presence, Roche's fifteen accepted novels also enjoyed a strong reprint and translation history. *The children of the abbey* is the most obvious example of Roche's popular success. With as many as 80 reprints over the course of the nineteenth century, *The children of the abbey* was 'one of the

THE GOTHIC NOVEL IN IRELAND

most frequently reprinted Irish novels of the nineteenth century'.[60] It enjoyed particular success in the USA, with editions published in New York (1798), Connecticut (1822), and Philadelphia (1845; 1850), while on the Continent it was translated into French (1797; 1807), Dutch (1802–10), German (1803), and Spanish (1807/08, 1818, 1828, 1832).[61] Comparison with the reprint history of novels published that same year is revelatory of *The children of the abbey*'s market dominance: of the 91 novels published in 1796, as counted by James Raven, only 27 – or, roughly 30 per cent – were reprinted at least once before 1801.[62]

Roche's subsequent novels, while not repeating *The children of the abbey*'s resounding success, nevertheless also fared well with both local and foreign readerships, as attested to by Figure 4.[63] Reprinted across Britain, Ireland, France, Holland, Germany, Spain, and the Americas, Roche's novels were widely disseminated and enjoyed what Piper terms in a different context, 'bibliographic everywhereness'.[64] The striking geographic spread of Roche's fiction owed much to the far-reaching network of the Minerva Press, which helped ensure the repeated re-production of Roche's novels abroad, particularly in the United States. Similar to the situation in

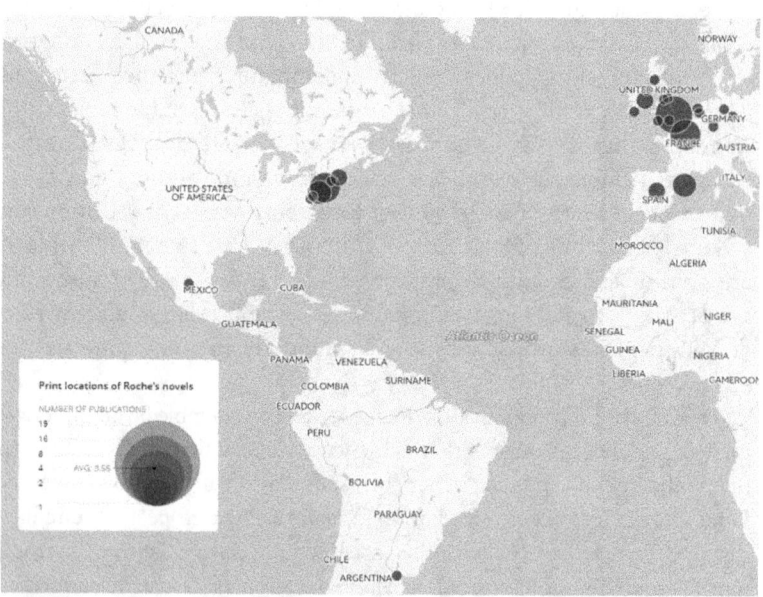

Figure 4 Map of the publication, reprint, and translation history of Roche's novels in the long nineteenth century

pre-Union Ireland, the fledgling print industry in eighteenth- and early nineteenth-century America was heavily reliant on reprints, and Minerva proved a lucrative source of publishable material, as Eve Tavor Bannet points out: 'a significant portion of the contemporary novels that were reprinted in the early Republic at the turn of the nineteenth century had first been issued in London by the Minerva Press. At this time, more Minerva Press novels were reprinted in America than novels issued by any other British or European publisher'.[65] As a result, Bannet argues, the Minerva Press critically facilitated 'the transatlantic migration of texts' in the Romantic period.[66]

Significantly, the successful transatlantic trade of Minerva Press titles was not simply the result of American publishers choosing, like their eighteenth-century Irish counterparts, to reprint and sell cheaper versions of 'the most readable and popular material from London publications'.[67] Instead, the dissemination and republication of Minerva Press works in the early Republic reflected Lane's ambitious expansion of the circulating library network he had already begun to establish in Britain and its colonies, including Jamaica and India.[68] From 1801, Lane had forged a business partnership with New York bookseller and French émigré, Hocquet Caritat, who became an official US agent for the Minerva Press and maintained a high proportion of Minerva titles at his circulating library.[69] He may also have supplied Lane with *Wieland* (1798) and other Charles Brockden Brown titles to be printed in London.[70] While Caritat returned to France in 1807, thereby ending his trade relationship with Lane, Lane's interests continued to be served by a variety of other booksellers, importers, and circulating library owners across the United States.[71]

Thanks to Lane's increasingly expansive bibliographic network, Roche appears to have been a household name in North America in the first three decades of the nineteenth century, appealing to a wide and diffuse readership. Tellingly, the *Missouri Republican* declared in its 1825 advertisement of the publication of *The castle chapel*, 'This lady is so well known among novel readers, that we doubt not her new work will be sought after with great avidity'.[72] Three years later, the *New England Weekly Review* named Roche as second only in literary fame to Walter Scott.[73] Even if Roche's fictions had been eclipsed by Scott's 'more masterly productions', American readers were still encouraged to buy and read new editions of Roche's novels, *The children of the abbey* in particular, until the end of the nineteenth century.[74] An 1891 edition of *The children of the abbey*, for instance, published in Chicago by A.C. McClurg & Co., was promoted as 'an attractive new edition of a tale that once charmed our grandmothers to tears'. Despite the narrative's 'quaintness', the edition was seen to 'well [repay] a reading'.[75] And, in April 1893, *The Daily Inter Ocean* advertised the sale of 'the *Gems* of the literature of the world', listing the names of authors whose works might be had for a very attractive 25 cents. Keeping Roche company in this catalogue of well-known and widely read authors is a diverse selection of eighteenth- and nineteenth-century British, Irish, American, and European authors, including Honoré de Balzac, Charlotte Brontë, William Carleton, Cervantes, James Fenimore Cooper, Charles Dickens, Thomas Hardy, Edgar Allan Poe, Walter Scott, and Jonathan Swift.[76]

THE NARRATOLOGICAL MANIFESTATIONS OF ROCHE'S BIBLIOGRAPHIC EVERYWHERENESS

The remarkable material circulation of Roche's novels indicates the very real advantages to be gleaned from loyalty to Lane, even if Roche's motives for publishing with Minerva remain unclear. We may not currently know how much Roche earned from her publications, or whether she lacked the business acumen to negotiate with a publisher other than Lane. She never mentions feeling constrained by critical opinion which, by the publication of *Trecothick bower; or, the lady of the west country* (1814), had effectively typecast her as the quintessential Minerva author, thus potentially dissuading her and/or other potential publishers from entering into a new publishing relationship.[77] Nor does she provide direct proof in her correspondence of a desire to foster a transatlantic and transcontinental literary career through continued publication with Lane. Nevertheless, her repeated acknowledgements to the reading public, coupled with internal evidence drawn from her novels themselves, suggest her very real awareness of the global circulation and appeal of her works as Minerva Press publications. Roche's often wry and playful commentary on the contemporary literary marketplace, the publication of popular gothic romances such as hers, and the worldwide distribution of these works thus invites further consideration. As an example, her 1813 novel, *The monastery of St Columb; or, the atonement*, features the hapless, would-be romance writer, Miss Elmere, who yearns to make a name for herself as an author. Having received from her friend a manuscript account of the 'haunted apartments' of the dilapidated Co. Wicklow estate of Greymount, Miss Elmere immediately recognises its literary potential: 'How delightful! … perhaps it may furnish me with a plot for my romance, and thus save me all further trouble on that head'.[78] Later, after reading the manuscript, she confirms her intent '[to] trouble herself no further to seek for a plot for her romance, but make use of the one which it had furnished her for the purpose, conceiving, with the embellishments she should bestow on it, there could not be a better' (*The monastery of St Columb*, vol. 2, p. 39).

A tongue-in-cheek parody of the average Minerva Press author as imagined by critics, Miss Elmere also happens to be a prototypical popular novel reader. As such, she conducts her life based on what she has read, dismissing as 'citizonic' the heroine's common-sense wish in the midst of a long walk 'that they had thought of bringing something [to eat and drink] along with them in a work-basket' (*The monastery of St Columb*, vol. 1, pp. 250, 251). Later, urging Greymount's current residents not to make any changes to the home, arguing that 'there is something so infinitely more impressive in ancient than modern decorations, from the recollections they revive', Miss Elmere specifically links her whimsical ways to her reading habits: 'the moment I find a heroine safely lodged in a snug chamber, I begin to yawn over her history; but as long as she continues the inmate of a desolate apartment, I feel an interest kept alive for her' (*The monastery of St Columb*, vol. 1, p. 268).

Indicative of the association of popular literature like that sold by the Minerva Press with 'debased taste, wasted time and delusion', Miss Elmere speaks to the 'dangers to domestic and social order [represented] by her asocial ("unfeminine") self-indulgence'.[79] Through her reading habits and her desire to publish her own gothic romance, Miss Elmere is explicitly linked to a licentious and immoral print industry that had rendered the Romantic-era novel an endlessly duplicated object with very little value, literary or otherwise, 'the disposable ephemera of an increasingly commercialized economy fed in no small measure by the mechanical printing press'.[80] The 'sly smile[s]' and gentle laughter with which Miss Elmere's assertions are met indicate Roche's recognition that her own Minerva Press novels could easily be dismissed as mere financially motivated imitations (*The monastery of St Columb*, vol. 1, p. 268). Tellingly, the novel evidences a singular attention to doubles, material – like Miss Elmere's intended retelling of the Greymount narrative – and otherwise. The hero, Lord Hexham, for instance, disguises himself as Villiers to escape the ill effects of a disadvantageous and disastrous marriage ended in divorce. As Villiers, he courts and secretly marries the novel's heroine, Angeline, only to renounce her after he has been duped into believing that she is just like his former wife – promiscuous, dishonest, and debased. Angeline later discovers her true parentage and identity via revelations that include two different instances of baby-swapping, allowing her to lay claim over the course of the novel to three different fathers, one of whom masquerades as De Burgh for much of the narrative, when, in fact, he is really St Ruth.[81] The novel fittingly concludes with a double marriage that sees Lord Hexham wedded to a veiled woman he believes to be Clora Frazer – who also happens to bear Angeline's *real* first name – but is revealed to be Angeline herself, not dead, as was believed, but very much alive. *The monastery of St Columb* thus takes to a near parodic extreme a 'concern with doubling, as forms of duplication both material and cultural' recently identified by Connolly in early nineteenth-century Irish fiction.[82]

Given the manner in which Roche's novels were routinely assessed as imitative and unoriginal, this interest in doubling and an 'emerging culture of the copy' more widely is hardly surprising.[83] As noted earlier in this chapter, Roche's gothic romances found themselves frequently condemned by critics both for their association with the Minerva Press and their perceived pandering to the unsophisticated tastes of circulating library readers. If *The children of the abbey* had been judged vastly superior to 'the quantity of trash that has issued from Leadenhall Street', Roche's subsequent novels were increasingly viewed as indistinguishable from the 'hundreds of novels which should never have met the light' regularly produced by Lane.[84] *Clermont* was understood as a paltry imitation of Radcliffe: 'This tale reminds us, without any great pleasure, of Mrs. Radcliffe's romances. In Clermont, mystery is heaped upon mystery, and murder upon murder, with little art, and great improbability.'[85] A decade or so later, *The monastery of St Columb* was reviewed relatively favourably by *La belle Assemblée* for the 'great spirit' with which its characters were drawn and the 'unaffected pathos' of its narrative style, one 'prov[ing] Mrs. Roche's power over the human heart'. Nevertheless, the review ultimately damned the novel with faint praise, proclaiming it a 'work [that] must rank high in the class of literature to which it belongs'.[86] More specific about the degraded 'class' of literature that Roche was seen to produce, *The Critical Review*'s assessment of *Trecothick bower* named Roche 'one of those ladies who assiduously feed the pig-stye of literature in Leadenhall-street'.[87] *The children of the abbey* may have enhanced Minerva's 'fame', but *Trecothick bower* was now dismissed sardonically as 'another monument of [Roche's] literary fame'.[88] Its prevailing features were summarised as 'grotesque and unnatural characters, improbable events arising from impossible causes, a wild and disjointed plot, and the most bombastic and inflated language'; its fate, *The Critical Review* predicted, would be momentarily to 'enjoy its circulation with its other kindred trash' before being consigned 'to that oblivion to which its dulness has impelled it'.[89]

Twentieth- and twenty-first-century scholarship of Roche's works has tended to echo Romantic-era criticism's ironically mimetic stereotyping of popular gothic fiction as dull, unnatural, debased, and endlessly repeatable. Revealingly, what limited attention has been paid to Roche has generally assessed her fiction by reference to Radcliffe and routinely found it lacking.[90] Even where Roche is given credit for deviating from Radcliffe's model, she is seen to turn to other, more financially and critically successful writers for inspiration, particularly in her fictive 'return' to Ireland in the 1820s, with works such as *The Munster cottage boy* (1820), *The tradition of the castle*, and *Contrast*.[91] Natalie Schroeder's pioneering scholarship on Roche in the 1970s and 1980s began to recover her *oeuvre* to view but was nonetheless based on the assumption that Roche was a 'minor novelist' whose works have failed the test of time due to their author's inability to forge an original creative identity: 'Throughout her long writing career, Mrs. Roche remained a follower rather than a leader of what was "fashionable" in fiction. After Ann Radcliffe, Mrs. Roche looked to Maria Edgeworth, Walter Scott, Lady Morgan, and a series of other popular novelists as her models'.[92]

Recycling the early nineteenth-century critical view of Roche's works, more recent scholarship has failed to give Roche credit for either her humorous and self-conscious treatment of the literary marketplace or the heavy intertextuality that reveals just how cleverly Roche situated her fiction amongst that of contemporaries. Indeed, throughout her *oeuvre* Roche repeatedly indulges in cutting reflections on the contemporary literary marketplace and the common understanding of popular novels like hers as, in Ina Ferris's terms, 'consumptive goods', the illegitimate offspring of a 'promiscuous' print industry trading in 'endless multiplication, anonymous circulation, [and] unfocused desire'.[93] She does so through author figures such as Miss Elmere and Eugene O'Neil as well as through subtle and not-so-subtle references to other texts and literary genres undoubtedly familiar to her readers. Both techniques function together not to condemn popular literature and gothic romances as falling short of 'an elite or high literature' as 'defin[ed] and valorize[ed]' by critics,[94] but instead to suggest, as in Austen's *Northanger Abbey*, that any threat to the reading public offered by such works had to do with how they were read.[95] In their sensitivity to and conscious reflections on literature as well as its production and circulation, Roche's novels insistently position themselves amongst the 'tranche of bibliographically oriented novels, or bookish books' produced by Romantic-era Irish writers.[96] As such, in Connolly's terms, 'they capture within themselves the splits and divisions of the worlds in which Irish books move', partially, as we have already seen, through attention to 'questions of reproduction and copying' as well as 'psychological plots of doubling'.[97]

The castle chapel provides an illuminating example of Roche's bibliographic consciousness. In that novel, O'Neil repeatedly finds himself in trouble on account of his misreading of both books and people. Before embarking on his literary career, O'Neil enters the Royal Navy but is quickly dismissed in the belief that he is 'of incompetent judgment' (*The castle chapel*, vol. 1, p. 109). This assessment is made in light of O'Neil's attempts to defend his assault on a commanding officer by reference to the theories of Franz Joseph Gall (1758–1828) and Johann Gaspar Spurzheim (1776–1832), which he has evidently misunderstood.[98] Following his failed military career, O'Neil finds himself imprisoned for treason after Mordaunt – disguised as the apparently benevolent Mr Wilkinson – tricks him into copying out a 'seditious' and 'inflammatory' radical tract (*The castle chapel*, vol. 2, p. 41). O'Neil nevertheless naively agrees moments afterwards to deliver a packet of 'papers of consequence' for Mordaunt to a bookseller (*The castle chapel*, vol. 2, p. 42). The receipt for this delivery bears O'Neil's name and is later used as evidence that he is the author of what he has so strenuously condemned, resulting in his incarceration.

O'Neil's imprisonment thanks to his production of a textual copy recalls the accusations of paltry imitation and even blatant plagiarism frequently levelled at Minerva Press authors such as Roche while also obliquely referring to the many false attributions Roche's transnational career and fame inspired.[99] While O'Neil's downfall might be blamed on his act of copying, though, Roche's emphasis falls on his worldly innocence and inability to read Mordaunt accurately. Just as he had earlier in the novel been misguided by his misreading of Gall and Spurzheim, here he falls prey to his miscomprehension of Wilkinson/Mordaunt. Something very similar happens in Roche's prolix 1807 tale *The discarded son; or, haunt of the banditti*, the very unsubtly named villain of which – Lord O'Sinister – indicates Roche's playfulness.[100] Like Mordaunt in *The castle chapel*, O'Sinister contrives to harass and oppress the virtuous Munroe family by way of several disguises, masquerading as both Mr Eaton and Mr Raymond at various points in the novel. It is in the form of Mr Raymond

GOTHIC MATERIALITIES

that O'Sinister is rescued from Italian banditti by Osmond Munroe, the young man whom he had earlier attempted to banish to Jamaica in order to seduce Osmond's sister, Elizabeth. Not recognising O'Sinister, who carefully keeps his face hidden from view, Osmond befriends Mr Raymond's wife and her romance-reading daughter. Terrified from her recent ordeal, Mrs Raymond explains that her daughter had

> [taken] it into her head, owing to the perusal of romances, to wish to find herself the inhabitant of some dilapidated mansion, where she would be likely to lose herself in old corridors, marble halls, and subterraneous passages – in short, have the sublime sensation of terror every instant awakened in her mind.[101]

Unlike Austen's Catherine Morland, who finds her expectations of such features and occurrences at Northanger Abbey disappointed, Miss Raymond appears to have had her romance fulfilled. '[N]o one will deny', her mother asserts, 'that this wish has been accomplished' (*The discarded son*, vol. 3, p. 303). Yet, Miss Raymond contends, in a manner that mirrors the enumeration of features in the many 'recipes' that appeared in the late eighteenth and early nineteenth centuries instructing readers in the preparation of their very own novel or gothic romance, 'to have rendered our adventures truly horrific and romantic, we should have seen a spectre, and met with a mutilated manuscript' (*The discarded son*, vol. 3, p. 303).[102] As it happens, even this has been provided for, as Osmond explains. Unable to '[raise] a spectre', he instead produces a manuscript discovered as the party fled from the titular 'haunt of the banditti' (*The discarded son*, vol. 3, p. 303). Together, he and his companions entertain themselves on their journey to Venosa reading of the treachery of the Marchese Montana toward his murdered wife, Isabella. As they read, Mrs Raymond remarks, 'I am not ambitious of figuring away again as a heroine of romance'; her daughter agrees that 'it is much pleasanter to read of, than to meet with adventures' (*The discarded son*, vol. 4, pp. 21–2). At the same time, Mrs Raymond suggests, her experiences have provided her with 'so complete a tale of wonder' with which to amuse her friends that she cannot 'much regret them' (*The discarded son*, vol. 4, p. 22).

In its self-conscious comparison of narrative romance – the manuscript – and the romance of real life – the Raymond family's adventures with the banditti – *The discarded son* situates itself amongst texts discussed in Chapter 2 of this book: *The convent* (1786), *The Irish heiress* (1797), *More ghosts!* (1798), *The heroine* (1813), and *Strathallan* (1816). Although not

173

as overtly parodic as many of these novels, *The discarded son* nevertheless repeatedly and insistently underlines issues of textuality as a way of critiquing the critical condemnation of popular romances and gothic fiction as socially disruptive, subliterary reading material. As in these texts, in *The discarded son*, *how* one reads is much more important than *what* one reads. The significance of discriminating reading is made apparent throughout the novel by the continued calamities introduced by the Munroe family's failure accurately to understand Lord O'Sinister and his motives. Unconcerned by O'Sinister's name or the dark rumours surrounding him, Captain Munroe willingly accepts a loan from O'Sinister in order to travel to Ireland as the steward of O'Sinister's estate near Donaghadee. He then fails to put two and two together when he is shot at and seriously injured by an unknown assailant in Ireland. Only when he returns to Scotland and finds his daughter, Elizabeth, just escaped from an abortive marriage ceremony with the mysterious Mr Eaton, who is revealed as O'Sinister in disguise, does Munroe realise the truth of O'Sinister's character. Even then, he remains in O'Sinister's power, due to the debt he owes him and to the fact that O'Sinister has promised to place Munroe's son, Osmond, in a lucrative living once he has taken orders. Later, Osmond, too, almost falls victim to his inability to comprehend O'Sinister. Told that the promised living has been taken out of O'Sinister's hands, Osmond is on the point of agreeing to an alternative living in Jamaica, when Elizabeth's fiancé, Delacour, accurately identifies O'Sinister's intent. '[D]o not flatter yourself with a hope of being able to impose on me', Delacour tells O'Sinister (*The discarded son*, vol. 2, p. 220).

Delacour's correct perception of O'Sinister depends, at least in part, on his travels as a captain in the Royal Navy. Threatening to publicise O'Sinister's 'real character', Delacour explains, 'I have been more than once at Jamaica, and know perfectly well the character of the gentleman to whom you intended to send Osmond Munroe; know well, that he has no such living in his gift as you speak of' (*The discarded son*, vol. 2, pp. 221, 220). It is the knowledge gleaned from Delacour's experiences abroad, the narrative suggests, that enables him accurately to interpret O'Sinister's motives and thereby put an end to his machinations. The significance of Delacour's travel-informed perspective is reinforced by his name. Recalling Edgeworth's reformed fashionable reader in *Belinda* (1801), Delacour manifests *The discarded son*'s keen interest in contemporary debates on 'appropriate' female reading. More than that, he conjures *Belinda*'s consideration of British colonial relations. Connolly has ably analysed the inherence of 'sentiment and power' in *that* novel's twinned discourses on sensibility and colonial politics.[103] The heroine's choice of Clarence Hervey over the Creole planter Mr Vincent, Connolly argues, relies not only on her beliefs about 'first love' but also on her discovery of his lack of feeling in his treatment of his servant, Juba.[104] Rejecting Mr Vincent, Belinda registers her disdain for 'the disgraceful extensions of sympathy characteristic of its mobilization within discourses of empire'.[105] She also effectively asserts her preference for her home in England over Mr Vincent's plantation in the West Indies, as underlined by Edgeworth's original title: 'Abroad and at home'.

Like Belinda, Roche's Delacour eventually chooses 'home' in Britain over military escapades 'abroad', settling with Elizabeth in Scotland after being named the heir apparent to his aunt's rich estates. While Edgeworth's equivalent travelling man, Mr Vincent is, as Connolly writes, 'tainted by his association with West Indian plantation slavery', it is precisely Delacour's exposure to Jamaican society that enables him to cleanse his native home of the effects of O'Sinister's hitherto unchallenged power.[106] Although placed at the heart of British imperial and commercial endeavours in the West Indies by way of his position in the Royal Navy, Delacour is not a symbol of exploitation as Mr Vincent is. Instead, in offering Osmond the position of chaplaincy on his ship, Delacour provides his future brother-in-law with the means to escape, at least temporarily, what the narrative presents as effective enslavement by O'Sinister. Tellingly, O'Sinister's attempt to 'banish' Osmond to Jamaica is couched in the language of liberty (*The discarded son*, vol. 4, p. 422). Refusing to obey O'Sinister's imperious commands, Osmond rejects his efforts to deprive him of intellectual independence, even if he can do nothing to prevent his imprisonment for debts due to O'Sinister: 'The liberty of which his lordship has deprived me is not half so estimable in my eyes, as that of which he seeks to rob me – the liberty of acting agreeably to the dictates of my reason' (*The discarded son*, vol. 4, p. 256).

The discarded son refrains from further reflections on colonial politics in the British West Indies, nimbly sidestepping questions of imperial rule. That it should rest the power of resolving the complicated interpersonal issues between the Munroe family and O'Sinister on a captain of the Royal Navy charged with protecting British commercial interests in Jamaica is nevertheless a suggestive reminder of the centrality of expanding Atlantic trade to the widespread circulation of popular fiction. As Hazel Bennett has observed, libraries in late eighteenth- and early nineteenth-century

Jamaica were generally short-lived and were often decried for supplying the same kind of lowbrow material for which circulating libraries at home had become infamous.[107] Still, they formed the basis for 'the development of an intellectual elite'.[108] Wealthy plantation owners also themselves imported books, once again relying on popular fiction to fill their personal libraries.[109] Helping to supply growing demand in Jamaica and the West Indies with reading material, popular presses such as Minerva were at the heart of an ever-increasing bibliographic world linked to British imperialistic agendas.

In this sense, to reference British colonial interests in the West Indies, as *The discarded son* does, is also to summon the trade routes followed by contemporary gothic romances, Roche's included. By so doing, the novel subtly stresses the bibliographic everywhereness of Roche's *oeuvre* and also points to the manner in which so many of her characters appear to trace the lines of trade by which her works were distributed across the British Isles, Continental Europe, North America, and further afield. These movements reflect, in part, Roche's own experience moving from Ireland to England and back again while also speaking to wider migration and emigration trends in the late eighteenth and early nineteenth centuries. More than that, though, in their frequent travels, Roche's heroes and heroines become themselves bookish entities, dispersed widely along the routes of literary trade then being established and solidified.[110] Think of *The children of the abbey*: in that novel, the heroine's angst-ridden journeys between England, Ireland, Scotland, and Wales, have been understood as indicative of Roche's nationalist intent. Identifying *The children of the abbey* as the first national tale, Miranda Burgess reads Amanda Fitzalan's 'wanderings' as a sign of her dispossession as well as an early vindication of Irish culture, partially by way of a concentration on English depravity.[111] Diane Long Hoeveler similarly called Amanda's movement 'a sort of endless hyper-nationalistic loop', in which the heroine searches 'for a home that eludes her until the end of this long novel'.[112] Far from parochial or inward-looking, as suggested by Hoeveler's arguments, Roche's descriptions of Amanda's travels point to the wider, increasingly global reach of the nineteenth-century Irish novel. When coupled with her brother's experiences serving in the British army in North America, Amanda's movements begin uncannily to resemble those of Roche's novels as they were re-published, translated, and re-packaged over the course of the nineteenth century. As such, Amanda's travels, much like those of characters in *The castle chapel* and *The discarded son*, evoke the centrality of the Romantic print trade and the circulation of books to the emergence of the modern nation-state and an associated, if apparently contradictory, transnational perspective.

ROCHE, IRISH GOTHIC FICTION, AND (TRANS)NATIONALISM

Narratologically replicating the bibliographic everywhereness Roche enjoyed throughout the long nineteenth century as a Minerva author, her novels enact in themselves the patterns of cultural exchange and encounter depicted in *The tradition of the castle* and elsewhere in Roche's *oeuvre* as essential to a modern Irishness shaped by transnationalism. In this, these works attest to the manner in which, as Piper puts it, the Romantic-era printed book both 'participated in the making of the imagined communities of nineteenth-century nation states' and 'facilitat[ed] the emergence of what Karl Guthke has called a "world-spanning consciousness" around 1800'.[113] On the one hand, Roche's works educated readers about Ireland, even when not specifically about the country, and engaged in the kind of translation of political consciousness and violence to 'cultural self-definition' now identified with the national tale.[114] On the other hand, in keeping with their heavy emphasis on travel as the key to re-imagined, post-Union identities, they chart a new map of Ireland that is less about the physical reclamation of native territory than it is about Irish integration into emergent global communities. This is evidenced, as argued in Chapter 3, in characters who, out of both necessity and choice, undertake widely varied, transatlantic, and transcontinental travels that finally enable recovered and renewed identities at home. It is also apparent in the material circulation of Roche's novels, which ensured an increasingly worldwide familiarity and interaction with Ireland. As Begoña Lasa Álvarez contends, 'a bit of Ireland ... travel[led] with each of the copies [of Roche's works] carried or published abroad'.[115]

Álvarez reads the act of cultural transfer performed by the dissemination of Roche's novels as accidental, but an attentiveness to Ireland is a hallmark of Roche's fiction, even in its early, putatively gothic, rather than national, phase.[116] *The children of the abbey*, for its part, is centrally concerned with an investigation of Irish identity and nationhood more commonly associated with the Irish national tale than the contemporary gothic novel.[117] *Clermont*, too, betrays a real interest in Ireland, particularly in its depiction of Lord Dunlere, the heroine's maternal grandfather and a native Irishman banished to the Continent thanks to 'his attachment to that unhappy Prince [James II]'.[118] Described as 'one of the most faithful and zealous supporters' of the Jacobite cause in Ireland, Lord Dunlere loses his 'considerable property' and is forced into exile upon James's defeat at the Battle of the Boyne (1690) (*Clermont*, p. 240). Although he is said to live his secluded life in 'the obscurity' of the Alps, 'looking back on the world he has left without regret', he nevertheless deeply feels the loss of the 'blessings' he once possessed in Ireland (*Clermont*, pp. 240, 305). He conjures his son-in-law 'to preserve one relique of the noble house of Dunlere' through careful guardianship of Dunlere's infant granddaughter, asserting his family's patrician descent and sketching the enviable beauties of Ireland:

> Yes, I repeat, noble was the house of Dunlere: and should any chance ever lead you to the isle in which it stands, you will find I have not been a vain boaster in calling it so. True, its honours are departed, its possessions are divided; but though its glory has set, it has set like yon bright orb, leaving a long tract of radiance behind it: 'tis on the flowery banks of the Shannon you would hear of the fame of my ancestors; 'tis there you would hear that they were ever foremost in the ranks of virtue and of valour; that their arms were never stretched against the feeble, nor their swords stained with the blood of innocence. (*Clermont*, p. 305)

Madeline ultimately never travels to Ireland, but her matrilineage connects her to the Flight of the Wild Geese and a history of Catholic dispossession that constructs her life in France as one of political exile.[119]

Roche's *Nocturnal visit* (1800) also features a brief but significant Irish interlude. Its heroine, the apparently orphaned Jacintha, discovers that her mother was the unfortunate Miss Decourcy, who, after being seduced by the nefarious Lord Gwytherin, had given birth to her illegitimate daughter in Ireland, in 'an ancient castle, near the celebrated Lakes of Killarney, which had long been in the possession of her family'.[120] Secrecy is ensured thanks to local legend: the castle is said to have been 'deserted by its possessors, in consequence of some dark and dreadful transactions which had taken place within it' (*Nocturnal visit*, vol. 3, p. 55). Miss Decourcy then allows family and friends to assume that the child is that of her soon-to-be sister-in-law, before marrying the Earl of Dunsane, 'the descendant of a noble Irish family; who, in consequence of their attachment to the cause of James the Second, lost the principal part of their property in Ireland; but, by splendid alliances in France, regained nearly an equivalent for it' (*Nocturnal visit*, vol. 2, p. 268). Years later, confronted with her abjured daughter, Lady Dunsane imprisons Jacintha in a remote castle in the Pyrenees, threatening her with fatal consequences should she reveal her parentage to anyone. Her fears finally prove unnecessary, as Jacintha is at last revealed to be Lady Eglantine Sinclair, daughter and heiress of the wealthy Scottish aristocrat, the Earl of Endermay, whose wife had been delivered of a baby on board the ship carrying her to confinement in a Continental convent in the false belief that she had committed adultery. Endermay's grasping half-siblings kidnap the child, intending to claim for themselves her inheritance, but her nurse, paying a visit to her sister in Ireland, secretly switches Eglantine with the recently deceased Jacintha.

Eglantine's discovery of her true identity deprives her of an Irish family line but allows for the repossession of the rightful Dunsane heir, long divested of his title and estates by 'the basest schemes' and raised in France as the son of indigent servants (*Nocturnal visit*, vol. 4, p. 362). While the novel briefly flirts with a marriage between Eglantine and the newly reinstated Lord Dunsane, thereby proposing an Irish-Scottish-French alliance too symbolic to be ignored in the immediate aftermath of the 1798 Rebellion, it ultimately weds her to her English suitor, Egbert Oswald, prompting Dunsane to return to France '[to triumph] over his hopeless passion' by way of the powers of 'reason' (*Nocturnal visit*, vol. 4, p. 393). Purposely recalling *The triumph of prudence over passion* (1781) but also arguably *The fair Hibernian* (1789), *Nocturnal visit* appears to offer a less stridently patriotic conclusion than either of these two novels. Its Anglo-Scottish union of hearts denies the calls for independence sounded by both of these novels, replacing them, in the year of the passage of the Act of Anglo-Irish Union, with an optimistic vision of national accord underwritten by historical precedence.[121]

Much like the other Rochean works discussed earlier in this book, both *Clermont* and *Nocturnal visit* attest to the overlap of gothic and national literary modes in this period. But they also, in their interest in the Flight of the Wild Geese as well as the diaspora occasioned by the failure of the Jacobite cause in Ireland, turn attention to the global movement of the Irish in the long eighteenth century. The centrality of mobility receives added reinforcement in both novels by the insistent detailing of the various travels undertaken by their characters. In *Nocturnal visit*, for instance, Egbert's father is sent to North America shortly after he elopes with his commanding officer's daughter; there he fights in the American War of Independence (1775-83) before returning to England with his wife and son. Egbert later inherits a fortune from his father's friend and confidant, Colonel Moreland, who has died in Jamaica. To claim this legacy and protect it from the designs of Moreland's agent, Egbert himself must venture to Jamaica and elsewhere in the West Indies, from whence

Jacintha's presumed mother, Mrs Decourcy, has recently returned with her husband after having earned their considerable wealth there. When the Decourcys later depart for Portugal, leaving Jacintha without a protector, she is forced to wend her perilous way through the English countryside, a French convent, and the Pyrenees before being reunited with Egbert and settling in Scotland. Far from the 'endless hyper-nationalist loop' Hoeveler identified in *The children of the abbey*, these journeys reflect contemporary patterns of short- and long-term Irish and English migration and emigration, colonial expansion, and popular tourism routes.

More importantly, at least in terms of this discussion, they speak to expanding bibliographic networks and the new transnational story of books themselves. Circulated throughout Britain, Europe, North and South America, and the British Empire, Roche's novels introduced readers to elements of Irish culture, history, politics, and geography, even when not explicitly about Ireland, as in the case of *Clermont* and *Nocturnal visit*. As they did so, they raised the questions of citizenship and national belonging so central to Irish Romantic literature as writers sought to make sense of political exile and increasing migration. In Roche's *oeuvre*, the act of moving and living outside of Ireland becomes, in Wright's terms, 'a register of transnational politics, a differential space in which "here" is always tacitly juxtaposed with "there", while "here" and "there" remain themselves contested categories ... to [be] define[d] and stabilize[d]'.[122] In their material circulation, Roche's works demonstrate a similar process of cultural encounter, comparison, and consolidation. Placed at the heart of the international and internationalising book trade sponsored by William Lane, Roche's novels became themselves productive sites of cultural exchange, contributing to attempts at self-definition at home and abroad over the course of the long nineteenth century and beyond. As such, they ably demonstrate the manner in which, as Wright points out, the Romantic print trade helped shape 'cooperative nationalist projects based not just on opposition to "them", but also on an expansion of "us" and with commensurately fluid notions of territory'.[123] This is perhaps most evident in the translation history of Roche's novels, details of which underline the importance of Piper's call for 'transnational accounts of the book' that move beyond a narrow concentration on the regional or national practices of a particular country or place to include a 'sense of the overlaps and interactions between ... bookish communities'. The various foreign language editions of Roche's works that appeared throughout the nineteenth century, in other words, elucidate how the expanding print trade encouraged what

Piper calls 'a transnational sensibility of local differences' – and indeed, similarities – in the Romantic period.[124]

This chapter has already touched upon the notable translation history of Roche's *oeuvre*, but it is worth revisiting in more detail here as revelatory of the key role her novels played in Romantic nationalist projects outside of Ireland. In particular, the repeated translation of Roche's novels into Spanish presents a persuasive case study, not least because Spain has often been understood not to have a gothic literary tradition, or, as in Ireland's case, to develop a late, largely derivative one.[125] Recent scholarship has begun to contest this lack of a gothic literary consciousness, partially through the recovery of translations by Roche, Radcliffe, Reeve, Lewis, and a number of other primarily Anglo- and Francophone writers.[126] In a compelling essay enumerating Spanish language editions of *The children of the abbey* in the nineteenth and early twentieth centuries, Álvarez points to the importance of the novel not just in the establishment of a gothic literary production in Spain but also in the discourse of Spanish linguistic unity and national singularity. An 1806 translation presented to Spanish authorities as *Los hijos de Fitzalán o Los niños de la Abadía* was rejected by lay censors both for its lack of literary appeal and its many Gallicisms.[127] The condemnation of the translation in terms of its genre – 'la lectura de esta clase de composciones interesa muy poco o nada a la felicidad y buena moral del hombre' – suggests a concern with popular literature similar to that evident in reviews of Minerva Press publications in Britain, indicating a desire to protect an elite literature linked, as the censor's further remarks make clear, to linguistic purity: 'El language no tiene nada de castizo, y en muchos pasajes de la obra la construcción es del todo francesa y acredita también que el traductor no está muy versado en este idoma'.[128]

No copy of the rejected work is now available, as Álvarez observes, but it seems likely that it was prepared using the French language summarisation of *The children of the abbey* that had appeared in 1797 in the fifth volume of the *Bibliothèque Britannique* (Geneva, 1796–1815). This was the case with the first Spanish translation to be cleared by censors: *Los niños de la Abadía*, published in a collection of various abridged texts brought out by Pedro Maria de Olive in Madrid in 1807.[129] The censor's denunciation of a Spanish translation of a French redaction of an English language popular novel, particularly with reference to the notion of 'lo castizo', which, as Alda Blanco points out, 'had historically denoted Spanish purity – racial, linguistic, and cultural', underlines concerns in the Romantic period over the importation of literature to Spain and its potential to disrupt what Benedict Anderson termed the 'vernacularly imagined community'.[130] For writers and critics later in the nineteenth century, it was precisely this dominance of foreign works in translation that was seen to have impeded the growth of an autochtonous writing tradition in Spain, and, concomitantly, a unified and secure nation-state. 'Haunted by the not-so-distant Napoleonic incursion as well as the memory of the "Frenchification" of Spain begun in the eighteenth-century, the copious amounts of translated literature, and the growing presence of foreign capital and culture', Blanco writes, mid-century critics envisioned Spain 'as a boundary-less nation subject to invasion and subjugation'.[131]

Despite concerns over perceived cultural contamination as well as regulations put in place in 1799 and 1805 that made the publication of novels more difficult, the translation of foreign language, particularly Francophone, fictions in the late eighteenth and early nineteenth centuries remained both popular and lucrative.[132] *The children of the abbey* itself was translated into Spanish more than ten times between 1807 and the early twentieth century in Madrid, Barcelona, Paris, and via printing conglomerates in Spanish South America, Buenos Aires and Mexico as well.[133] *Clermont* and *The monastery of St Columb* also appeared in Spanish translation in 1831 and 1839, respectively.[134] These translations, like those of other English- and French-language gothic romances, may be taken simply as representative of the lowbrow tastes of the early nineteenth-century Spanish reader, a stance assumed in the censorship of *Los hijos de Fitzalán o Los niños de la Abadía*.[135] They may further indicate the dominance of an imitative literary technique that prevented the development of a national Spanish literature – gothic or otherwise – well into the century, as was the opinion of many nineteenth-century critics. Yet, as Rocío Rodtjer points out in her review of Miriam López Santos's *La novela gótica en Espanã (1788–1833)*, Spanish translations of works such as Roche's so altered their source texts to satisfy state and religious censors as to produce new fictions that spoke directly to the Spanish social, cultural, and political contexts in which they were published.[136] These then contributed directly to the development of an 'original' Spanish gothic literature in the 1830s by way of what López Santos calls 'transfer of genre'.[137]

Exegesis of the Spanish translations of Roche's novels promises to shed light on the potential ideological agendas of authors, translators, and publishers, akin to that identified by Terry Hale in his analysis of Jean Cohen's 1821 French translation of *Melmoth the wanderer*.[138] This is not the place for such a consideration, but it is worth observing the manner in which even this brief analysis of the translation history of Roche's works into Spanish places her prominently upon what Rodtjer calls 'Spain's Gothic atlas'.[139] Also noteworthy is Roche's centrality to a process of literary exchange that incorporated Spain into a wider European cultural consciousness and material production at the same time that it asserted the distinctiveness of Spanish traditions. As Rodtjer puts it, 'The study of Gothic motifs in Spanish literature brings the country closer to a European literary tradition from which it has occasionally felt excluded. Yet it simultaneously highlights Spain's difference, not only in its socio-economic trajectory and chronology, but also in its scholastic tradition and the scope of theory.'[140]

Rodtjer's comments about the twinned processes of European integration and Spanish national definition enacted through the production, reception, and criticism of gothic fiction call to mind a wider Romantic reality. Benedict Anderson powerfully wrote of the centrality of print-capitalism to the formation of the modern nation-state; it is through the transnational and transatlantic circulation of print, he suggested, 'that the unstable, imagined worlds' of emergent national communities were created. Against Herderian privileging of land and territory as the basis of national identity, Anderson contended that it is mobility – of people and print – rather than geographical rootedness that produces the cultural and linguistic 'hybridity' from which emerge '[n]ationalism's purities'.[141] The modern nation-state's foundation in hybridity allows for diasporic nationalism or, in Anderson's words, 'long-distance nationalism', by which exiled or migrant communities might feel a part of a 'home' country at a distance. At the same time, it recognises the manner in which, as Nancy Vogeley observes, the developing print trade encouraged an awareness of the 'porous[ness]' of national borders – a reality manifest in the publication and circulation of translations – and a concomitant transnational understanding of 'a larger humanity and universality'.[142] In the Romantic period, Monika Class and Terry F. Robinson assert, 'inter/transcultural issues' vitally informed literary production, as writers 'confront[ed] affiliations and differences between self and other, near and far, the familiar and the foreign'. Considering specifically English literary production, Class and Robinson contend that increasing migration, colonial expansion, widespread political unrest across Europe and North America, and the rapid development of a global literary marketplace ensured a constant physical and imaginative interaction 'with domestic and distant others'. The result, they suggest, is the 'blur[ring of] distinctions between England and other nations', even as these cultural encounters reveal the dialogic reciprocity essential to contemporary definitions of Englishness.[143]

A more detailed consideration of the translation of Roche's works across Europe as well as the various cultural, historical, and political contexts in which they were produced would nuance this argument and its applicability to other countries in this period. This is beyond the scope of this book. But, as Piper points out, the proliferation of translations in the Romantic period both 'helped consolidate the collective identities of those audiences' throughout Europe and North America and functioned 'to estrange, to draw readers' attention somewhere else', thus helping 'to foster an alternative international literary imaginary' that moved beyond 'local and locatable boundaries'.[144] The material history of Roche's novels, then, speaks directly to the transnational account of books demanded by Piper. Frequently translated into French, German, and Spanish in the last decade of the eighteenth century and the first three decades of the nineteenth, Roche's fiction encourages us to think about both national *and* world literature in this period.[145] As it does so, it strikingly underlines the transnational element of Irish gothic romances produced by the Minerva Press as well as the flow of culture fostered by Lane's enterprise: in the expansive bibliographic network established by Lane, supported by a number of Irish authors at home and abroad, and mirrored in the migratory patterns of authors and fictional characters alike, we begin to see the real transnational spread and impact of nineteenth-century Irish gothic fiction.

CONCLUSION

Combined with the analysis Roche's novels presented in this and previous chapters, the truncated translation history traced here aptly sketches the transnational element of Roche's *oeuvre*. In their delineation of the importance of travel to modern Irish nationhood and their narratological revelation of what Michael Wiley calls 'a *migratory disposition*', Roche's novels chart the expansion of Irish cultural and economic borders.[146] As they do so, they offer a method of imaginatively, if not physically (re)-claiming Roche's homeland even as she herself remained abroad for much of her adult life, precisely by plotting a new transnational and transcultural map of Ireland. Her fiction ably exemplifies, in other words, the sense of 'long-distance nationalism' referred to by Benedict Anderson, negotiating, even in texts apparently unconcerned with Ireland, an adaptable notion of 'Irishness' reliant not on physical proximity to the land, but on individual and material mobility instead.¹⁴⁷ Relatedly, her works reveal the manner in which popular gothic romances such as hers functioned in the cultural nationalist projects of other emergent nation-states. Catering to a rapidly expanding, multi-lingual audience, Roche's novels contribute to discourses of national purity and distinctiveness on the one hand and, on the other, a growing awareness of cultural interconnectedness. Far from the marginal, derivative, sub-literary fictions of traditional scholarly opinion, Roche's gothic romances, like those of her fellow Irish Minerva Press authors, invite new attention. Not only do they constitute what we might call, in Moretti-inspired terms, the canon of the market or the canon of the read, they are also positioned centrally in the development of nineteenth-century cultural nationalisms and a new transnationalism powered by print.¹⁴⁸

NOTES

1 Clíona Ó Gallchoir, *Maria Edgeworth: women, enlightenment, and nation* (Dublin: University College Dublin Press, 2005), pp. 13, 100–2. For similar readings of Lord Glenthorn's adoption of his wife's surname, see Murphy, *Maria Edgeworth and romance*, pp. 161–2, and Elizabeth Kowaleski-Wallace, *Their fathers' daughters: Hannah More, Maria Edgeworth, and patriarchal complicity* (Oxford: Oxford University Press, 1991), pp. 164–5.
2 Regina Maria Roche, *The castle chapel; a romantic tale*, 3 vols (London: A.K. Newman & Co., 1825), vol. 2, p. 217. Further references are to this edition and are given in parentheses in the text.
3 Delamere's journey to India contrasts with that undertaken by Lady Geraldine and Cecil Devereux in *Ennui* in that it works not, as Marilyn Butler has suggested, to indicate the role to be played by post-Union Ireland in British colonial endeavours, but instead to highlight the manner in which temporary sojourns abroad could enhance, develop, and contribute to a more broadly conceived network of international cultural exchange with Ireland – or more accurately, Irish people and products – at its heart. See Marilyn Butler, 'Introduction', in Maria Edgeworth, Castle Rackrent *and* Ennui, ed. Marilyn Butler (London: Penguin, 1992), pp. 44–5.
4 Here again, Roche reveals an apparent indebtedness to Maturin, whose *Melmoth the wanderer*, published only five years prior to *The castle chapel*, features an Englishman named Stanton tricked into a lengthy stay at an asylum.
5 Karen O'Brien, 'Introduction', in Garside and O'Brien (eds), *The Oxford history of the novel*, p. xviii.
6 Piper, *Dreaming in books*, p. 14.
7 *Ibid.*

8 Lane had begun trade as a printer and circulating library owner as early as 1763, and his press was active by 1784; he only adopted the name of 'Minerva Press' in 1790, however. Deborah McLeod, 'The Minerva Press', Ph.D. dissertation (University of Alberta, 1997), p. 4.

9 Roche's accepted publications include *The vicar of Lansdowne; or, country quarters* (1789); *The maid of the hamlet* (1793); *The children of the abbey* (1796); *Clermont* (1798); *Nocturnal visit* (1800); *The discarded son; or haunt of the banditti* (1807); *The houses of Osma and Almeria; or, the convent of St Ildefonso* (1810); *The monastery of St Columb; or, the atonement* (1813); *Trecothick bower; or, the lady of the west country* (1814); *The Munster cottage boy* (1820); *Bridal of Dunamore; and Lost and won* (1823); *The tradition of the castle; or, scenes in the Emerald Isle* (1824); *The castle chapel* (1825); *Contrast* (1828); and *The nun's picture* (1836). Spurious attributions include *Anna; or, Edinburgh* (London, 1815), *London tales; or, reflective portraits* (London, 1814), *Melinda, or the victim of seduction* (Danbury, CT, 1804), and *Plain tales* (London, 1814). *Alvondown vicarage* (London, 1807) is also often attributed to Roche but, as Anthony Mandal demonstrates, probably was not written by her; 'Revising the Radcliffean model: Regina Maria Roche's *Clermont* and Jane Austen's *Northanger Abbey*', *Cardiff Corvey: reading the Romantic text*, 3 (1999), n.p., www.romtext.org.uk/articles/cc03_n03/, accessed 4 October 2016. For a differing opinion on the authorship of *Alvondown vicarage*, see Natalie Schroeder, 'Regina Maria Roche, popular novelist, 1789-1834: the Rochean canon', *Papers of the Bibliographical Society of America*, 73 (1979), 464.

10 As Adrian Johns notes, Lane's Minerva Press produced 'a third of all new novel titles to appear' in the 1790s and remained 'the leading novel producer until 1826, when Henry Colburn ... came into his own'; 'Changes in the world of publishing', in James Chandler (ed.), *The Cambridge history of English Romantic literature* (Cambridge: Cambridge University Press, 2009), p. 383.

11 Piper, *Dreaming in books*, p. 3; Deirdre Lynch, 'Transformations of the novel – I', in Chandler (ed.), *The Cambridge history of English Romantic literature*, p. 452. On the quantitative rise of the novel, see also Clifford Siskin, *The work of writing: literature and social change in Britain, 1700-1830* (Baltimore, MD and London: The Johns Hopkins University Press, 1998), especially Chapter 6, 'Periodicals, authorship, and the Romantic rise of the novel', pp. 155-71 and James Raven, *Judging new wealth: popular publishing and responses to commerce in England 1750-1800* (Oxford: Clarendon Press, 1992), pp. 31-41.

12 Blakey, *The Minerva Press*, p. 1.

13 See, for instance, reviews of Irish Minerva Press novels *Charles Henley; or, the fugitive restored* (1790), *Court intrigue* (1799), and *Arrivals from India* (1812) in *The Critical Review*, 70 (August 1790), 219; *The Critical Review*,

2nd ser., 28 (January 1800), 116; *The Critical Review*, 4th ser., 2 (September 1812), 332, respectively.
14 McLeod, 'The Minerva Press', p. 13.
15 *Ibid.*, p. 144.
16 *Ibid.*, p. 145. Added emphasis.
17 See Aileen Douglas, '"Whom gentler stars unite": fiction and union in the Irish novel', *Irish university review*, 41.1 (2011), 183–95.
18 Edward Copeland, *Women writing about money: women's fiction in England, 1790-1820* (Cambridge: Cambridge University Press, 1995), p. 5.
19 See Eve Tavor Bannet, 'Charles Brockden Brown and England: of genres, the Minerva Press, and the early Republican print trade', in Kevin Hutchings and Julia M. Wright (eds), *Transatlantic literary exchanges, 1790-1870: gender, race, and nation* (Farnham: Ashgate, 2011), pp. 133–52, and Melissa J. Homestead and Camryn Hansen, 'Susannah Rowson's transatlantic career', *Early American literature*, 45.3 (2010), 619–54.
20 Roche published *The vicar of Lansdowne* and *The maid of the hamlet* with London publishers Joseph Johnson and H. Long, respectively.
21 For biographical details of Roche's life, see Loeber and Loeber, *A guide to Irish fiction*, pp. 1133–4 and Jim Shanahan, 'Roch[e], Regina Maria Dalton', *Dictionary of Irish biography*, eds James McGuire and James Quinn (Cambridge: Cambridge University Press, 2009), http://dib.cambridge.org, accessed 4 October 2016.
22 Regina Maria Dalton, *The vicar of Lansdowne; or, country quarters: a tale*, 2 vols (London: J. Johnson, 1789), vol. 1, [pp. iv–v]; *Monthly Review*, 2nd ser., 1 (February 1790), 223. Original emphasis.
23 Roche, *Contrast*, vol. 1, p. xv.
24 Edward Popham and Cornelius Bolton to [Joseph Snow], 23 February 1827; British Library MS1077, Reel 17, Item 2.
25 Pollard, *Dublin's trade in books*, p. 67.
26 Richard Cargill Cole, *Irish booksellers and English writers, 1740-1800* (London: Mansell Publishing, 1986), p. 194.
27 Connolly, 'The national tale', p. 223.
28 O'Neil's participation in the Greek War of Independence (1821–32) indicates *The castle chapel*'s contemporary setting.
29 These dispossessions are said to occur under Henry VIII and Cromwell.
30 On the experience of Irish female writers in London, in particular, see Rolf Loeber and Magda Stouthamer-Loeber, 'Literary absentees: Irish women authors in nineteenth-century England', in Belanger (ed.), *The Irish novel in the nineteenth century*, pp. 167–86.
31 O'Brien, 'Introduction', p. xxi.
32 For Lane's own advertisement stating that he would pay 'Five to One Hundred Guineas' for manuscripts, see *Adeline; or, the orphan*, 3 vols (London: W. Lane,

1790), vol. 3, [p. 248]. Indicative of the wealth Lane accumulated through his literary enterprise, his estate was valued at approximately £17,500 at his death; Blakey, *The Minerva Press*, p. 21.
33 Blakey, *The Minerva Press*, p. 73.
34 See William St Clair, *The reading nation in the Romantic period* (Cambridge: Cambridge University Press, 2004), p. 173.
35 Blakey, *The Minerva Press*, p. 74; St Clair, *The reading nation*, p. 173.
36 Mrs Smith, *The Caledonian bandit; or, the heir of Duncaethal* (London: A.K. Newman and Co., 1811); quoted in Blakey, *The Minerva Press*, p. 75.
37 St Clair, *The reading nation*, p. 162.
38 Roche to Joseph Snow, 19 November 1831; British Library MS1077, Reel 17, Item 16.
39 These works are *The Munster cottage boy*; *Bridal of Dunamore*; and *Lost and won*; *The tradition of the castle; or, scenes in the Emerald Isle*; *The castle chapel*; and *Contrast*.
40 Michelle Levy, 'Women and print culture, 1750–1830', in Jacqueline M. Labbe (ed.), *The history of British women's writing, 1750–1830*, vol. 5 (Basingstoke and New York: Palgrave Macmillan, 2010), pp. 35, 38.
41 Schroeder, 'Regina Maria Roche, popular novelist', 462.
42 'Maria Regina Roche [sic]', *The New England weekly review*, 35 (10 November 1828), n.p., *Nineteenth-century U.S. newspapers*. www.gale.com/c/19th-century-us-newspapers, accessed 5 March 2015. This comment was made specifically of *The children of the abbey*, but, as discussed later in this chapter, Roche's *oeuvre* as a whole enjoyed an enviable material dissemination that ensured her novels a truly global reach.
43 Blakey, *The Minerva Press*, p. 119.
44 *Ibid.*, p. 123.
45 William Lane, *An address to the public, on circulating libraries* (London, 1795), p. 2. Original italics.
46 *The correspondents, an original novel, in a series of letters* (1775; London: T. Becket and William Lane, 1784), [p. 247].
47 Lane, *An address to the public*, p. 2.
48 *Ibid.*
49 *Ibid.*
50 Christopher Skelton-Foord, 'To buy or to borrow? Circulating libraries and novel reading in Britain, 1778–1828', *Library review*, 47.7 (1998), 349.
51 Lane, *An address to the public*, p. 4.
52 Franz J. Potter, *The history of gothic publishing, 1800–1835: exhuming the trade* (Basingstoke and New York: Palgrave, 2005), p. 22.
53 See the library information in entries for individual authors in Peter Garside, Jacqueline Belanger, and Sharon Ragaz, *British fiction, 1800–1829: a database of production, circulation and reception*, designer, Anthony Mandal,

www.british-fiction.cf.ac.uk, accessed 4 October 2016. The database includes 24 libraries across England, Ireland, Scotland, and Wales, providing what the compilers believe is 'a representative picture of library holdings' in early nineteenth-century Britain; see Garside, Belanger, and Ragaz, 'Guide to contemporary libraries', in Garside, Belanger, and Ragaz, *British fiction, 1800–1829*, www.british-fiction.cf.ac.uk/guide/libraries.html, accessed 19 October 2016.

54 See Morin, *Charles Robert Maturin* and Jim Kelly, *Charles Maturin: authorship, authenticity and the nation* (Dublin: Four Courts Press, 2011).

55 Charles Robert Maturin, *Women; or, pour et contre*, 3 vols (Edinburgh and London: Archibald Constable and Co., and Longman, Hurst, Rees, Orme and Brown, 1818), vol. 1, p. iii.

56 *Ibid.*

57 On this often overlooked legacy, see Morin, *Charles Robert Maturin*, particularly the conclusion.

58 See, in particular, Colin B. Atkinson and Jo Atkinson, 'Sydney Owenson, Lady Morgan: Irish patriot and first professional woman writer', *Éire-Ireland*, 15 (1980), 60–90, and Mary Campbell, *Lady Morgan: the life and times of Sydney Owenson* (London: Pandora, 1988). More recent scholarship includes Jacqueline Belanger, *Sydney Owenson, Lady Morgan: critical receptions* (Palo Alto, CA: Academica Press, 2007), and Donovan, *Sydney Owenson, Lady Morgan*.

59 See also Roche's dedication to the public in the second edition of *The vicar of Lansdowne*, where she declares, 'The Author of the following work gladly embraces the present opportunity of returning her most grateful acknowledgments to the Public, for the high favour and patronage it has already experienced from them'; *The vicar of Lansdowne; or, country quarters*, 2 vols (2nd edn; London: William Lane, 1800), vol. 1, p. i.

60 Loeber and Loeber, *A guide to Irish fiction*, p. 1136.

61 *Ibid.* For a more extensive account of Spanish translations, including further publications in 1837, 1859, 1868, 1872, 1880, 1882, 1889, c. 1901, and c. 1910/11, see Begoña Lasa Álvarez, 'Regina Maria Roche, an eighteenth-century Irish writer on the continent and overseas', in Marisol Morales Ladrón and Juan F. Elices Agudo (eds), *Glocal Ireland: current perspectives on literature and the visual arts* (Newcastle-upon-Tyne: Cambridge Scholars Publishing, 2011), pp. 51–61, and Miriam López Santos, *La novela gótica en Espanã (1788–1833)* (Pontevedra: Editorial Academia del Hispanismo, 2010), pp. 290–1.

62 Raven, 'Historical introduction', p. 35.

63 The republication and translation information on which this figure is based was gathered from Garside, Belanger, and Ragaz, *British fiction, 1800–1829*; Lasa Álvarez, 'Regina Maria Roche'; Loeber and Loeber, *A guide to Irish fiction*, pp. 1133–41; and López Santos, *La novela gótica*. See also Loeber and Loeber, *A guide to Irish fiction*, Figure 13, 'The republication of Regina

Maria Roche's novels (first published in London) in Ireland, France, Holland, Germany, and the United States', p. xcvi.
64 Piper, *Dreaming in books*, p. 65. On my use of this phrase in contrast to Piper's, see p. 24, note 49.
65 Bannet, 'Charles Brockden Brown and England', p. 134.
66 *Ibid.*, p. 135.
67 Pollard, *Dublin's trade in books*, p. v. As Rosalind Remer points out, publishers and printers in colonial and early republican America were cautious of undertaking the costs involved in producing reprints for an unreliable and developing market and, thus, were more inclined to import British publications for circulation; *Printers and men of capital: Philadelphia in the New Republic* (Philadelphia: University of Pennsylvania Press, 1996), pp. 12, 15–16.
68 Blakey indicates that Minerva Press titles had found their way to circulating libraries in Jamaica and India by the first decade of the nineteenth century; *The Minerva Press*, p. 123. For further information on the British book trade in India and the West Indies, see Wil Verhoeven, 'The global British novel', in Garside and O'Brien (eds.), *The Oxford history of the novel in English*, pp. 577–80.
69 Blakey, *The Minerva Press*, p. 43.
70 Blakey suggests that Lane's reprinting of Brown's six novels may have been unauthorised, but Bannet more recently demonstrates that Brown had a transatlantic strategy that pivoted on his works being reprinted by the Minerva Press; see Blakey, *The Minerva Press*, p. 43, and Bannet, 'Charles Brockden Brown and England', p. 135.
71 Blakey, *The Minerva Press*, pp. 44, 123.
72 'Literary intelligence', *Missouri Republican*, 165 (23 May 1825), 670, Nineteenth-century U.S. Newspapers. www.gale.com/c/19th-century-us-newspapers, accessed 25 May 2015.
73 'Maria Regina Roche [sic]', *New England weekly review* (10 November 1828), *Nineteenth-century U.S. newspapers*. n.p., www.gale.com/c/19th-century-us-newspapers, accessed 25 May 2015.
74 *Ibid.*
75 'Brief review of new books', *The Milwaukee Sentinel* (3 January 1892), 11, *Nineteenth-century U.S. newspapers*. www.gale.com/c/19th-century-us-newspapers, accessed 25 May 2015.
76 'Multiple classified adverts', *The daily inter ocean* (23 April 1893), 5, *Nineteenth-century U.S. newspapers*. www.gale.com/c/19th-century-us-newspapers, accessed 25 May 2015.
77 See below, pp. 170–1, for a discussion of the reviews of Roche's works.
78 Regina Maria Roche, *The monastery of St Columb; or, the atonement. A novel*, 5 vols (London: A.K. Newman, 1813), vol. 1, pp. 264, 266–7. Further references are to this edition and are given in parentheses in the text.

79 Ina Ferris, 'Transformations of the novel – II', in Chandler (ed.), *The Cambridge history of English Romantic literature*, p. 474.
80 *Ibid.*
81 Angeline De Burgh is actually Clora Clanronel, though she has been raised by an adoptive father St Ruth/De Burgh, who believed her to be the daughter of the nefarious Roscrea and his beautiful wife, Elvira.
82 Claire Connolly, 'A bookish history of Irish Romanticism', in Porscha Fermanis and John Regan (eds), *Rethinking British Romantic history, 1770–1845* (Oxford: Oxford University Press, 2014), p. 282.
83 Piper, *Dreaming in books*, p. 57.
84 W.H. Ireland, *Scribbleomania; or, the printer's devil's polichronicon* (1815), p. 157; quoted in Blakey, *The Minerva Press*, p. 59.
85 *The Critical Review*, n.s., 24 (November 1798), 356.
86 *La belle Assemblée*, n.s., 6 (1812), 371.
87 *The Critical Review*, 4th ser., 5 (January 1814), 99.
88 *Ibid.*
89 *Ibid.*, 101.
90 See Natalie Schroeder, '*The mysteries of Udolpho* and *Clermont*: the Radcliffean encroachment on the art of Regina Maria Roche', *Studies in the novel*, 12 (1980), 131–43 and Mandal, 'Revising the Radcliffean model'.
91 Natalie Schroeder, 'Regina Maria Roche and the early nineteenth-century Irish novel', *Eire-Ireland*, 19.2 (1984), 116.
92 Schroeder, '*The mysteries of Udolpho* and *Clermont*', 131, 143.
93 Ferris, 'Transformations of the novel – II', pp. 474.
94 McLeod, 'The Minerva Press', p. 85.
95 See Chapter 2, pp. 91–6.
96 Connolly, 'A bookish history of Irish Romanticism', p. 281.
97 *Ibid.*, pp. 281, 282.
98 Gall is known today as the founder of phrenology and developed what he referred to as '*Schädellehre*' or 'doctrine of the skull' in early works such as *Philosophisch-medicinische untersuchungen über natur und kunst im kranken und gesunden zustande des menschen* (1791; *Philosophical-medical investigations of nature and artifice in man's diseased and healthy conditions*) and public lectures delivered in Vienna from 1796. His connection with Spurzheim began in 1804, when Gall hired him as an assistant. Spurzheim accompanied Gall on his lecture tour through Germany, Denmark, the Netherlands, Switzerland, and France beginning in 1805. Together, Gall and Spurzheim published two of four volumes of *Anatomie et psychologie du système nerveux en general, et du cerveau en particulier, avec des observations sur las possibilité de reconnoître plusieurs dispositions intellectuelles et morales de l'homme et des animaux, par la configuration de leurs têtes* (1810–19), but they parted ways in Paris in 1813. Gall subsequently published two further volumes of *Anatomie et psychologie*,

while Spurzheim went to Britain to lecture on a modified system of phrenology. Although, as John van Wyhe observes, the early reception of Gall's system in Britain from 1800 to 1805 was enthusiastic, by 1806, 'the tide of British opinion [had] turned against him'. Spurzheim's arrival in Britain in 1814, then, was not accorded the same applause that Gall's original European tour had garnered. Indeed, by 1808, Gall and Spurzheim's ideas were 'uncontroversially considered absurd'; John van Wyhe, *Phrenology and the origins of Victorian scientific naturalism* (Aldershot: Ashgate, 2004), pp. 25, 26.

99 See p. 186, note 9 above on spurious attributions. Other works, including *Eliza; or, the pattern of women; a moral romance* (Lancaster, PA, 1802) and *Le père coupable, ou, les malheurs de la famille Lewison* (Paris, 1821) clearly attempted to cash in on Roche's fame by falsely advertising themselves as translations of Roche's works.

100 O'Sinister is by far the most transparent name in the pantheon of Roche's villains and villainesses, who also include Father Jerome (*The houses of Osma and Almeria*); Morcar (*Trecothick bower*); Lady Jane Morley and O'Callaghan/don Callan (*The tradition of the castle*); Mr Mordaunt (*The castle chapel*); and Sir Osbert Henley (*Contrast*).

101 Regina Maria Roche, *The discarded son; or, haunt of the banditti. A tale*, 5 vols (London: Lane, Newman, and Co., 1807), vol. 3, p. 303. Further references are to this edition and are given in parentheses in the text.

102 Examples of these 'recipes' include 'Recipe for dressing up novels *ad libitum*', *Monthly Review*, 2nd ser., 5 (July 1791), 338 and 'Terrorist novel writing', in E.J. Clery and Robert Miles (eds), *Gothic documents: a sourcebook 1700–1820* (Manchester: Manchester University Press, 2000), p. 184. The latter is itself a riff on Pope's 'A receipt to make an epic poem', published in *Memoirs of Martin Scriblerus* (1741). I am grateful to Ian Campbell Ross for pointing out the similarities between Pope's piece and 'Terrorist novel writing' to me.

103 Connolly, *A cultural history of the Irish novel*, p. 103.

104 *Ibid.*, p. 104.

105 *Ibid.* Connolly here is working from the arguments of Jonathan Lamb; see 'Modern metamorphoses and disgraceful tales: eighteenth-century fictional "it-narratives"', *Critical inquiry*, 28.1 (2001), 133–66.

106 Connolly, *A cultural history of the Irish novel*, p. 104.

107 Hazel Bennett, 'Private and subscription libraries in Jamaica before 1879', *Journal of library history*, 3 (1968), 246.

108 *Ibid.*, 243.

109 Joseph A. Boromé, 'Origin and growth of the public libraries of Dominica', *Journal of library history*, 3 (1970), 201.

110 This is also the case for several of Roche's Irish contemporaries publishing with the Minerva Press. For more extensive discussions of these authors and

their works, see Morin, 'At a distance from [my] country', and Morin, 'Irish gothic goes abroad'.
111 Burgess, 'Violent translations', p. 43.
112 Hoeveler, 'Regina Maria Roche's *The children of the abbey*', 141.
113 Piper, *Dreaming in books*, p. 6.
114 Burgess, 'Violent translations', 36.
115 Lasa Álvarez, 'Regina Maria Roche', p. 58.
116 *Ibid.*
117 See Burgess, 'Violent translations'; Hoeveler, 'Regina Maria Roche's *The children of the abbey*'; and Morin, ' "Gothic" and "national"?'.
118 Regina Maria Roche, *Clermont; a tale*, ed. Natalie Schroeder (1798; Chicago, IL: Valancourt Books, 2006), p. 240. Further references are to this edition and are given in parentheses in the text.
119 The 'Wild Geese' were members of the Irish Jacobite army who left Ireland in the wake of their defeat at the Battle of the Boyne in 1690 and the subsequent negotiation of the Treaty of Limerick in 1691. They joined armies abroad, particularly that of France's Louis XIV, and, as Éamonn Ó Ciardha notes, 'remained pivotal to Irish Jacobite hopes and Protestant fears', as did their eighteenth-century successors in the Irish Brigades in France and Spain; *Ireland and the Jacobite cause, 1685–1766; a fatal attachment* (Dublin: Four Courts Press, 2002), p. 32.
120 Regina Maria Roche, *Nocturnal visit; a tale*, 4 vols (London: Minerva Press, 1800), vol. 3, p. 54. Further references are to this edition and are given in parentheses in the text.
121 The Anglo-Scottish Union (1707) was frequently taken as a point of comparison by both pro- and anti-Unionists in the debates surrounding Anglo-Irish Union at the close of the eighteenth century. See James Livesey, 'Acts of union and disunion: Ireland in Atlantic and European contexts', in Dáire Keogh and Kevin Whelan (eds), *Acts of union: the causes, contexts, and consequences of the Act of Union* (Dublin: Four Courts Press, 2001), pp. 95–105.
122 Wright, *Representing the national landscape*, p. 98.
123 *Ibid.*, p. xxiv.
124 Piper, *Dreaming in books*, p. 6.
125 As Ann Davies writes, 'Spain does not apparently have a Gothic tradition. With the rise of Anglophone Gothic in the eighteenth century, Spain appeared to serve at best as part of a Southern European location for Anglophone encounters with the Gothic other … Spanish culture was able to create a Gothic context but unable to recognize it as such'; 'Spanish gothic cinema: the hidden continuities of a hidden genre', in Elena Oliete-Aldea, Beatriz Oria, and Juan A. Tarancón (eds), *Global genres, local films: the transnational dimension of Spanish cinema* (London and New York: Bloomsbury Academic, 2016), p. 115.

126 See Xavier Aldana Reyes, *Spanish gothic: national identity, collaboration and cultural adaptation* (Basingstoke and New York: Palgrave Macmillan, 2017); Abigail Lee Six, *Gothic terrors: incarceration, duplication, and bloodlust in Spanish narrative* (Lewisburg, PA: Bucknell University Press, 2010); and López Santos, *La novela gótica*.
127 Lasa Álvarez, 'Regina Maria Roche', p. 55.
128 Spanish National Archive, AHN, Consejos, 5567/17; quoted in Lasa Álvarez, 'Regina Maria Roche', pp. 55, 125. The two passages translated read as follows: 'reading this kind of composition offers little or nothing to the happiness and good morals of man'; 'The language is not authentic, and in many passages of the work the construction is in French and also proves that the translator is not well versed in this language'. My thanks to Dr Jaele Rollins-McColgan for her help in translating these passages.
129 Lasa Álvarez, 'Regina Maria Roche', pp. 53-4.
130 Alda Blanco, 'Gender and national identity: the novel in nineteenth-century Spanish literary history', in Lou Charnon-Deutsch and Jo Labanyi (eds), *Culture and gender in nineteenth-century Spain* (Oxford: Clarendon Press, 1995), p. 125; Benedict Anderson, *Imagined communities: reflections on the origin and spread of nationalism* (rev. edn; London and New York: Verso, 2006), p. 79.
131 Blanco, 'Gender and national identity', p. 123. See also Elisa Martí-López, 'The market conditions in a peripheral literary space', *Borrowed words: translation, imitation, and the making of the nineteenth-century novel in Spain* (Lewisburg, PA: Bucknell University Press, 2002), pp. 33-44.
132 Rebecca Haidt, 'The Enlightenment and fictional form', in Harriet Turner and Adelaida López de Martínez (eds), *The Cambridge companion to the Spanish novel from 1600 to the present* (Cambridge: Cambridge University Press, 2003), p. 38.
133 See Lasa Álvarez, 'Regina Maria Roche', p. 61 and López Santos, *La novela gótica*, pp. 290-1.
134 López Santos, *La novela gótica*, p. 291.
135 See *ibid.*, pp. 280-91 for an extensive list of gothic romances in translation.
136 Rocío Rodtjer, 'The Spanish gothic', *Journal of romance studies*, 12.1 (2002), 87.
137 *Ibid.* López Santos's term is 'transferencia génerica'.
138 Terry Hale, 'Translation in distress: cultural misappropriation and the construction of the gothic', in Avril Horner (ed.), *European gothic: a spirited exchange 1760-1960* (Manchester: Manchester University Press, 2002), pp. 17-38.
139 Rodtjer, 'The Spanish gothic', p. 86.
140 *Ibid.*, p. 93.
141 Benedict Anderson, *The spectre of comparisons: nationalism, Southeast Asia, and the world* (London: Verso, 1998), p. 62. See also, Johann Gottfried Herder,

Outlines of a philosophy of the history of man, trans. T. Churchill (London: J. Johnson, 1800).
142 Nancy Vogeley, 'Translation studies: the novel and other Enlightenment crossings', *Eighteenth-century studies*, 44:2 (2011), 292.
143 Monika Class and Terry F. Robinson, 'Introduction', in Monika Class and Terry F. Robinson (eds), *Transnational England: home and abroad, 1780–1860* (Newcastle upon Tyne: Cambridge Scholars Publishing, 2009), p. 1.
144 Piper, *Dreaming in books*, p. 155.
145 See Moretti, 'Conjectures on world literature'.
146 Michael Wiley, *Romantic migrations: local, national, and transnational dispositions* (Basingstoke and New York: Palgrave Macmillan, 2008), p. 2. Original emphasis.
147 See Anderson, *The spectre of comparisons*, pp. 58–74.
148 See Moretti, 'The slaughterhouse of literature'.

Conclusion

Recent scholarship has begun to rehabilitate Minerva Press publications such as Roche's, arguing for a new academic approach that moves beyond traditional denunciations of these fictions as unoriginal and imitative. In her research, Elizabeth A. Neiman traces the manner in which Minerva authors actively responded in their texts to the accusations of derivativeness so often levelled at them by critics and, in so doing, 'developed their own model of collective authorship'. Only by reading their novels together, Neiman suggests, will we have a full sense of the impact of Minerva Press publications and their engagement with a wide range of contemporary debates.[1] Elsewhere, Edward Copeland, Jennie Batchelor, and Cheryl Turner have brought attention to the insights afforded by the careers and works of Minerva authors to questions of female authorship in the Romantic period.[2] Meanwhile, illuminating research by Eve Tavor Bannet, Melissa J. Homestead, and Camryn Hansen has illustrated Minerva's transnational presence by way of the circulation of texts, linking the press's provision of a dispersed readership to the cultivation of successful and financially lucrative international careers by particularly savvy authors.[3]

The evidence of Roche's lasting fame and influence presented in Chapter 4 draws attention to the many overlooked Irish novelists who published with Lane in the Romantic period.[4] It also underlines the importance of readers in the determination of literary relevance and impact. As Franco Moretti aptly puts it, 'Readers, not professors, make canons'. There is '[a] space outside the school', Moretti suggests, 'where the canon is selected', and that space is 'the market'.[5] As is clear from the material history of Roche's works, she was a major figure in this canon, exerting a cultural influence hitherto denied to her and, in the process, attesting to the international prominence of Irish gothic fiction in the late eighteenth and early nineteenth centuries. In addition to highlighting the importance of renewed consideration of Minerva Press publications, therefore, Roche's works invite a continuation of the research presented here: an interrogation, in other words, of the critical assumptions shaping our current understanding of both Irish and gothic literary production in this period.

Relevant and timely work by the team behind the Leverhulme-funded *Lady's magazine* (1770–1818) project has added weight to the appeal for scholarship made here. What Jennie Batchelor calls 'the Minerva Press fiction of the Romantic periodical marketplace', the *Lady's magazine* offered its many readers a wide range of literary and cultural delights each month, including short and serialised fiction, some of it excerpts from gothic romances published by popular presses such as Minerva, and much of it closely resembling them in style and mode.[6] Indicatively, as Jenny DiPlacidi documents, there was considerable overlap between the authors publishing gothic tales within the pages of the *Lady's magazine* and those producing novels with Minerva and other popular publishers.[7] One such writer was Miss Kitty or Catherine Cuthbertson, whose novels include *Romance of the Pyrenees* (1803), *Santa Sebastiano* (1806), *The forest of Montalbano* (1810), *Adelaide; or, the countercharm* (1813), *Rosabella; or, a mother's marriage* (1817), *The hut and the castle* (1823), and *Ethelbert* (1830).[8] Like Roche, Cuthbertson was generally viewed as a Radcliffean imitator and, accordingly, has been given short shrift in scholarship of the Romantic period. Yet, also like Roche, Cuthbertson's gothic romances were extremely widely read throughout the nineteenth century, with Cuthbertson remaining a recognisable name long after her death, despite the fact that she published most of her work anonymously.[9]

The same might be said of a considerable number of gothic fiction writers in this period. What makes Cuthbertson a particularly interesting figure in the context of this study is Batchelor's recent discovery of her Irish birth, a finding that brings Roche and Cuthbertson even closer together. Born in Dublin in or around 1775, Cuthbertson relocated to London some time before 1803, specifically for professional reasons: to 'wr[i]te romances'.[10] Over the next three decades or so, Cuthbertson would produce seven novels, many of which remained familiar to readers at least until the early twentieth century but which have been largely ignored by literary criticism. Like Roche, then, Cuthbertson represents the migration of Irish literary production at the start of the nineteenth century and is indicative of the systematic erasure of so much popular fiction from the annals of (Irish) Romantic literature. The relegation of gothic romance writers such as Roche, Cuthbertson, and many of the other authors included in this study to the margins of literary history not only denies the significance of their long-lasting, transnational appeal, but it also emphasises the limitations of accepted accounts of 'canonical' Romantic-era literature. As Batchelor writes,

> Cuthbertson, like so many *Lady's Magazine* authors, is an important figure in literary history, not just because of what she wrote, how many people fainted in her novels' pages, or because people like [Thomas Babington] Macaulay read her. She is important because her persistent popularity and claim on readers' imagination makes clear that so many things we once thought we knew about literary history – about who was read and remembered – don't always chime with reality.[11]

If Batchelor's exciting discovery of Cuthbertson's birth threatens to plunge us even further into 'the sublime of literary history' noted in the Introduction, it also emphatically stresses how incomplete and often misguided our understanding of Irish gothic literary production in this period is. As detailed in the preceding chapters, our assumptions about late eighteenth-and early nineteenth-century gothic literature in Britain lead to a deceptively smooth account of what appears to be a largely Anglo-centric phenomenon typified by defined formal, generic, stylistic, and narratological boundaries. Within this scenario, contemporary Irish gothic cultural production is marginalised as delayed and derivative, a secondary development of an English tradition, the norms of which it never successfully replicated thanks to the conditions and consequences of its own cultural specificity.

The texts discussed here – some of which have never before benefited from serious scholarly consideration – demonstrate the inaccuracy of these ideas, illustrating that Irish authors actively produced an adaptable, cross-generic, cross-cultural gothic literature reflective of contemporary understandings of the term gothic, not as the codified formal or generic heading it has become. Exploring historical example, continuity, and change, the authors of eighteenth- and nineteenth-century Irish gothic literature produced a diverse body of fiction that probed questions of modernity, progress, and enlightenment from a variety of different angles. Many of these works adopt the conventions we associate with 'the Gothic novel' and 'Irish Gothic', e.g., medievalism; Catholic Continental settings; overt supernaturalism. But, as evidenced here, many of them do not, preferring instead contemporary time periods, local geography, and a more generalised recourse to romance. Attention to the apparent deviations and exceptions to the norm highlights the heterogeneous breadth that is eighteenth- and nineteenth-century Irish gothic literature. As it does so, it re-integrates the gothic into mainstream British and Irish literary history, revealing the striking overlaps between gothic fictions and apparently distinct forms such as the historical novel and the national tale, and positioning the literary gothic not as the disreputable, popular output of hack writers unworthy of cultural memory but as an invaluable body of widely read literature vital to the transnational development of nineteenth-century literature and culture.

The aim of this book has been to outline a new model of gothic literary production reflective of these realities without falling prey either to the trap of unnecessarily limiting definitions or to the appeal of canon-making. Quantitative analysis has been useful in avoiding these pitfalls, clearly enumerating the literary and material facts on which this book's claims are built. The various maps and graphs draw into stark relief the broad, formally and generically porous approach to the literary gothic held by eighteenth- and nineteenth-century writers. And, if the discussion of these works has necessarily been reliant on a representative selection, these figures sketch out and begin to add contour to a revised and expanded map of Irish gothic fiction that accurately situates it formally, generically, narratologically, ideologically, and geographically within the contexts of Irish, British, and European literary output. Alongside the more traditional qualitative analysis included here, these 'graphs, maps, and trees' provide an innovative and transformative account of Irish gothic fiction that not only reframes scholarship of 'the Gothic novel' and 'Irish Gothic' but also reworks conventional perceptions of the literary gothic's place within and impact upon Romantic-era culture. At the same time, in keeping with Moretti's suggestion that 'graphs, maps, and trees place the literary field literally in front of our eyes – and show us how little we still know about it', the statistical illustrations included here gesture towards the rich, Irish gothic terrain yet to be explored.[12] Opening up the study of Romantic literary history, this work invites continued interrogation of individual cases such as those with which this conclusion began, as well as more collective bodies of Irish and gothic literary production in order further to develop and refine the literary cartography presented here.

NOTES

1 Elizabeth A. Neiman, 'A new perspective on the Minerva Press's "derivative" novels: authorizing borrowed material', *European Romantic review*, 26.5 (2015), 634, 635.

2 See Jennie Batchelor, *Women's work: labour, gender, authorship, 1750–1830* (Manchester: Manchester University Press, 2010); Copeland, *Women writing about money*; and Cheryl Turner, *Living by the pen: women writers in the eighteenth century* (1992; London and New York: Routledge, 1994).
3 See Bannet, 'Charles Brockden Brown and England', and Homestead and Hansen, 'Susannah Rowson's transatlantic career'.
4 For discussion of some of these other authors, see Morin, 'Irish gothic goes abroad' and Morin, 'At a distance from my country'.
5 Moretti, 'The slaughterhouse of literature', p. 209.
6 Jennie Batchelor, 'The *Lady's* magazine and the Minerva Press', *The Lady's magazine (1770–1818): understanding the emergence of a genre*, 29 July 2015, https://blogs.kent.ac.uk/ladys-magazine/2015/07/29/the-ladys-magazine-and-the-minerva-press/, accessed 14 October 2016. See also Jennie Batchelor, Jenny DiPlacidi, and Koenraad Claes, 'Welcome to the *Lady's magazine*: understanding the emergence of a genre', *The Lady's magazine (1770–1818): understanding the emergence of a genre*, 29 October 2014, http://blogs.kent.ac.uk/ladys-magazine/2014/10/, accessed 18 October 2016; and Jenny Di Placidi, 'C.D.H. or Catharine Day Haynes: a gothic author for the Lady's magazine and the Minerva Press', *The Lady's magazine (1770–1818): understanding the emergence of a genre*, 19 August 2015, https://blogs.kent.ac.uk/ladys-magazine/2015/08/19/c-d-h-or-catharine-day-haynes-a-gothic-author-for-the-ladys-magazine-and-the-minerva-press/, accessed 18 October 2016.
7 Di Placidi, 'C.D.H. or Catharine Day Haynes'.
8 Cuthbertson's novels were not originally published by the Minerva Press, but, as Batchelor notes, there clearly was 'authorial migration' between Minerva and the *Lady's magazine*, as is clear in the case of C.D.H or Catharine Day Haynes; 'The *Lady's magazine* and the Minerva Press'. See also Di Placidi, 'C.D.H. or Catharine Day Hayes'.
9 Jennie Batchelor, 'Finding the mysterious Miss Cuthbertson in the *Lady's Magazine*', *The Lady's magazine (1770–1818): understanding the emergence of a genre*, 17 April 2016, http://blogs.kent.ac.uk/ladys-magazine/2016/04/17/finding-the-mysterious-miss-cuthbertson-and-the-ladys-magazine/, accessed 14 October 2016.
10 William Ball Wright, 'Note', *Notes and queries*, 77 (17 June 1911), 475; quoted in Batchelor, 'Finding the mysterious Miss Cuthbertson'.
11 Batchelor, 'Finding the mysterious Miss Cuthbertson'.
12 Moretti, *Graphs, maps, trees*, p. 2.

Appendix: A working bibliography of Irish gothic fiction, c. 1760–1829

As suggested by the term 'working', this bibliography is not intended to be exhaustive or definitive, but rather indicative. It represents revisions to various existing bibliographies, including those offered by Loeber and Stouthamer-Loeber, Potter, and Summers.[1] Texts that have appeared in these previous works are noted below, as indicated in the following key. Doing so helps to situate these works within existing gothic criticism. Texts that have not appeared in these earlier works are those identified as representative of the cross-generic, cross-formal, cross-cultural gothic literary production in Ireland analysed in previous chapters.

KEY

L   appeared in Loeber and Stouhamer-Loeber, 'The publication of Irish novels and novelettes'
P   appeared in Potter, *The history of gothic publishing*
S   appeared in Summers, *A gothic bibliography*

Underlined text in the title of a work indicates the primary generic identifiers used in Figure 1.

Bold type in the title of a work indicates the marketing cues on which Figure 3 is based.

Novels included in the sampling on which Figure 4 is based are indicated by an asterisk (*) following the title. For these titles, geographical settings are included.

Works personally consulted in the preparation of this monograph are indicated by an obelisk (†) following the title.

NOTES

1 See Loeber and Stouthamer-Loeber, 'The publication of Irish novels and novelettes', Table 5, The development of Irish gothic fiction in the context of English gothic fiction, pp. 37–8; Potter, *The history of gothic publishing*, Appendix 1, 'Gothic novels, 1800–1824', pp. 152–65, and Appendix 3, 'Gothic tales, 1800–1834', pp. 179–89; and Montague Summers, *A gothic bibliography* (1940; New York: Russell & Russell, 1964).

APPENDIX

Date	Author	Novel title	Settings	Notes
1762	Thomas Leland	**Longsword, Earl of Salisbury**; <u>an historical romance</u>*†	England, France	L, S
1764	Elizabeth Griffith	**Amana**; a dramatic poem*†	Egypt	S
1769	Elizabeth Griffith	The delicate distress, <u>a novel</u>. In letters*†	England, France, Italy	
1771	Elizabeth Griffith	The <u>history of Lady Barton</u>, a novel. In letters*†	Ireland, England, France	S
1776	Elizabeth Griffith	The <u>story of Lady Juliana Harley</u>, a novel, in letters*†	England, Ireland, 'the Continent'	S
1780	Elizabeth Griffith	'Conjugal fidelity; or, female fortitude'*† (in *Novellettes, selected for the use of young ladies and gentlemen*)	Ireland	
1780	Elizabeth Griffith	'Story of Lady Fanny Beaumont and Lord Layton'*† (in *Novellettes, selected for the use of young ladies and gentlemen*)	England	
1786	Anne Fuller	The **convent**; or, the history of Sophia Nelson*†	England, France	S
1787	Anne Fuller	**Alan Fitz-Osborne**, <u>an historical tale</u>*†	England, Scotland, 'the Holy Land'	L, S
1789	Anne Fuller	The **son of Ethelwolf**, <u>an historical tale</u>*†	England, Denmark, Iceland	S
1789	Regina Maria Roche	The **vicar** of Lansdowne; or, country quarters. <u>A tale</u>*†	England, Scotland	S
1789	James White	**Earl Strongbow**; or, <u>the history of Richard de Clare and the beautiful Geralda</u>*†	Wales, Ireland	L, S
1789	James White	Conway Castle; a poem*†	Wales	S
1790	Mrs Sarah Green	**Charles Henley**; or, the fugitive restored		S
1790	James White	The **adventures of John of Gaunt, Duke of Lancaster***†	England	S
1791	James White	The <u>Adventures of King Richard Coeur-de-Lion</u>; to which is added, The death of Lord Falkland: a poem*†	Continental Europe (various), Asia, Siberia, England	S

203

Date	Author	Novel title	Settings	Notes
1793	Anna Milliken	**Corfe Castle**; or, <u>historic tracts. A novel</u>*†	England, Sweden, Hungary, Scotland	L, S
1793	Regina Maria Roche	**The maid of the hamlet**; <u>a tale</u>*†	England, Ireland	L, S
1794	Stephen Cullen	The haunted priory: or, the fortunes of the house of Rayo. <u>A romance, founded partly on historical facts</u>*†	Spain, Portugal	
1795	Anna Milliken	Eva; <u>an old Irish story</u>*†[2]	Ireland	
1796	Stephen Cullen	The castle of Inchvalry; <u>a tale – alas! too true</u>*†	Ireland, England, Portugal	S
1796	Regina Maria Roche	**The children of the abbey**; <u>a tale</u>*†	England, Ireland, Wales, Scotland, North America	S
1797	Mrs F.C. Patrick	**The Irish heiress**; <u>a novel</u>*†	Ireland, France	S
1797	Catharine Selden	**The count de Santerre**; <u>a romance</u>*†	France	S
1797	Catharine Selden	The English nun; <u>a novel</u>*†	England, Portugal	S
1798	Mrs F.C. Patrick	More ghosts!*†	England, France	L, S
1798	Regina Maria Roche	**Clermont**; <u>a tale</u>*†	France	S
1799	Mrs Sarah Green	Court intrigue; or, **the victim** of constancy. <u>An historical romance</u>*†	England, France	S
1799	Mrs F.C. Patrick	**The Jesuit**; or, <u>the history of Anthony Babington, Esq., an historical novel</u>*†	England	S

2 This novel was originally published anonymously but has been identified as written by Milliken; Loeber and Loeber, *A guide to Irish fiction*, p. 901.

APPENDIX

Date	Author	Novel title	Settings	Notes
1800	Maria Edgeworth	*Castle Rackrent; an Hibernian tale. Taken from facts, and from the manner of the Irish squires, before the year 1782**†	Ireland	
1800	Regina Maria Roche	*Nocturnal visit; a tale**†	England	P, S
1800	Catharine Selden	*Serena; a novel**†	Portugal	S
1801	Anon.	*The monastery of Gondolfo; a romance*	Italy[3]	L, P
1801	Mrs Saran Green	*The private history of the court of England*	England	S
1802	Anna Milliken	*Plantagenet; or, secrets of the house of Anjou. A tale of the twelfth century*	France[4]	L, P, S
1803	Catherine Cuthbertson	*Romance of the Pyrenees**†	Italy, France, Spain	P, S
1803	Sydney Owenson	*St Clair; or, the heiress of Desmond**†	Ireland	S
1804	Anna Milliken	*The rival chiefs; or, battle of Mere. A tale of ancient times*	Ireland	P, S
1804	Henrietta Rouvière Mosse	*Lussington Abbey; a novel**†	Wales	P, S
1805	Revd. Luke Aylmer Conolly	*The friar's tale; or, memoirs of the Chevalier Orsino, with other narratives*†	Italy, Austria, Poland, Germany, England[5]	L, S
1805	Catharine Selden	*Villa Nova; or, the ruined castle. A romance*†	Southern Europe[6]	L, P, S
1806	Catherine Cuthbertson	*Santo Sebastiano; or, the young protector. A novel**†	England, Italy, France	P, S

3 Loeber and Loeber, *A guide to Irish fiction*, p. 1391.
4 *Ibid.*, p. 901.
5 *Ibid.*, p. 289.
6 *Ibid.*, p. 1176.

Date	Author	Novel title	Settings	Notes
1806	Marianne Kenley	**The cottage of the Appenines**, or, the Castle of Novina; a romance*†	Italy	L
1806	Henrietta Rouvière Mosse	**The heirs** of Villeroy; a romance*†	England, Italy	S
1806	Sydney Owenson	**The novice** of Saint Dominick*†	France	L, P, S
1806	Sydney Owenson	The wild Irish girl; a national tale*†	Ireland	P, S
1807	Charles Robert Maturin	The fatal revenge; or, the family of **Montorio**. A romance*†	Italy	L, P,S
1807	Henrietta Rouvière Mosse	A peep at our ancestors; **an historical romance***†	England	S
1807	Regina Maria Roche	**The discarded son**; or, haunt of the banditti. A tale*†	Scotland, England, Ireland, Spain, Italy	P, S
1808	Mrs Sarah Green	Tankerville family	Ireland, England	S
1808	Charles Robert Maturin	The wild Irish boy*†	Ireland, England	P, S
1808	Henrietta Rouvière Mosse	**The old Irish baronet**; or, manners of my country*†	Ireland, Spain	S
1808	Elizabeth Plunkett	The exile of Erin; a novel*†	Ireland, England, Wales, North America	S
1809	Maria Edgeworth	Ennui; or memoirs of the Earl of Glenthorn*† (in Tales of fashionable life)	Ireland, England	
1809	Mrs Sarah Green	Tales of **the manor***†	England, Italy, France	S

APPENDIX

Date	Author	Novel title	Settings	Notes
1809	Sydney Owenson	*Woman; or, Ida of Athens**†	Greece, England	S
1810	Anon.	The **soldier** of *Pennaflor: or, a season in Ireland**†	England, Wales, Ireland	P, S
1810	Catherine Cuthbertson	**The forest of Montalbano**; *a novel*		P, S
1810	Mrs Sarah Green	*The festival of* **St Jago**; *a Spanish romance**†	Spain	P, S
1810	Mrs Sarah Green	*The reformist!!! A serio-comic-political* <u>novel</u>⁷	England⁸	S
1810	Mrs Sarah Green	*Romance readers and romance writers; a satirical* <u>novel</u>*†	England	S
1810	Mrs Sarah Green	*The* **royal exile**; *or, victims of human passions. An historical romance of the sixteenth century**†	France, England	S
1810	John Hamilton Roche	*A Suffolk* <u>tale</u>; *or,* **the perfidious guardian**⁹	Ireland, England, Canada¹⁰	P, S
1810	Regina Maria Roche	*The houses of Osma and Almeria; or,* **the convent of St Ildefonso**, *a tale**†	Spain	P, S
1811	Mrs Sarah Green	*Good men of modern date; a satirical* <u>tale</u>†	England¹¹	S
1811	Sydney Owenson	**The missionary**; *an Indian* <u>tale</u>*†	India	S
1811	Charles Phillips	*The loves of* **Celestine and St Aubert**; *a romantic tale*		S
1812	Maria Edgeworth	*The absentee* (in <u>Tales</u> *of fashionable life*)*†	Ireland, England	S

7 This title was republished as *Percival Ellingford; or, the reformist* (1816).
8 McLeod, 'The Minerva Press', p. 395.
9 For Roche's identification as Irish, see Loeber and Loeber, *Guide to Irish fiction*, p. 1133.
10 Loeber and Loeber, *A guide to Irish fiction*, p. 1133
11 *Ibid.*, p. 506.

Date	Author	Novel title	Settings	Notes
1812	Charles Robert Maturin	The **Milesian chief**; _a romance_*†	Ireland, England, Italy	P, S
1812	Henrietta Rouvière Mosse	Arrivals from India; or, time's a great master. _A novel_		S
1813	Eaton Stannard Barrett	The **heroine**; or, _adventures of a fair romance reader_*†	England	S
1813	Catherine Cuthbertson	Adelaide; or, the countercharm		P
1813	Mrs Sarah Green	Deception; a fashionable _novel_ … _founded on facts_	England[12]	P
1813	Regina Maria Roche	The **monastery of St Columb**; or, the atonement. _A novel_*†	Ireland, England, Spain,	P, S
1814	Mrs Sarah Green	The **Carthusian friar**; or, the mysteries of Montanville; a posthumous _romance_		P
1814	Mrs Sarah Green	The **fugitive**; or, family incidents		S
1814	Sydney Owenson	O'Donnel; _a national tale_*†	Ireland, England	S
1814	Regina Maria Roche	**Trecothick bower**; or, the lady of the west country. _A tale_*†	England, France	S
1814	Robert Torrens	The **victim of intolerance**; or, **the hermit** of Killarney. A Catholic _tale_†	Ireland[13]	S
1816	Lady Caroline Lamb	Glenarvon; _a tale_†	Ireland[14]	P, S
1816	Alicia Le Fanu	**Strathallan***†	England	S

12 Ibid.
13 See Wright, _Representing the national landscape_, pp. 37–43 on _The victim of intolerance_ and its twinned use of gothic and national modes.
14 Loeber and Loeber, _A guide to Irish fiction_, p. 720.

APPENDIX

Date	Author	Novel title	Settings	Notes
1817	Nugent Bell	*Alexena; or, the castle of Santa Marco, <u>a romance</u>*†	Spain[15]	P
1817	Catherine Cuthbertson	*Rosabella; or, a mother's marriage*		S
1817	Henrietta Rouvière Mosse	*A **bride** and no wife; <u>a novel</u>*†	Scotland[16]	S
1817	Catharine Selden	*Villasantelle; or, the curious impertinent. <u>A romance</u>*†	Spain[17]	P, S
1818	Alicia Le Fanu	*Helen Monteagle*		S
1818	Charles Robert Maturin	*Women; or, pour et contre. <u>A tale</u>*†	Ireland, France	S
1818	Sydney Owenson	*Florence Macarthy; an Irish <u>tale</u>*†	Ireland	S
1819	Alicia Le Fanu	*Leolin **Abbey**; <u>a novel</u>*		S
1820	Charles Robert Maturin	*Melmoth **the wanderer**; <u>a tale</u>*†	Spain, Ireland, England, India	L, P, S
1820	Regina Maria Roche	*The Munster cottage boy; <u>a tale</u>*†	Ireland, England	S
1822	Mrs Sarah Green	*Who is the bridegroom? or, nuptial discoveries. <u>A novel</u>*		S
1823	Catherine Cuthbertson	*The hut and **the castle**; <u>a romance</u>*		S
1823	Mrs Sarah Green	*Gretna Green marriages; or, the nieces. <u>A novel</u>*		S
1823	Lady Caroline Lamb	***Ada Reis**; <u>a tale</u>*		P, S

15 *Ibid.*, p. 136.
16 McLeod, 'The Minerva Press', p. 397.
17 *Ibid.*, p. 1176.

Date	Author	Novel title	Settings	Notes
1823	Alicia Le Fanu	**Don Juan de las Sierras**; or, el empecinado. A romance		S
1823	Alicia Le Fanu	The **outlaw** (in Tales of a tourist)†	Ireland[18]	S
1823	Regina Maria Roche	The bridal of **Dunamore**; and Lost and won. Two tales*†	Ireland, England	S
1824	John Banim	Revelations of the **dead-alive***†	England	
1824	Mrs Sarah Green	Scotch novel reading; or, modern quakery. A novel really founded on facts		
1824	Charles Robert Maturin	**The Albigenses**; a romance*†	France	S
1824	Regina Maria Roche	The tradition of **the castle**; or, scenes in the Emerald Isle*†	Ireland, England	S
1825	John and Michael Banim	'The **fetches**' (in Tales by the O'Hara family)*†	Ireland	
1825	Mrs Sarah Green	Parents and wives; or, inconsistency and mistakes. A novel		S
1825	Charles Robert Maturin	'**Leixlip Castle**: an Irish family legend'*†	Ireland	P, S
1825	Henrietta Rouvière Mosse	A father's love and a woman's friendship; or, the widow and her daughters. A novel		S
1825	Regina Maria Roche	**The castle chapel**; a romantic tale*†	Ireland, England, Wales	S
1826	Alicia Le Fanu	Henry the fourth of **France**; a romance		S
1826	Henrietta Rouvière Mosse	Gratitude, and other tales		S

18 Loeber and Loeber, A guide to Irish fiction, p. 737.

APPENDIX

Date	Author	Novel title	Settings	Notes
1827	Henrietta Rouvière Mosse	Woman's wit and man's wisdom; or, intrigue. A novel		S
1827	Sydney Owenson	The O'Briens and the O'Flahertys; a national tale*†	Ireland	S
1828	Revd. George Croly	*Salathiel; a story of the past, the present, and the future*		L, P
1828	Regina Maria Roche	Contrast*†	Ireland, Italy, Wales, England	S
1829	Henrietta Rouvière Mosse	The Blandfords; or, fate and fortune		S

211

Select bibliography

MANUSCRIPT SOURCES

Archives of the Royal Literary Fund, *1790–1918*, British Library.
British Library 41996/27, letter from Maturin to Hurst, Robinson & Co, 25 June 1821.
The Walter Scott manuscript collection, National Library of Scotland.

NEWSPAPERS AND JOURNALS

The British Critic and Quarterly Theological Review
The Critical Review
The Daily Inter-Ocean
Edinburgh Review
Gentleman's Magazine
The Guardian
La belle Assemblée
The Milwaukee Sentinel
Missouri Republican
The Monthly Mirror
Monthly Review
New England Weekly Review

OTHER PRIMARY SOURCES

Adeline; or, the orphan. 3 vols. London: W. Lane, 1790.
A late lord. *Reginald Du Bray: an historick tale. By a late lord, greatly admired in the literary world.* Dublin, 1779.

SELECT BIBLIOGRAPHY

A late nobleman. *Reginald Du Bray: an historic tale. By a late nobleman.* Dublin, 1784.

Austen, Jane. *Northanger Abbey.* 1818. Eds James Kinsley and John Davie. Introd. Claudia L. Johnson. Oxford: Oxford University Press, 2003.

Banim, John. *Revelations of the dead-alive.* London: W. Simpkin & R. Marshall, 1824.

—— and Michael Banim, *The fetches. Tales by the O'Hara family.* By John and Michael Banim. Volume 2. London: W. Simpkin and R. Marshall, 1825. 111–392.

Barrett, Eaton Stannard. *The heroine, or, adventures of a fair romance reader.* 1813. Eds Avril Horner and Sue Zlosnik. Kansas City, MO: Valancourt Books, 2011.

Beattie, James. *Dissertations moral and critical.* London, 1783.

The correspondents, an original novel, in a series of letters. 1775. London: T. Becket and William Lane, 1784.

Dalton, Regina Maria [Roche]. *The vicar of Lansdowne; or, country quarters: a tale.* 2 vols. London: J. Johnson, 1789.

—— *The vicar of Lansdowne; or, country quarters.* 2 vols. 2nd edn. London: William Lane, 1800.

Edgeworth, Maria. *The absentee.* 1812. Eds W.J. McCormack and Kim Walker. Oxford: Oxford University Press, 2001.

Fielding, Henry. *The history of the adventures of Joseph Andrew and of his friend Mr. Abraham Adams.* 1742. Ed. Douglas Brooks-Davies. Introd. Thomas Keymer. Oxford: Oxford University Press, 2008.

Finberg, Melinda C., ed. *Eighteenth-century women dramatists.* Oxford: Oxford University Press, 2001.

Fuller, Anne. *Alan Fitz-Osborne, an historical tale.* 2 vols. London, [1787].

—— *The convent: or, the history of Sophia Nelson.* 2 vols. London, [1786].

—— *The son of Ethelwolf; an historical tale.* Dublin, [1789].

Griffith, Elizabeth. *Amana. A dramatic poem.* London, 1764.

—— 'Conjugal fidelity: or, female fortitude', in Griffith and Goldsmith (eds), *Novellettes*, pp. 179–91.

—— *The delicate distress, a novel: in letters.* 1769. 2 vols. Dublin, 1787.

—— *The delicate distress,* eds Cynthia Booth Ricciardi and Susan Staves. Lexington, KY: The University Press of Kentucky, 1997.

—— *The history of Lady Barton, a novel, in letters.* 3 vols. London, 1771.

—— 'Story of Lady Fanny Beaumont and Lord Layton', in Griffith and Goldsmith (eds), *Novellettes*, pp. 192–202.

—— *The story of Lady Juliana Harley, a novel. In letters.* 2 vols. Dublin, 1776.

—— and Oliver Goldsmith, eds. *Novellettes, selected for the use of young ladies and gentlemen.* London, 1780.

Herder, Johann Gottfried. *Outlines of a philosophy of the history of man.* Trans. T. Churchill. London: J. Johnson, 1800.

Jeffrey, Francis. Review of *Marmion; a tale of Flodden Field*. *Edinburgh Review*, 12.23 (1808), 1–35.
Lane, William. *An address to the public, on circulating libraries*. London, [1795?].
Le Fanu, Alicia. *Strathallan*. 1816. Ed. Anna M. Fitzer. London: Pickering & Chatto, 2008.
Leland, Thomas. *Longsword, Earl of Salisbury: an historical romance*. 2 vols. Dublin, 1762.
—— *Longsword, Earl of Salisbury*. London, 1762.
—— *Longsword, Earl of Salisbury*. 2nd edn. London, 1763.
Maturin, Charles Robert. 'Leixlip Castle: an Irish family legend'. *The literary souvenir; or, cabinet of poetry and romance*. London: Hurst, Robinson, & Co., 1825.
—— 'Leixlip Castle: an Irish family legend'. 1825. *Twelve gothic tales*. Ed. Richard Dalby. Oxford: Oxford University Press, 1998, pp. 1–13.
—— *The Milesian chief; a romance*. 4 vols. London: Henry Colburn, 1812.
—— *Women; or, pour et contre*. 3 vols. Edinburgh and London: Archibald Constable and Co., and Longman, Hurst, Rees, Orme and Brown, 1818.
Melville, Theodore. *The White Knight, or the monastery of Morne. A romance*. 3 vols. London: Crosby & Letterman, 1802.
Milliken, Anna. *Corfe Castle; or, historic tracts. A novel, in two volumes*. Cork: James Haly, 1793.
The moral miscellany; or, a collection of select pieces, in prose and verse, for the instruction and entertainment of youth. Dublin, 1774.
Mosse, Henrietta Rouvière. *The old Irish baronet; or, manners of my country. A novel*. 3 vols. London: Lane, Newman & Co., 1808.
The new polite instructor; or universal moralist. London, 1771.
Owenson, Sydney. *O'Donnel: a national tale*. 3 vols. London: Colburn, 1814.
—— *The wild Irish girl: a national tale*. 1806. Ed. Kathryn Kirkpatrick. Oxford: Oxford University Press, 1999.
Patrick, Mrs F.C. *The Irish heiress, a novel, in three volumes*. London, 1797.
—— *The Jesuit; or, the history of Anthony Babington, Esq., an historical novel*. 3 vols. Bath, 1799.
—— *More ghosts! In three volumes*. London, 1798.
Ratchford, Fannie E., and Wm H. McCarthy, Jr., eds. *The correspondence of Sir Walter Scott and Charles Robert Maturin, with a few other allied letters*. Austin, TX: University of Texas Press, 1937.
Reeve, Clara. *The old English baron*. 1778. Ed. James Trainer. Introd. James Watt. Oxford: Oxford University Press, 2008.
—— *The progress of romance, through times, countries, and manners; with remarks on the good and bad effects of it, on them respectively; in a course of evening conversations*. 1785. *Bluestocking feminism: writings of the Bluestocking Circle, 1738–1785*, Volume 6: Sarah Scott and Clara Reeve. Ed. Gary Kelly. London: Pickering & Chatto, 1999, pp. 160–275.

SELECT BIBLIOGRAPHY

The rival friends; or, the noble recluse: a novel. London: T. Vernor, 1776.
Rizzo, Betty, ed. *Eighteenth-century women playwrights. Volume 4: Elizabeth Griffith.* London: Pickering & Chatto, 2001.
Roche, Regina Maria. *The castle chapel. A romantic tale.* 3 vols. London: A.K. Newman & Co., 1825.
—— *The children of the abbey.* 1796. New York: Thomas Crowell & Co., no date.
—— *Clermont; a tale.* 1798. Ed. Natalie Schroeder. Chicago, IL: Valancourt Books, 2006.
—— *Contrast.* 3 vols. London: A.K. Newman & Co., 1828.
—— *The discarded son; or, haunt of the banditti. A tale.* 5 vols. London: Lane, Newman, and Co., 1807.
—— *The monastery of St Columb; or, the atonement. A novel.* 5 vols. London: A.K. Newman, 1813.
—— *Nocturnal visit; a tale.* 4 vols. London: Minerva Press, 1800.
—— *The tradition of the castle; or, scenes in the Emerald Isle.* 4 vols. London: A.K. Newman & Co., 1824.
—— *Trecothick Bower; or, the lady of the west country: a tale.* 3 vols. London: A.K. Newman, 1814.
—— [née Dalton]. *The vicar of Lansdowne; or, country quarters: a tale.* 2 vols. London: J. Johnson, 1789.
—— [née Dalton]. *The vicar of Lansdowne; or, country quarters.* 2 vols. 2nd edn. London: William Lane, 1800.
Scott, Sir Walter. *The bride of Lammermoor.* 1819. Ed. Fiona Robertson. Oxford: Oxford University Press, 1991.
—— *Lives of the novelists.* 2 vols. Philadelphia, PA, 1825.
—— Review of *Women; or, pour et contre*, by Charles Robert Maturin. *Edinburgh Review*, 30.59 (1818), 234–57.
—— *Waverley; or, 'tis sixty years since.* 1814. Ed. Claire Lamont. Oxford: Clarendon Press, 1981.
Selden, Catharine. *The English nun: a novel.* London: William Lane, 1797.
'Terrorist novel writing', in *Gothic documents: a sourcebook 1700–1820*. Eds E.J. Clery and Robert Miles. Manchester: Manchester University Press, 2000, pp. 182–4.
Walpole, Horace. *The castle of Otranto.* 1764. Ed. W.S. Lewis, introd. E.J. Clery. London: Oxford University Press, 1964.
White, James. *The adventures of John of Gaunt, Duke of Lancaster.* 3 vols. London, 1790.
—— *Conway Castle: a poem.* London, 1789.
—— *Earl Strongbow: or, the history of Richard de Clare and the beautiful Geralda.* 2 vols. Dublin, 1789.
Woolley, David, ed. *The correspondence of Jonathan Swift, D.D.* 4 vols. Frankfurt am Main: Peter Lang, 1999–2007.

HISTORICAL AND CRITICAL STUDIES

Adair, Charlene. 'The trial of Lord Maguire and "print culture"', in Eamon Darcy, Annaleigh Margey, and Elaine Murphy (eds), *The 1641 depositions and the Irish Rebellion*. London: Pickering & Chatto, 2012, pp. 169–83.

Aldana Reyes, Xavier. *Spanish gothic: national identity, collaboration and cultural adaptation*. Basingstoke and New York: Palgrave Macmillan, 2017.

Anderson, Benedict. *Imagined communities: reflections on the origin and spread of nationalism*. Rev. edn. London and New York: Verso, 2006.

— — *The spectre of comparisons: nationalism, Southeast Asia, and the world*. London: Verso, 1998.

Atkinson, Colin B. and Jo Atkinson. 'Sydney Owenson, Lady Morgan: Irish patriot and first professional woman writer', *Éire-Ireland*, 15 (1980), 60–90.

Backus, Margot Gayle. *The gothic family romance: heterosexuality, child sacrifice, and the Anglo-Irish colonial order*. Durham, NC: Duke University Press, 1999.

Bakhtin, Mikhail. *The dialogic imagination: four essays*. Ed. Michael Holquist. Trans. Caryl Emerson and Michael Holquist. Austin, TX: University of Texas Press, 1981.

Baldick, Chris and Robert Mighall. 'Gothic criticism', in Punter (ed.), *A companion to the gothic*, pp. 209–28.

Bannet, Eve Tavor. 'Charles Brockden Brown and England: of genres, the Minerva Press, and the early Republican print trade', in Kevin Hutchings and Julia M. Wright, eds, *Transatlantic literary exchanges, 1790–1870: gender, race, and nation*. Farnham: Ashgate, 2011, pp. 133–52.

Barnard, Toby. 'The uses of 23 October 1641 and Irish Protestant celebrations', *English historical review*, 106 (1991), pp. 889–920.

Batchelor, Jennie. 'Finding the mysterious Miss Cuthbertson in the *Lady's Magazine*', *The Lady's magazine (1770–1818): understanding the emergence of a genre*, 17 April 2016. http://blogs.kent.ac.uk/ladys-magazine/2016/04/17/finding-the-mysterious-miss-cuthbertson-and-the-ladys-magazine/, accessed 14 October 2016.

— — 'The *Lady's magazine* and the Minerva Press', *The Lady's magazine (1770–1818): understanding the emergence of a genre*, 29 July 2015. https://blogs.kent.ac.uk/ladys-magazine/2015/07/29/the-ladys-magazine-and-the-minerva-press/, accessed 14 October 2016.

— — *Women's work: labour, gender, authorship, 1750–1830*. Manchester: Manchester University Press, 2010.

— —, Jenny DiPlacidi, and Koenraad Claes, 'Welcome to the *Lady's magazine*: understanding the emergence of a genre', *The Lady's magazine (1770–1818): understanding the emergence of a genre*, 29 October 2014. http://blogs.kent.ac.uk/ladys-magazine/2014/10/, accessed 18 October 2016.

SELECT BIBLIOGRAPHY

Belanger, Jacqueline. 'Introduction', in Belanger (ed.), *The Irish novel in the nineteenth century*, pp. 11-33.

—— 'Some preliminary remarks on the production and reception of fiction relating to Ireland, 1800-1829', *Cardiff Corvey: reading the Romantic text*, 4.2 (2000), 1-31. www.cf.ac.uk/encap/corvey/articles/cc04_n02.html, accessed 15 June 2017.

—— *Sydney Owenson, Lady Morgan: critical receptions*. Palo Alto, CA: Academica Press, 2007.

——, ed. *The Irish novel in the nineteenth century: facts and fictions*. Dublin: Four Courts Press, 2005.

Bennett, Hazel. 'Private and subscription libraries in Jamaica before 1879', *Journal of library history*, 3 (1968), 242-9.

Blakey, Dorothy. *The Minerva Press 1790-1820*. London: The Bibliographical Society at the University Press, Oxford, 1939.

Blanco, Alda. 'Gender and national identity: the novel in nineteenth-century Spanish literary history', in Lou Charnon-Deutsch and Jo Labanyi (eds), *Culture and gender in nineteenth-century Spain*. Oxford: Clarendon Press, 1995, pp. 120-36.

Boromé, Joseph A. 'Origin and growth of the public libraries of Dominica', *Journal of library history*, 3 (1970), 200-36.

Burgess, Miranda. 'The national tale and allied genres, 1770s-1840s', in Foster (ed.), *The Cambridge companion to the Irish novel*, pp. 39-59.

—— 'Violent translations: allegory, gender, and cultural nationalism in Ireland, 1796-1806', *Modern language quarterly*, 59.1 (1998), 33-70.

Butler, Marilyn. 'Introduction', in *Castle Rackrent and Ennui*, by Maria Edgeworth. Ed. Marilyn Butler. London: Penguin, 1992, pp. 1-56.

—— *Jane Austen and the war of ideas*. 1975. Oxford: Clarendon Press, 2002.

Cahalan, James. *Great hatred, little room: the Irish historical novel*. Dublin: Gill and Macmillan, 1983.

Campbell, Mary. *Lady Morgan: the life and times of Sydney Owenson*. London: Pandora, 1988.

Chandler, James, ed. *The Cambridge history of English Romantic literature*. Cambridge: Cambridge University Press, 2009.

Chard, Chloe. *Pleasure and guilt on the Grand Tour: travel writing and imaginative geography, 1600-1830*. Manchester: Manchester University Press, 1999.

Class, Monika and Terry F. Robinson. 'Introduction', *Transnational England: home and abroad, 1780-1860*. Newcastle upon Tyne: Cambridge Scholars Publishing, 2009, pp. 1-20.

Clery, E.J. 'The genesis of "Gothic" fiction', in Hogle (ed.), *The Cambridge companion to gothic fiction*, pp. 21-40.

—— 'Introduction', in *The castle of Otranto*, by Horace Walpole. Ed. W.S. Lewis. London: Oxford University Press, 1964, pp. vii-xvi.

—— *The rise of supernatural fiction, 1762–1800.* Cambridge, Cambridge University Press, 1995.
Cole, Richard Cargill. *Irish booksellers and English writers, 1740–1800.* London: Mansell Publishing, 1986.
Connolly, Claire. 'A bookish history of Irish Romanticism', in Porscha Fermanis and John Regan (eds), *Rethinking British Romantic history, 1770–1845.* Oxford: Oxford University Press, 2014, pp. 271–324.
—— *A cultural history of the Irish novel, 1790–1829.* Cambridge: Cambridge University Press, 2011.
—— 'Irish Romanticism, 1800–1829', in Kelleher and O'Leary (eds), *The Cambridge history of Irish literature*, pp. 407–48.
—— 'The national tale', in Garside and O'Brien (eds), *The Oxford history of the novel in English*, pp. 216–33.
Connolly, Sean. 'Patriotism and nationalism', in Alvin Jackson (ed.), *The Oxford handbook of modern Irish history.* Oxford: Oxford University Press, 2014, pp. 27–44.
Copeland, Edward. *Women writing about money: women's fiction in England, 1790–1820.* Cambridge: Cambridge University Press, 1995.
Cox, Jeffrey. *Seven gothic dramas, 1789–1825.* Ohio: Ohio University Press, 1992.
Davies, Ann. 'Spanish gothic cinema: the hidden continuities of a hidden genre', in Elena Oliete-Aldea, Beatriz Oria, and Juan A. Tarancón (eds), *Global genres, local films: the transnational dimension of Spanish cinema.* London and New York: Bloomsbury Academic, 2016, pp. 115–26.
Day, William Patrick. *In the circles of fear and desire.* Chicago: University of Chicago Press, 1985.
Di Placidi, Jenny. 'C.D.H. or Catharine Day Haynes: a gothic author for the Lady's magazine and the Minerva Press', *The Lady's magazine (1770–1818): understanding the emergence of a genre*, 19 August 2015. https://blogs.kent.ac.uk/ladys-magazine/2015/08/19/c-d-h-or-catharine-day-haynes-a-gothic-author-for-the-ladys-magazine-and-the-minerva-press/, accessed 18 October 2016.
Donovan, Julie. *Sydney Owenson, Lady Morgan and the politics of style.* Palo Alto, CA: Academica Press, 2009.
Donovan, Kellie A. 'Imprisonment in *Castle Rackrent*: Maria Edgeworth's use of gothic conventions', in Lynch, Fischer, and Coates (eds), *Back to the present*, pp. 145–56.
Doody, Margaret Anne. 'Introduction', in *The female Quixote*, by Charlotte Lennox. Oxford: Oxford University Press, 2008, pp. xi–xxxii.
Douglas, Aileen. 'The novel before 1800', in Foster (ed.), *The Cambridge companion to the Irish novel*, pp. 22–38.
—— '"Whom gentler stars unite": fiction and union in the Irish novel', *Irish university review*, 41.1 (2011), 183–95.

———, Moyra Haslett, and Ian Campbell Ross, eds. *Irish fiction, 1660-1830*, special issue of *Irish university review*, 41.1 (2011).

Duff, David. *Romanticism and the uses of genre*. Oxford: Oxford University Press, 2009.

Duffy, Seán. *Brian Boru and the Battle of Clontarf*. 2013. Dublin: Gill & Macmillan, 2014.

Duncan, Ian. *Modern romance and transformations of the novel: the gothic, Scott, Dickens*. Cambridge: Cambridge University Press, 1992.

——— 'Walter Scott, James Hogg and Scottish gothic', in David Punter (ed.), *A companion to the gothic* (London: Blackwell, 2001), pp. 70-80.

Eagleton, Terry. *Heathcliff and the Great Hunger: studies in Irish culture*. London: Verso, 1995.

Edwards, Elizabeth. 'Iniquity, terror and survival: Welsh gothic, 1789-1804', *Journal for eighteenth-century studies*, 35.1 (2012), 119-33.

Fay, Elizabeth. *Romantic medievalism: history and the Romantic literary ideal*. Basingstoke and New York: Palgrave Macmillan, 2002.

Ferris, Ina. *The achievement of literary authority: gender, history, and the Waverley Novels*. Ithaca, NY: Cornell University Press, 1991.

——— *The Romantic national tale and the question of Ireland*. Cambridge: Cambridge University Press, 2002.

——— 'Transformations of the novel – II', in Chandler (ed.), *The Cambridge history of English Romantic literature*, pp. 473-89.

Fitzer, Anna M. 'Introduction', in *Strathallan*, by Alicia Le Fanu. London: Pickering & Chatto, 2008, pp. vii–xxii.

Flanagan, Thomas. *The Irish novelists, 1800-1850*. New York: Columbia University Press, 1958.

Fogarty, Anne. 'Imperfect concord: spectres of history in the Irish novels of Maria Edgeworth and Lady Morgan', in Kelleher and Murphy (eds), *Gender perspectives in nineteenth-century Ireland*, pp. 116-26.

Foster, John Wilson, ed. *The Cambridge companion to the Irish novel*. Cambridge: Cambridge University Press, 2006.

Foster, Roy. *Paddy and Mr Punch: connections in Irish and English history*. London: Penguin, 1995.

Frye, Northrop. *The secular scripture: a study of the structure of romance*. Cambridge, MA: Harvard University Press, 1976.

Gamer, Michael. *Romanticism and the gothic: genre, reception, and canon formation*. Cambridge: Cambridge University Press, 2000.

Garside, Peter. 'Authorship', in Garside and O'Brien (eds), *The Oxford history of the novel in English*, pp. 29-52.

——— 'Popular fiction and national tale: hidden origins of Scott's *Waverley*', *Nineteenth-century literature*, 46.1 (1991), 30-53.

——, Jacqueline Belanger, and Sharon Ragaz. *British fiction, 1800–1829: a database of production, circulation and reception*. Designer, Anthony Mandal. www.british-fiction.cf.ac.uk, accessed 4 October 2016.

—— and Karen O'Brien. *The Oxford history of the novel in English; volume 2: English and British fiction, 1750–1820*. Oxford: Oxford University Press, 2015.

Gillespie, Niall. 'Irish Jacobin gothic, c. 1796–1825', in Morin and Gillespie (eds), *Irish gothics*, pp. 58–73.

Gilroy, Amanda and Wil Verhoeven, 'The Romantic-era novel: a special issue', *Novel: a forum on fiction*, 34.2 (2001), 147–62.

Gordon, Scott Paul. 'The space of romance in Lennox's *Female Quixote*', *Studies in English literature 1500–1900*, 38.3 (1998), 499–516.

Haidt, Rebecca. 'The Enlightenment and fictional form', in Harriet Turner and Adelaida Lóez de Martínez (eds), *The Cambridge companion to the Spanish novel from 1600 to the present*. Cambridge: Cambridge University Press, 2003, pp. 31–46.

Hale, Terry. 'French and German gothic: the beginnings', in Hogle (ed.), *The Cambridge companion to gothic fiction*, pp. 63–84.

—— 'Translation in distress: cultural misappropriation and the construction of the gothic', *European gothic: a spirited exchange 1760–1960*. Ed. Avril Horner. Manchester: Manchester University Press, 2002, pp. 17–38.

Hamblyn, Richard. 'Notes from underground: Lisbon after the earthquake', *Romanticism*, 14.2 (2008), 108–18.

Hammond, Brean and Shaun Regan. *Making the novel: fiction and society in Britain, 1660–1789*. Basingstoke and New York: Palgrave Macmillan, 2006.

Hand, Derek. *A history of the Irish novel*. Cambridge: Cambridge University Press, 2011.

Haslam, Richard. 'Irish gothic', in Catherine Spooner and Emma McEvoy (eds), *The Routledge companion to gothic*. London: Routledge, 2007, pp. 83–94.

—— 'Maturin's Catholic heirs: expanding the limits of Irish gothic', in Morin and Gillespie (eds), *Irish gothics*, pp. 113–29.

Hester, Nathalie C. 'Geographies of belonging: Italian travel writing and Italian identity in the age of early European tourism', *Annali d'Italianistica*, 21 (2003), 287–300.

Hoeveler, Diane Long. *Gothic riffs: secularizing the uncanny in the European imaginary, 1780–1820*. Columbus, OH: Ohio State University Press, 2010.

—— 'Regina Maria Roche's *The children of the abbey*: contesting the Catholic presence in female gothic fiction', *Tulsa studies in women's literature*, 31.1/2 (2012), 137–58.

Hogle, Jerrold E., ed. *The Cambridge companion to gothic fiction*. Cambridge: Cambridge University Press, 2002.

Homestead, Melissa J. and Camryn Hansen. 'Susannah Rowson's transatlantic career', *Early American literature*, 45.3 (2010), 619–54.

SELECT BIBLIOGRAPHY

Horner, Avril and Sue Zlosnik. 'Introduction', in *The heroine, or, adventures of a fair romance reader*, by Eaton Stannard Barrett. Kansas City, MO: Valancourt Books, 2011, pp. vii–xxxi.

Ingelbien, Raphaël. 'Paradoxes of national liberation: Lady Morgan, O'Connellism, and the Belgian Revolution', *Éire-Ireland*, 42.3&4 (2007), 104–25.

Johns, Adrian. 'Changes in the world of publishing', in Chandler (ed.), *The Cambridge history of English Romantic literature*, pp. 377–402.

Kalter, Barrett. 'DIY gothic: Thomas Gray and the medieval revival', *ELH*, 70.4 (2003), 989–1019.

Kauffman, Linda S. *Discourses of desire: gender, genre, and epistolary fictions*. Ithaca, NY: Cornell University Press, 1986.

Kelleher, Margaret and James M. Murphy, eds. *Gender perspectives in nineteenth-century Ireland: public and private spheres*. Dublin: Irish Academic Press, 1997.

—— and Philip O'Leary, eds. *The Cambridge history of Irish literature: volume 1, to 1890*. Cambridge: Cambridge University Press, 2006.

Kelly, Gary, ed. *Varieties of female gothic*. 6 vols. London: Pickering & Chatto, 2002.

Kelly, James. *Charles Maturin: authorship, authenticity and the nation*. Dublin: Four Courts Press, 2011.

—— 'Gothic and the Celtic Fringe, 1750–1850', in Glennis Byron and Dale Townshend (eds), *The gothic world*. London: Routledge, 2013, pp. 38–50.

——, ed. *Ireland and Romanticism: publics, nations and scenes of cultural production*. Basingstoke and New York: Palgrave Macmillan, 2011.

Kilfeather, Siobhán. 'The gothic novel', in Foster (ed.), *The Cambridge companion to the Irish novel*, pp. 78–96.

—— 'Origins of the Irish female gothic', *Bullán*, 1.2 (1994), 34–45.

—— 'Sex and sensation in the nineteenth-century Irish novel', in Kelleher and Murphy (eds), *Gender perspectives in nineteenth-century Ireland*, pp. 83–92.

—— '"Strangers at home": political fictions by women in eighteenth-century Ireland'. Ph.D. dissertation, Princeton University Press, 1989.

—— 'Terrific register: the gothicization of atrocity in Irish Romantic writing'. *boundary 2*, 31.1 (2004), 49–71.

——, 'The profession of letters, 1700–1810', in Angela Bourke, Siobhán Kilfeather, Maria Luddy, Margaret Mac Curtain, Gerardine Meaney, Máirín Ní Dhonnchadha, Mary O'Dowd, and Clair Wills (eds), *The Field Day anthology of Irish writing*, vol. 5. Cork: Cork University Press, 2002, pp. 772–832.

Killeen, Jarlath. *The emergence of Irish gothic fiction: history, origins, theories*. Edinburgh: Edinburgh University Press, 2014.

—— *Gothic Ireland: horror and the Irish imagination in the long eighteenth century*. Dublin: Four Courts Press, 2005.

Kowaleski-Wallace, Elizabeth. *Their fathers' daughters: Hannah More, Maria Edgeworth, and patriarchal complicity*. Oxford: Oxford University Press, 1991.

Kramer, Dale. *Charles Robert Maturin*. New York: Twayne, 1973.

Lamb, Jonathan. 'Modern metamorphoses and disgraceful tales: eighteenth-century fictional "it-narratives"', *Critical inquiry*, 28.1 (2001), 133–66.

Lasa Álvarez, Begoña. 'Regina Maria Roche, an eighteenth-century Irish writer on the continent and overseas', in Marisol Morales Ladrón and Juan F. Elices Agudo (eds), *Glocal Ireland: current perspectives on literature and the visual arts*. Newcastle-upon-Tyne: Cambridge Scholars Publishing, 2011, pp. 51–61.

Leerssen, Joep. *Mere Irish and Fíor-Ghael: studies in the idea of Irish nationality, its development and literary expression prior to the nineteenth century*. Cork: Cork University Press and Field Day, 1996.

Lee Six, Abigail. *Gothic terrors: incarceration, duplication, and bloodlust in Spanish narrative*. Lewisburg, PA: Bucknell University Press, 2010.

Levy, Michelle. 'Women and print culture, 1750–1830', in Jacqueline M. Labbe (ed.), *The history of British women's writing, 1750–1830*, vol. 5. Basingstoke and New York: Palgrave Macmillan, 2010, pp. 29–46.

Livesey, James. 'Acts of union and disunion: Ireland in Atlantic and European contexts', in Dáire Keogh and Kevin Whelan (eds), *Acts of union: the causes, contexts, and consequences of the Act of Union*. Dublin: Four Courts Press, 2001, pp. 95–105.

Loeber, Rolf and Magda, with Anne Mullin Burnham. *A guide to Irish fiction, 1650–1900*. Dublin: Four Courts Press, 2006.

Loeber, Rolf and Magda Stouthamer-Loeber. 'Literary absentees: Irish women authors in nineteenth-century England', in Belanger (ed.), *The Irish novel in the nineteenth century*, pp. 167–86.

—— 'The publication of Irish novels and novelettes, 1750–1829: a footnote on Irish gothic fiction', *Cardiff Corvey: reading the Romantic text*, 10 (2003), 17–44. www.romtext.org.uk/articles/cc10_n02, accessed 4 October 2016.

López Santos, Miriam. *La novela gótica en Espanā (1788–1833)*. Pontevedra: Editorial Academia del Hispanismo, 2010.

Lougy, Robert E. *Charles Robert Maturin*. Lewisburg, PA: Bucknell University Press, 1975.

Lukács, Georg. *The historical novel*. 1937. Trans. Hannah and Stanley Mitchell. Lincoln, NE: University of Nebraska Press, 1983.

Lynch, Deirdre. 'Transformations of the novel – I', in Chandler (ed.), *The Cambridge history of English Romantic literature*, pp. 451–472.

Lynch, Patricia A., Joachim Fischer, and Brian Coates, eds. *Back to the present, forward to the past: Irish writing and history Since 1798*, vol. 1. Amsterdam: Rodopi, 2006.

McCormack, W.J. *Ascendancy and tradition in Anglo-Irish literary history from 1789 to 1939*. Oxford: Oxford University Press, 1985.

—— 'Irish gothic and after (1820–1945)', in Seamus Deane (ed.), *The Field Day anthology of Irish writing*, vol. 2. Derry: Field Day, 1991, pp. 831–949.

MacFadyen, Heather. 'Lady Delacour's library: Maria Edgeworth's *Belinda* and fashionable reading', *Nineteenth-century literature*, 48.4 (1994), 423–39.
McLeod, Deborah. 'The Minerva Press', Ph.D. dissertation, University of Alberta, 1997.
Mack, Ruth. 'Horace Walpole and the objects of literary history', *ELH*, 75.2 (2008), 367–87.
Mandal, Anthony. *Jane Austen and the popular novel: the determined author.* Basingstoke and New York: Palgrave Macmillan, 2007.
—— 'Revising the Radcliffean model: Regina Maria Roche's *Clermont* and Jane Austen's *Northanger Abbey*', *Cardiff Corvey: reading the Romantic text*, 3 (1999), 1–13. www.romtext.org.uk/articles/cc03_n03/, accessed 4 October 2016.
Martí-López, Elisa. *Borrowed words: translation, imitation, and the making of the nineteenth-century novel in Spain.* Lewisburg, PA: Bucknell University Press, 2002.
Matthews-Kane, Bridget. 'Gothic excess and political anxiety: Lady Morgan's *The wild Irish girl*', *Gothic studies*, 5.2 (2003), 7–19.
Maxwell, Richard, and Katie Trumpener, eds. *The Cambridge companion to fiction in the Romantic period.* Cambridge: Cambridge University Press, 2008.
—— 'The historical novel', in Maxwell and Trumpener (Eds), *The Cambridge companion to fiction in the Romantic period*, pp. 65–87.
—— 'The historiography of fiction in the Romantic period', in Maxwell and Trumpener (eds), *The Cambridge companion to fiction in the Romantic period*, pp. 7–21.
Mighall, Robert. *A geography of Victorian gothic fiction: mapping history's nightmares.* Oxford: Oxford University Press, 1999.
Miles, Robert. *Gothic writing, 1750–1820: a genealogy.* London: Routledge, 1993.
—— 'The 1790s: the effulgence of gothic', in Hogle (ed.), *The Cambridge companion to gothic fiction*, pp. 41–62.
Miller, Julia Anne. 'Acts of union: family violence and national courtship in Maria Edgeworth's *The absentee* and Sydney Owenson's *The wild Irish girl*', in Kathryn Kirkpatrick (ed.), *Border crossings: Irish women writers and national identities.* Tuscaloosa, AL and London: University of Alabama Press, 2000, pp. 13–37.
Moers, Ellen. *Literary women.* 1963. London: The Women's Press, 1978.
Molloy, Frank. 'Thomas Campbell's "Exile of Erin": English poem, Irish reactions', in Lynch, Fischer, and Coates (eds), *Back to the present*, pp. 43–53.
Moretti, Franco. *Atlas of the European novel, 1800–1900.* London: Verso, 1998.
—— 'Conjectures on world literature', *New left review*, 1 (2000), 54–68.
—— *Graphs, maps, trees: abstract models for literary history.* 2005. London: Verso, 2007.
—— *The novel.* 2 vols. London: Verso, 2005.
—— 'The slaughterhouse of literature', *MLQ: modern language quarterly*, 61.1 (2000), 207–27.

Morin, Christina. '"At a distance from [my] country": Henrietta Rouvière Mosse, the Minerva Press, and the negotiation of Irishness in the Romantic literary marketplace', *European Romantic review*, 28.4 (2017), 447–60.

—— *Charles Robert Maturin and the haunting of Irish Romantic fiction*. Manchester: Manchester University Press, 2011.

—— '"Gothic" and "national"? Challenging the formal distinctions of Irish Romantic fiction', in Kelly (ed.), *Ireland and Romanticism*, pp. 172–87.

—— 'Irish gothic goes abroad: cultural migration, materiality, and the Minerva Press', in Marguérite Corporaal and Christina Morin (eds), *Traveling Irishness in the long nineteenth century*. Basingstoke and New York: Palgrave Macmillan, 2017, pp. 185–203.

—— 'Theorizing "gothic" in eighteenth-century Ireland', in Morin and Gillespie (eds), *Irish gothics*, pp. 13–33.

—— and Niall Gillespie. 'Introduction: de-limiting the Irish gothic', in Morin and Gillespie (eds), *Irish gothics*, pp. 1–12.

—— and Niall Gillespie, eds. *Irish gothics: genres, forms, modes and traditions*. Basingstoke and New York: Palgrave Macmillan, 2014.

—— and Jarlath Killeen. 'The new adventures of Miss Sophia Berkley: revisiting Ireland's "first" gothic novel', *Eighteenth-century Ireland*, 29 (2014), 155–63.

Moynahan, Julian. *Anglo-Irish: the literary imagination in a hyphenated culture*. Princeton, NJ: Princeton University Press, 1995.

Murphy, Sharon. *Maria Edgeworth and romance*. Dublin: Four Courts Press, 2004.

Neiman, Elizabeth A. 'A new perspective on the Minerva Press's "derivative" novels: authorizing borrowed material', *European Romantic review*, 26.5 (2015), 633–58.

Nolan, Emer. 'Banim and the historical novel', in Belanger (ed.), *The Irish novel in the nineteenth century*, pp. 80–93.

—— *Catholic emancipations: Irish fiction from Thomas Moore to James Joyce*. Syracuse, NY: Syracuse University Press, 2007.

O'Brien, Karen. 'Introduction', in Garside and O'Brien (eds), *The Oxford history of the novel in English*, pp. xvii–xxix.

Ó Ciardha, Éamonn. *Ireland and the Jacobite cause, 1685–1766; a fatal attachment*. Dublin: Four Courts Press, 2002.

Ó Gallchoir, Clíona. 'Celtic Ireland and Celtic Scotland: Ossianism and *The wild Irish girl*', in David Duff and Catherine Jones (eds), *Scotland, Ireland, and the Romantic aesthetic*. Lewisburg, PA: Bucknell University Press, 2007, pp. 114–30.

—— *Maria Edgeworth: women, enlightenment, and nation*. Dublin: University College Dublin Press, 2005.

O'Halloran, Clare. *Golden ages and barbarous nations: antiquarian debate and cultural politics in Ireland, c. 1750–1800*. Cork: Cork University Press and Field Day, 2004.

Pearson, Jacqueline. 'Masculinizing the novel: women writers and intertextuality in Charles Robert Maturin's *The wild Irish boy*', *Studies in Romanticism*, 36.4 (1997), 635-50.

Perry, Ruth. *Women, letters, and the novel*. New York: AMS Press, 1980.

Piper, Andrew. *Dreaming in books: the making of the bibliographic imagination in the Romantic Age*. Chicago: University of Chicago Press, 2009.

Pittock, Murray. *Scottish and Irish Romanticism*. Oxford: Oxford University Press, 2008.

Pollard, Mary. *Dublin's trade in books, 1550-1800*. Oxford: Clarendon Press, 1989.

Potter, Franz J. *The history of gothic publishing, 1800-1835: exhuming the trade*. Basingstoke and New York: Palgrave, 2005.

Powell, Martyn J. *Britain and Ireland in the eighteenth-century crisis of empire*. Basingstoke and New York: Palgrave Macmillan, 2003.

Price, Fiona. 'Ancient liberties? Rewriting the historical novel: Thomas Leland, Horace Walpole and Clara Reeve', *Journal for eighteenth-century studies*, 34.1 (2011), 19-38.

Punter, David. *The literature of terror*. 2 vols. 2nd edn. London: Longman Group, 1996.

Purves, Maria. *The gothic and Catholicism: religion, cultural exchange and the popular novel, 1785-1829*. Cardiff: University of Wales Press, 2009.

Raven, James. 'The anonymous novel in Britain and Ireland, 1750-1830', in Robert J. Griffin (ed.), *The faces of anonymity: anonymous and pseudonymous publication from the sixteenth to the twentieth century*. Basingstoke and New York: Palgrave Macmillan, 2003, pp. 141-66.

—— 'Historical introduction: the novel comes of age', in Raven and Forster (eds), with Bending, *The English novel 1770-1829: a bibliographical survey of prose fiction published in the British Isles. Vol. 1, 1770-1799*, pp. 15-121.

—— *Judging new wealth: popular publishing and responses to commerce in England 1750-1800*. Oxford: Clarendon Press, 1992.

—— and Antonia Forster, with Stephen Bending. *The English novel 1770-1829: a bibliographical survey of prose fiction published in the British Isles. Vol. 1, 1770-1799*. Oxford: Oxford University Press, 2000.

Regan, Shaun. 'Locating Richard Griffith: genre, nation, canon', *Irish university review*, 41.1 (2001). 95-114.

Remer, Rosalind. *Printers and men of capital: Philadelphia in the New Republic*. Philadelphia: University of Pennsylvania Press, 1996.

Rintoul, Suzanne. 'Gothic anxieties: struggling with a definition'. *Eighteenth-century fiction*, 17.4 (2005), 701-9.

Robertson, Fiona. *Legitimate histories: Scott, gothic, and the authorities of fiction*. Oxford: Clarendon Press, 1994.

Rodtjer, Rocío. 'The Spanish gothic', *Journal of romance studies*, 12.1 (2002), 85-93.

Ross, Ian Campbell. 'Fiction to 1800', in Seamus Deane (ed.), *The Field Day anthology of Irish Writing*, vol. 1. Derry: Field Day Publications, 1991, pp. 682–759.

—— 'Irish fiction before the Union', in Belanger (ed.), *The Irish novel in the nineteenth century*, pp. 34–51.

—— 'Mapping Ireland in early fiction', *Irish university review*, 41.1 (2011), 1–20.

—— 'Prose in English, 1690–1800: from the Williamite Wars to the Act of Union', in Kelleher and O'Leary (eds), *The Cambridge history of Irish literature*, pp. 232–81.

—— Review of *A guide to Irish fiction*, *Eighteenth-century Ireland*, 22 (2007), 223–6.

St Clair, William. *The reading nation in the Romantic period*. Cambridge: Cambridge University Press, 2004.

Schroeder, Natalie. '*The mysteries of Udolpho* and *Clermont*: the Radcliffean encroachment on the art of Regina Maria Roche', *Studies in the novel*, 12 (1980), 131–43.

—— 'Regina Maria Roche and the early nineteenth-century Irish novel', *Éire-Ireland*, 19.2 (1984), 116–30.

—— 'Regina Maria Roche, popular novelist, 1789–1834: the Rochean canon', *Papers of the Bibliographical Society of America*, 73 (1979), 462–8.

Shanahan, Jim. 'Charles Lever, Walter Scott, and the Irish national tale', in Paddy Lyons, Willy Maley, and John Miller (eds), *Romantic Ireland: from Tone to Gonne; fresh perspectives on nineteenth-century Ireland*. Newcastle upon Tyne: Cambridge Scholars Publishing, 2013, pp. 298–309.

—— 'Escaping from Barrett's moon: recreating the Irish literary landscape in the Romantic period', in Kelly (ed.), *Ireland and Romanticism*, pp. 188–203.

Siskin, Clifford. *The work of writing: literature and social change in Britain, 1700–1830*. Baltimore, MD and London: The Johns Hopkins University Press, 1998.

Skelton-Foord, Christopher. 'To buy or to borrow? Circulating libraries and novel reading in Britain, 1778–1828', *Library review*, 47.7 (1998), 348–54.

Steele, Karen 'Irish incognitos: transnational mobility in the national tales of Maria Edgeworth and Sydney Owenson', *Éire-Ireland*, 50.3/4 (2015), 94–112.

Stevens, Anne H. *British historical fiction before Scott*. Basingstoke and New York: Palgrave Macmillan, 2010.

Stewart, Carol. *The eighteenth-century novel and the secularization of ethics*. Farnham: Ashgate, 2010.

Stones, Graeme, ed. *Parodies of the Romantic Age. Volume 1: the anti-Jacobin*. London: Pickering & Chatto, 1999.

Summers, Montague. *A gothic bibliography*. 1940. New York: Russell & Russell, 1964.

—— *The gothic quest: a history of the gothic novel*. 1938. New York: Russell & Russell, 1964.

Sweet, Rosemary. *Antiquaries: the discovery of the past in eighteenth-century Britain*. London: Hambledon and London, 2004.

Tompkins, J.M.S. 'James White, Esq. A forgotten humourist', *Review of English studies*, 3 (1927), 146–56.

Tracy, Robert. 'Maria Edgeworth and Lady Morgan: legality versus legitimacy', *Nineteenth-century fiction*, 40.1 (1985), 1–22.

Trumpener, Katie. *Bardic nationalism: the Romantic novel and the British Empire*. Princeton, NJ: Princeton University Press, 1997.

Turner, Cheryl. *Living by the pen: women writers in the eighteenth century*. 1992. London and New York: Routledge, 1994.

Van Wyhe, John. *Phrenology and the origins of Victorian scientific naturalism*. Aldershot: Ashgate, 2004.

Verhoeven, Wil. 'The global British novel', in Garside and O'Brien (eds), *The Oxford history of the novel in English*, pp. 566–88.

Vogeley, Nancy. 'Translation studies: the novel and other Enlightenment crossings', *Eighteenth-century studies*, 44.2 (2011), 292–8.

Warwick, Alexandra. 'Feeling gothicky?', *Gothic studies*, 9:1 (2007), 5–19.

Watson, Nicola J. *Revolution and the form of the British novel, 1790–1825: intercepted letters, interrupted seductions*. Oxford: Clarendon Press, 1994.

Watt, James. *Contesting the gothic: fiction, genre and cultural conflict, 1764–1832*. Cambridge: Cambridge University Press, 1999.

Wein, Toni. *British identities, heroic nationalisms, and the gothic novel, 1764–1824*. Basingstoke and New York: Palgrave Macmillan, 2002.

Wiley, Michael. *Romantic migrations: local, national, and transnational dispositions*. Basingstoke and New York: Palgrave Macmillan, 2008.

Williams, Anne. *Art of darkness: a poetics of gothic*. Chicago: The University of Chicago Press, 1995.

Wright, Julia M. 'Introduction', in *The missionary: an Indian tale*, by Sydney Owenson, Lady Morgan. Ed. Julia M. Wright. Ontario: Broadview Press, 2002, pp. 9–57.

—— '"The nation begins to form": competing nationalisms in Morgan's *The O'Briens and the O'Flahertys*', *ELH*, 66 (1999), 339–65.

—— *Representing the national landscape in Irish Romanticism*. Syracuse, NY: Syracuse University Press, 2014.

Index

Note: literary works can be found under authors' names.

Act of Anglo-Irish Union (1800) 160
    see also Anglo-Irish Union
Addison, Joseph 97, 109n59
The adventures of Miss Sophia Berkley 24n40
    see also *The history of Amanda*
Alfred the Great 129
American War of Independence (1775–83) 179
Anglo-Irish Union (1801) 15, 51, 77, 98, 117, 132, 142, 139, 155, 160, 179, 193n121
Anglo-Scottish Union (1707) 193n121
    see also Act of Anglo-Irish Union (1800)
Ashe, Captain Thomas 157
Austen, Jane 158
    Northanger Abbey 76, 78, 84, 92, 96, 108n46, 171, 173

Balzac, Honoré de 168
Banim, John 160
    The Boyne water 59–60
    imitation of Walter Scott and 59–60
    The Nowlans 59–60
    Revelations of the dead-alive 72
Banim, John and Michael 11, 56, 160

The fetches 59–62
    Tales by the O'Hara family 59
Baretti, Joseph
    Journey from England to Genoa 136–7
Barrett, Eaton Stannard 157
    The heroine, or adventures of a fair romance reader 76, 77–9, 80, 84–5, 87, 90, 91, 97, 105, 108n46, 173
Battle of the Boyne (1690) 178, 193n119
Battle of Clontarf (1014) 131
Beattie, James
    Dissertations moral and critical 74–5
Boru, Brian 131, 142, 144, 145
Boyle, Henry, 3rd Earl of Shannon 132
Brontë, Charlotte 168
Brown, Charles Brockden 158, 167, 190n70
    Wieland 167
Bürger, Gottfried August
    'Lenora' 95, 109n56
Burke, Edmund 48, 123, 160
Burney, Frances 87
    Evelina 79
Burns, Robert
    'Address to Edinburgh' 161–2
Byron, George Gordon, Lord 98

INDEX

Calprenède, Gauthier de Costes de la 74
Cassandre 74, 85
Campbell, Thomas 152n98
Caritat, Hocquet 167
Carleton, William 168
Catholic Emancipation (1829) 18, 25n70, 103
Cervantes 168
Don Quixote 84
Colburn, Henry 160, 186n10
Coleridge, Samuel Taylor 53
Conolly, Reverend Luke Aylmer
The friar's tale; or, memoirs of the chevalier Orsino 117
Cooper, James Fenimore 168
Copyright Act (1709) 160
The correspondents 164
Croker, Thomas Crofton
Fairy legends and traditions of the south of Ireland 58
Croly, Reverend George
Salathiel; a story of the past, the present, and the future 81
Cromwell, Oliver 125, 187n29
Cullen, Stephen
The castle of Inchvally 66n59, 100, 114
The haunted priory; or, the fortunes of the house of Rayo 117
Cuthbertson, Catherine (Miss Kitty) 197–8
Adelaide; or, the countercharm 197
Ethelbert 197
The forest of Montalbano 197
The hut and the castle 197
Romance of the Pyrenees 197
Rosabella; or, a mother's marriage 197
Santa Sebastiano 197

Dalrymple, William
Travels through Spain and Portugal, in 1774 137
David II 73
Dickens, Charles 168

Edgeworth, Maria 11, 111n76, 113, 114, 160, 161, 165, 171
The absentee 16, 101, 110n66, 119, 139, 142, 144
Belinda 87, 90, 174–5
Castle Rackrent 15, 45, 77, 98, 100, 114, 152n97
Ennui 98, 154, 185n3
Tales of fashionable life 78
Edward, the Black Prince 73
Edward I 44
Edward IV 48, 49–50
Elizabeth I 1, 130
Ennis, Alice Margaret 157
Ethelred the Unready 131–2
'The Exile of Erin' 145
contested authorship of 152–3n98

The fair Hibernian 138, 179
False appearances 160
female authorship 17–18, 25n64, 196
'masculinisation' of the novel and 18, 25n66, 83
Fielding, Henry 74, 78, 87
Joseph Andrews 74
on the novel's superiority to romance 74
Flight of the Wild Geese 178, 179, 193n119
French Revolution (1789) 19, 79, 89, 90, 93, 131
Fuller, Anne 38–48 *passim*, 52, 96, 129
Alan Fitz-Osborne 13, 30, 41–3, 47, 51, 63n7, 66n60, 81, 115, 117, 131
The convent; or the history of Sophia Nelson 15, 76, 85–8, 91, 94, 97, 105, 117, 118, 133–4, 137, 141, 150n72, 173
The son of Ethelwolf 63n7, 81, 117, 118, 129, 130–1, 132, 133, 141

∼ 229

INDEX

Gall, Franz Joseph and Spurzheim, Johann Gaspar 172, 191–2n98
George III 37, 39, 68n76, 148n37
George IV 51, 68n77
Godwin, William 98, 128
Goethe, Johann Wolfgang von
   The sorrows of young Werther 110n69
Goldsmith, Oliver 160
   The vicar of Wakefield 78
gothic
   constitution 5, 65n43, 123
      see also Swift: on Britain's Gothic constitution
   eighteenth-century understandings of 2–3, 5, 19–20, 28–30, 38, 122, 198
   'female' 18, 99, 115, 153n102
   as generic descriptor 5–6, 7, 22n23, 27, 32, 41, 76, 115–16, 129, 150n52
   past 5, 9, 13, 14, 15, 30, 31–8 *passim*, 41, 47, 53, 62, 100, 122, 129
   romance and 5–7, 77–84 *passim*
      see also romance: revival of; Walpole, Horace: *The castle of Otranto*: revival of romance and
   see also 'the Gothic novel'; 'Irish Gothic'
'the Gothic novel'
   anti-Catholicism and 28, 108n49, 130, 136
   Catholic Continental settings and 3, 13, 16, 113–19, 136–7, 158, 198
   'Celtic Fringe' and 13, 16, 115, 122, 126, 129, 137, 143, 146
   conventional understandings of 1–2, 3, 7–9, 13–14, 19, 27–8, 115–16, 198–9
   as a term used in this book 19–20, 21n3
   see also gothic

Green, Sarah 13, 157
   Charles Henley; or, the fugitive restored 186n13
   Court intrigue 186n13
   The festival of St Jago; a Spanish romance 98
   The royal exile; or victims of human passions 81
Griffin, Gerald 18, 160
Griffith, Elizabeth 105, 117, 119–28 *passim*, 141, 160
   Amana 122–3
   'Conjugal fidelity' 1–5, 6–7, 9, 118, 127
   The delicate distress 120, 121–2, 123, 149n40
   The double mistake 119
   The history of Lady Barton 81, 118, 123–5, 126, 127, 143
   The platonic wife 119
   The school for rakes 119
   'Story of Lady Fanny Beaumont and Lord Layton' 127–8
   The story of Lady Juliana Harley 81, 118, 123, 125–6
   A wife in the right 119
Griffith, Elizabeth and Goldsmith, Oliver
   Novellettes, selected for the use of young ladies and gentlemen 1, 126–7
Griffith, Elizabeth and Griffith, Richard
   A series of genuine letters between Henry and Frances 120–1
   Two novels in letters 120
Griffith, Richard 120
   The Gordian knot 148n25

Haly, James 132
Hardy, Thomas 168
Henry III 28, 37, 39, 40, 41–2, 43, 66–7n60
Henry VII 49, 50
Henry VIII 187n29

INDEX

historical novel 14, 15, 16, 18, 97, 98, 100, 198
  gothic literature and 13–14, 30–1, 52–6
  by Irish authors 30–1, 51–2, 56–7, 62
  Sir Walter Scott and the inauguration of 14, 29
  see also Scott, Sir Walter
The history of Amanda 24n40
  see also *The adventures of Miss Sophia Berkley*
Hogg, James 53, 98

'Irish Gothic'
  conventional understandings of 1–2, 3–4, 7–8, 98, 99–100, 198–9
  terminological debate and 7–8, 23n32
  as a term used in this book 19–20, 21n3
  see also gothic
Irish Jacobitism 22n15, 57, 59, 178, 179, 193n119
Irish patriot politics, Irish 3, 4, 22n15, 122–3, 130
Irish print industry 150n69, 155, 160
  application of English copyright law to Ireland and 155
Isdell, Sarah
  The vale of Louisiana; an American tale 160

Jacobite Rebellion (1745) 22n15
Jamaica 173, 174, 175, 179, 190n68
  circulating libraries in 167, 175–6
Jardine, Alexander
  Letters from Barbary, France, Spain, Portugal 137
Jeffrey, Francis 69n110
  on Walter Scott 54–6, 69n108
John of Gaunt 73, 82
Johnson, Joseph 160, 187n20

Kelly, Hugh 160
Kelly, Isabella 158
Kenley, Marianne
  The cottage of the Appenines, or, the Castle of Novina 117

Lady's magazine 197–8
Lane, William 98, 156, 186n8
  An address to the public, on circulating libraries 164
  circulating libraries and 164–5, 167
  payments to authors 162–3, 187–8n32
  personal wealth 187–8n32
  transnational literary marketplace and 163–8 *passim*, 180
  see also Minerva Press
Lee, Sophia
  The recess 115
Le Fanu, Alicia 157, 173
  Strathallan 76, 80, 94–7, 105, 115, 173
Le Fanu, Sheridan 2, 19
Leland, Thomas 129, 31–8 *passim*
  A history of the life and reign of Philip, King of Macedon 31
  Longsword, Earl of Salisbury 10, 13, 18, 27, 35–8, 39–41, 47, 51, 75, 76, 115, 117, 122, 131, 133
  adapted as *The Countess of Salisbury* 27
  reception of 31, 33–5, 39
  The Philipic orations of Demosthenes 31
Lennox, Charlotte
  The female Quixote 74, 76, 84, 85, 90, 95, 108n43, 108n52
Lever, Charles
  The O'Donoghue 153n101
Lewis, Matthew 3, 7, 72, 181
  The bravo of Venice 78
  'The grim white woman' 109n56
'loyalist Gothic romance' 40, 66n59, 122, 130

231

INDEX

Mangan, James Clarence 18–19
Mangin, Edward
  Essay on light reading, as it may be supposed to influence moral conduct on literary taste 80
Martin, Richard 163
Maturin, Charles Robert 11, 114, 160, 165
  The Albigenses 56–7
  Bertram; or, the castle of St Aldobrand 57, 70n120
  The fatal revenge; or, the family of Montorio 98, 109n56 117
  imitation of Walter Scott and 56–7, 70n119
  'Leixlip Castle: an Irish family legend' 57–9, 62
  Melmoth the wanderer 2, 7, 16, 98, 143, 152n95, 165, 182, 185n4
  The Milesian chief 15, 56, 77, 99, 102, 103, 105, 114, 115, 119, 147n7, 152n95
  The wild Irish boy 88, 119
  Women; or, pour et contre 70n120, 165
Melville, Theodore 115, 157
  The Irish chieftain, and his family 114
  The White Knight, or the monastery of Morne 113–14
Milliken, Anna 157
  Corfe Castle; or historic tracts 81, 117, 118, 131–3, 141
  Plantagenet; or, secrets of the house of Anjou 15, 83
Minerva Press 13, 16, 18, 98, 138, 154–85 *passim*, 186n10, 196–7
  American print industry and 166–7
  critical perceptions of 168–9, 170–1, 172
  see also Lane, William; Newman, A.K.

The moral miscellany; or, a collection of select pieces, in prose and verse, for the instruction and entertainment of youth 109
More, Hannah
  Coelebs in search of a wife 78
Mosse, Henrietta Rouvière 13, 157
  Arrivals from India 186n13
  Lussington Abbey 98
  The old Irish baronet; or, manners of my country 119, 139–42, 144, 145, 152n86, 154
Murphy, Arthur 160

national tale 4, 15, 16, 77, 97–105 *passim*, 113, 119, 120, 123, 132, 137–9, 142, 144, 146, 161, 176, 177, 199
  gothic literature and 15–16, 77, 97–105 *passim*, 137–45 *passim*
  Sydney Owenson and the inauguration of 77, 98–9
  see also Owenson, Sydney (Lady Morgan)
Netterville, John, 2nd Viscount Netterville of Dowth 139–40
Newman, A.K. 156, 159
  see also Minerva Press
The new polite instructor; or universal moralist 109n59

O'Callaghan, Cornelius, 1st Baron Lismore 140
O'Halloran, Sylvester 139
O'Keeffe, John 160
Owenson, Sydney (Lady Morgan) 11, 77, 113, 147n7, 160, 161, 165, 171

Florence MacCarthy 99
'Glorvina solution' and 98, 103,
    110n67, 110n73, 139
The missionary 94, 99, 138,
    151n81
The novice of Saint Dominick 99,
    138
The O'Briens and the O'Flahertys
    99
O'Donnel 77, 101–5
The princess; or, the Béguine 99
St Clair; or, the heiress of Desmond
    99, 110n69, 160
The wild Irish girl 4, 15, 16, 77,
    98–9, 100–1, 102,
    113–14, 119, 125, 139,
    143, 144
see also national tale: Sydney
    Owenson and the
    inauguration of

Patrick, Mrs F.C. 13, 157
The Irish heiress 76, 79–80, 84,
    91–4, 97, 105, 106n20,
    173
The Jesuit 130
More ghosts! 76, 84, 88–90, 91, 92,
    97, 108n49, 173
Peck, Frances 157
Percy, Elizabeth, Countess of
    Northumberland 122–3
Pery, Edmond 122–3
Phillips, Charles
*The loves of Celestine and St
    Aubert* 83
Pilkington, Laetitia
*The memoirs of Mrs Laetitia
    Pilkington* 121
Poe, Edgar Allan 168

Radcliffe, Ann 3, 7, 69n108, 72, 76,
    88, 89, 103, 113, 115,
    150n72, 158, 170, 171,
    181, 197
The castles of Athlin and Dunbayne
    111n76, 115

'explained supernatural' and 89
The Italian 77, 78, 106n17, 128
The mysteries of Udolpho 77, 78,
    109n56, 128
Rebellion, 1641 1, 3, 7, 127, 140
    historiography of 3
Rebellion, 1798 97, 117, 130, 132,
    139, 152n98, 179
Reeve, Clara 181
The old English baron 22n23, 40,
    41, 64n14, 89, 115, 122,
    129, 150n52
The progress of romance 6, 83
Reginald Du Bray: an historick tale
    66n54
    see also *The rival friends; or, the
        noble recluse*
Reynolds, George Nugent 152n98
Richardson, Samuel 74, 78, 90
The rival friends; or, the noble recluse
    66n54
    see also *Reginald Du Bray: an
        historick tale*
Robinson, George 162
Robinson, Mary
'The haunted beach' 95, 109n56
Roche, Ambrose 159, 163
Roche, Regina Maria 13, 16, 154–85
    passim, 196–8
    accepted publications 186n9
The castle chapel 154–6, 161–2,
    167, 172, 176
The children of the abbey 15, 83,
    100–1, 102, 114, 126,
    143, 158, 163, 165–6,
    167–8, 170, 176–7, 180,
    181–2
Clermont 158, 159, 170, 177–8,
    179, 180, 182
Contrast 159, 171
correspondence with the Royal
    Literary Fund 158,
    159–60, 162–3, 165
*The discarded son; or, haunt of
    the banditti* 15, 98,
    172–7

∼ 233

The houses of Osma and Almeria; or, the convent of St Ildefonso 83
The maid of the hamlet 159
The monastery of St Columb; or, the atonement 168–70, 171, 182
The Munster cottage boy 171
Nocturnal visit 178–80
The nun's picture 159
religious views of 153n102
spurious attributions 186n9, 192n99
The tradition of the castle; or, scenes in the Emerald Isle 119, 139, 142–5, 154, 171, 177
translation of her novels into Spanish 181–4
Trecothick bower; or, the lady of the west country 14, 48–51, 62, 80, 168, 170–1
The vicar of Lansdowne; or, country quarters 159, 189n59
romance
the novel and 6, 14–15, 74–7
revival of 6–7, 75, 77–84 passim
see also gothic: romance and; Walpole, Horace: *The castle of Otranto*: revival of romance and
Rousseau, Jean-Jacques 89, 92–3
Confessions 92
Rowson, Susannah 158

Saunders & Otley 160
Scott, Sir Walter 155, 158, 167, 168
The black dwarf 98
The bride of Lammermoor 56, 58, 59, 105
Castle Dangerous 98
'The eve of St John' 95
Guy Mannering 54
Ivanhoe 56
The lay of the last minstrel 95
Marmion 54
The monastery 98
romance and 52–7, 62
Waverley 14, 29, 48, 54, 56, 72, 88, 99
see also historical novel: Sir Walter Scott and the inauguration of
Scudéry, Madeleine de 74
Artamène; ou le grand Cyrus 74
Second Barons' War (1264–65) 41–2
Selden, Catharine 157
The English nun 118, 134–7, 141
Villa Nova; or, the ruined castle 15, 83, 98
Villasantelle; or, the curious impertinent 98
Shakespeare, William
Romeo and Juliet 127–8
Shelley, Mary 98
Sheridan, Elizabeth
The triumph of prudence over passion 179
Sheridan, Frances 120
Sheridan, Richard Brinsley 160
Smith, Mrs
The Caledonian bandit 162
Southey, Robert
'Donica' 95 109n56
Spain
gothic literary production of 181–4
Steele, Richard 109n59
Stoker, Bram 2, 19
Strongbow 44–7, 73
Subligny, Perdou de
The mock-Clelia 84
Swift, Jonathan 168
Gulliver's travels 73
on Britain's Gothic constitution 38, 65n43
see also gothic: constitution

Temple, Sir John
The Irish rebellion 3–4, 21n11
travel writing 119, 123, 136, 137, 151n77

Twiss, Richard
 Travels through Portugal and Spain 136–7

Walpole, Horace 122
 The castle of Otranto 2, 5–6, 10, 13, 15, 27, 38–9, 80, 95, 133
  reception of 32–3, 38
  revival of romance and 5–7, 75
  see also gothic: romance; romance: revival of
  Sir Walter Scott on 29
Warner, Richard
 Netley Abbey 129
White, James 13, 30, 38, 43–8 *passim*, 129
 The adventures of John of Gaunt, Duke of Lancaster 43, 73–4, 115
 The adventures of King Richard Coeur de Lion 43
 Conway Castle 43–4
 Earl Strongbow 15, 30, 44–8, 72–3
 Hints for a specific plan for an abolition of the slave trade and for the relief of negroes in the British West Indies 43
 The history of the revolution of France 43
 Speeches of M. de Mirabeau 43
Wilde, Oscar 2, 19

EU authorised representative for GPSR:
Easy Access System Europe, Mustamäe tee 50,
10621 Tallinn, Estonia
gpsr.requests@easproject.com

www.ingramcontent.com/pod-product-compliance
Lightning Source LLC
Chambersburg PA
CBHW070237240426
43673CB00044B/1829